POWERFUL SOCIAL STUDIES for ELEMENTARY STUDENTS

Jere Brophy
Michigan State University

Janet Alleman
Michigan State University

Harcourt Brace College Publishers

Fort Worth   Philadelphia   San Diego   New York   Orlando   Austin   San Antonio
Toronto   Montreal   London   Sydney   Tokyo

Publisher	Ted Buchholz
Editor in Chief	Christopher P. Klein
Acquisitions Editor	Jo-Anne Weaver
Project Editor	Christopher Nelson
Editorial Assistant	Dana Rodes
Production Manager	Debra A. Jenkin
Art Director	Vicki Whistler
Cover Designer	Melinda Welch
Cover Illustrator	Rhonda Voo
Digital Composition	Paul G. Zinn

ISBN: 0-15-502104-4

Library of Congress Catalog Card Number: 95-77463

Address for Editorial Correspondence: Harcourt Brace College Publishers, 301 Commerce Street, Suite 3700, Fort Worth, TX 76102.

Address for Orders: Harcourt Brace & Company, 6277 Sea Harbor Drive, Orlando, FL 32887-6777. 1-800-782-4479, or 1-800-433-0001 (in Florida).

Printed in the United States of America

5 6 7 8 9 0 1 2 3 4 039 0 9 8 7 6 5 4 3 2 1

Copyright Acknowledgements CHAPTER 6: The content for the exercise on pages 105–110 is from *From Sea to Shining Sea,* Teacher's Edition, in *Houghton Mifflin Social Studies* by Armento et al. Copyright © 1991 by Houghton Mifflin Company. Reprinted by permission of Houghton Mifflin Company. All rights reserved. CHAPTER 9: The questions on page 157 are from "Is Curriculum Integration a Boon or a Threat to Social Studies?" by Janet Alleman and Jere Brophy, in *Social Education,* Volume 57, Number 6, pp. 288–291. Copyright © 1993 by the National Council for the Social Studies. Reprinted by permission. CHAPTER 12: The description of changes in clothing on pages 199–203 is from *18th Century Clothing* and *19th Century Clothing,* Historic Community Series, Crabtree Publishing Co., 350 5th Ave., Ste. 3308, New York, NY 10118. Copyright 1993. PHOTOS appear courtesy of Harcourt Brace & Company Photo Studio.

*For Arlene Pintozzi Brophy
and George Trumbull*

ABOUT THE AUTHORS

Jere Brophy is a University Distinguished Professor of Teacher Education at Michigan State University. Author, coauthor, or editor of more than 20 books and 250 scholarly articles, chapters, and technical reports, he is well-known for his research on teacher expectations, teacher–student relationships, teacher effects on student achievement, classroom management, student motivation, and, most recently, elementary social studies curriculum and instruction. Dr. Brophy was a member of the Task Force on Social Studies Teaching and Learning that prepared the National Council for the Social Studies' position statement entitled "A Vision of Powerful Teaching and Learning in the Social Studies: Building Social Understanding and Civic Efficacy."

Janet Alleman is a professor in the Department of Teacher Education at Michigan State University. She is author and coauthor of a range of publications including an elementary social studies textbook series, a social studies methods text, and numerous journal articles. Dr. Alleman has been a contributor to the Stanford Achievement Tests and a consultant to the Educational Testing Service. She has served as the chair for the National Council for the Social Studies Testing Committee and currently is a member of the NCSS Committee for Advanced Certification of Social Studies Teachers. She is on the Advisory Board for the Elemtary Section of *Social Education,* and a consultant for Harcourt Brace on elementary social studies. Dr. Alleman is a member of the State Social Studies Framework Committee and recently has been appointed by the State Superintendent to become a member of the Michigan Curriculum Frameworks Joint Steering Committee. She has been a classroom and television teacher, actively works in school settings, and has taught at over a dozen international sites.

PREFACE

This book is intended for preservice and inservice elementary teachers and for social studies teacher educators. It offers a perspective on the nature and functions of elementary social studies, then presents principles and illustrative examples designed to help teachers plan social studies instruction that is coherently organized and powerful in producing desired student outcomes. It is not a conventional methods text that surveys a broad range of topics. Instead, it treats in depth selected issues that we consider crucial for teachers to work through if they are to develop powerful social studies programs in their classrooms.

The book is designed to accomplish two primary purposes. First, we seek to help elementary teachers develop a clear sense of social studies as a coherent school subject organized to accomplish social understanding and civic efficacy goals. Teachers need to understand the nature and purposes of social studies in order to plan and teach the subject effectively. Second, we seek to prepare elementary teachers to identify significant social education goals that are appropriate for their students and then use these goals to guide them in selecting content, developing it through classroom discourse, and using it in authentic application activities. To illustrate the applications of our suggested guidelines, we have included extended examples in the form of detailed plans for topically organized curricular units structured around powerful ideas. In addition, the book addresses issues of assessment and curricular integration as they apply to social studies teaching, and it suggests ways to encourage classes of students to begin to function as learning communities engaged in the social construction of knowledge.

To date, elementary social studies has not received much scholarly attention. Most of the work done so far has involved surveying teaching practices, criticizing instructional materials, or suggesting substitutions for the expanding communities scope and sequence that has become the de facto national curriculum. The principles elaborated in this book reflect our positions on the key issues addressed in this scholarly literature.

Although we recognize several problems with the expanding communities framework, we believe that it has endured, despite many attacks, because it incorporates better content choices for introducing elementary students to social studies than do the alternatives proposed by its critics. Consequently, we believe that the best way to improve elementary social studies is to build on the strengths and eliminate the weaknesses of the expanding communities framework, rather than replace it with something else. The strengths of this framework do not lie primarily in the "expansion" sequencing that has received so much attention (i.e., starting with the child in the here and now and gradually moving backward in time and outward in space). Instead, the strengths of the expanding communities framework lie in the topics that provide the basis for curriculum units.

In particular, universal human needs and social experiences (food, clothing, shelter, families, communities, government, transportation, communication, occupations, recreation, etc.) are ideal topics for units intended to introduce children to social studies. These topics represent the most fundamental and universal categories of social experience, and topic-focused curriculum units provide a basis for instruction that elementary students can understand and appreciate. Consequently, elementary social studies teaching will be made more powerful by continuing to address most of the same general topics that have been addressed traditionally, but doing so in ways that feature more consistent focus on key social studies goals and greater coherence in structuring the teaching around powerful ideas that students can apply in their lives outside of school. This involves retaining most features of the expanding communities framework, but shifting the focus of instructional planning from the expanding communities sequencing scheme to the key ideas involved in introducing children to the fundamentals of human social experience.

Our approach will appeal to elementary teachers for three reasons. First, it respects the limitations in elementary students' cognitive capacities and prior knowledge, so it avoids advocating premature instruction in abstract concepts. It emphasizes curricular power and coherence within developmentally appropriate content and teaching methods. Second, it takes the social understanding and civic efficacy goals of social studies seriously, but it interprets and applies them in ways suited to the needs of elementary-grade children. Third, it avoids ill-considered notions about junking the elementary social studies curriculum and replacing it with a mixture of history, myth, lore, and fable. Instead, it calls for retaining the most important topics that have been emphasized traditionally (for good reason), and for teaching about these topics in more coherent and powerful ways. The overall goal is to help students to understand how the social system works, how and why it got to be that way, how it varies across locations and cultures, and what this may mean for personal, social, and civic decision making.

Our book reflects recent classroom research on teaching school subjects for understanding, appreciation, and application. It also reflects recent position statements by the National Council for the Social Studies concerning the purposes and goals of social studies as a school subject and the principles involved in teaching it with coherence and power. Finally, although it deals in depth with fundamental issues, the book casts teachers in the role of key decision makers in planning, implementing, and assessing powerful social studies instruction. We encourage teachers to be proactive in identifying suitable social studies goals for their students, in adapting or supplementing the content, questions, and activities that their textbook series offer, and in exploiting local resources (including students' home cultures and personal experiences) as sources of content and sites for application of social studies learning. Our intention is that teachers who study this book thoughtfully will emerge from it with clear conceptions of the nature and purposes of social studies and usable knowledge about how to plan their social studies teaching with social understanding and civic efficacy goals in mind.

ACKNOWLEDGMENTS

This book was completed in part while Jere Brophy was on sabbatical leave from Michigan State University and in residence as a Fellow at the Center for Advanced Study in the Behavioral Sciences. He wishes to thank both of these institutions for their financial support during that sabbatical year. In addition, he wishes to thank the Spencer Foundation, which provided part of the funds for the support he received through the Center for Advanced Study in the Behavioral Sciences.

Some of the research that led to the writing of this book was done under the auspices of the Center for the Learning and Teaching of Elementary Subjects, located in the College of Education at Michigan State University. That center was funded primarily by the Office of Educational Research and Improvement, U.S. Department of Education. Author Brophy wishes to express his appreciation for this support, and also to note that opinions expressed in this publication do not necessarily reflect the position, policy, or endorsement of the Office or Department.

Both authors wish to thank the colleagues, students, and teachers who have collaborated with our work and enriched our understanding of social studies. In particular, we want to express our appreciation to Donna Anderson, Ruth Bell, Nancy Bredin, Jan Paul, Laura Docter Thornburg, and Bruce VanSledright.

Finally, we wish to express our appreciation to June Benson, who has been our secretary throughout our collaborations in social studies scholarship and research. June has made enormous contributions to our work, not only by consistently handling manuscript preparation and other normal secretarial tasks with efficiency and good humor, but in addition by producing remarkably complete and accurate transcriptions of our observational field notes and our interviews with teachers and students. She has made our work both easier and better, and we are most grateful for her help.

CONTENTS

Chapter 7

Social Studies in the Intermediate Grades   111

Chapter 8

Building a Learning Community in Your Classroom   137

Chapter 9

Chapter 10

Part Three: Representative Unit Plans   173

Chapter 11

PART ONE

Issues and Problems in Elementary Social Studies

Chapter 1
ELEMENTARY SOCIAL STUDIES: WHAT IS IT? WHAT MIGHT IT BECOME?

Chapter 2
LIMITATIONS OF TEXTBOOK SERIES AS PRIMARY BASES FOR
SOCIAL STUDIES CURRICULA

Serious concerns and dissatisfactions have been expressed about elementary social studies curriculum and instruction. Some of the concerns are rooted in fundamental disagreements about what should be the primary goals and content emphases in the subject, especially in the primary grades. Much of the dissatisfaction is focused on the elementary social studies series offered by the major publishers. Complaints focus not just on the parade-of-facts content in the textbooks but also on the reading/recitation/seatwork/test curriculum that results when teachers depend heavily on these textbooks not only for content but also for suggestions about questions to use as a basis for structuring classroom discourse, learning activities and assignments, and assessment methods.

These issues and problems are introduced in Chapter 1 and then exemplified in Chapter 2 through a case study of a popular elementary social studies series. By bringing to your attention the major issues involved in controversies about the purposes and goals of elementary social studies as a school subject, and by alerting you to the limitations of elementary social studies series as bases for curriculum and instruction, the chapters of Part One underscore the need for you to clarify and prioritize the goals of your social studies teaching and use these goals to guide your planning of social studies curriculum, instruction, and assessment.

Chapter 1

ELEMENTARY SOCIAL STUDIES: WHAT IS IT? WHAT MIGHT IT BECOME?

Social studies is the hardest thing you could ever ask me to explain. I guess social studies is a class where you learn about different things that happen around the world, and do reports on stuff that happens around the world, or things like that.

—A FIFTH GRADER QUOTED BY STODOLSKY, SALK, & GLAESSNER, 1981, P. 98

My general approach is to introduce geographic ideas to lay a foundation—create a sense of what geography is that can be built on later. The students also work on self, family, and Michigan awareness (during Michigan Week). Other than that, though, social studies is basically geography. Another part is teaching students to get along with one another and fulfill the student role. My emphasis is on centers and hands-on activities. The room includes a "mystery country of the week" bulletin board that features a map, photos, and artifacts (stamps, coins, flags, etc.) from the mystery country that students can use as clues to guess what the country is by the end of the week. Around the room are posters of international flags and a variety of different types and sizes of flags, globes, and maps. Students each have pretend passports that gradually get filled up as they "visit" each mystery country.

—A FIRST-GRADE TEACHER

My approach follows district policy. The content focuses on map skills, self, families, and communities. There is a unit on Native Americans of the region and on feelings and autobiography (linked with language arts, in which students write their own biographies). The emphasis is on commonalities among people and the acceptance of different cultures in food, shelter, family life, affection, and learning. We also talk about famous Americans throughout the year and discuss current events each morning. Social studies is not what is in books, but what is all around you. You have to be aware of that and share it with the children. I couldn't come in here and teach without doing the news. That is what life is all about and what the children are talking about.

—A SECOND-GRADE TEACHER

Social studies is people in the community, the world, living with each other, working with and learning about each other. It is also a sense of how history plays a part in the present and future. It is more than just helping students to understand a map or differences in language; it needs to be made real to students, something they become actively involved with and can apply to their lives. I have found that if I keep my students involved and thinking, I can make it meaningful to them. For example, some aren't much interested in government or how it influences them, but if you talk about laws that affect them personally, you can make it real to them.

—A THIRD-GRADE TEACHER

Social studies is taught for knowledge and awareness of the society, the world, and its geographical and physical makeup. It's the world that students live in. It's their life. This includes getting along with others that you interact with socially, as well as history (you bring all of your background with you into your social interactions). Another aspect is awareness and acceptance of other cultures. This starts at the grass-roots level—acceptance of one another. Then it can go out to acceptance of different cultures. Also, environmental awareness, not only of geography and land forms but environmentally safe practices and conservation. There is all of the history that I teach too, but that is just part of social studies.

—A FIFTH-GRADE TEACHER

As these quotations illustrate, elementary school teachers and students often are confused about the nature of social studies as a school subject. Lacking a clear sense of social education purposes and goals, many teachers are uncertain about how to teach social studies (Thornton, 1991). Often they downgrade its importance in the curriculum or offer fragmented programs because they select activities for convenience or student interest rather than for their value as means of accomplishing clearly formulated social education goals.

Such confusion is readily understandable. The history of social studies has been marked by ongoing debates over the nature, scope, and definition of the field (Lybarger, 1991). Curriculum developers disagree both on the general purposes of social studies and on how to accomplish particular goals effectively. Consequently, social studies instructional materials differ considerably, not only in the general kinds of content included (history, geography, etc.), but also in their approach to topics covered in common (which tribes are covered in units on Native Americans, which countries in units on geographical regions, etc.).

Fortunately, however, most competing points of view can be understood as combinations of a few basic ideas about the purposes and goals of social education. Once teachers understand these ideas, they can clarify their own positions, recognize the thinking behind social studies curriculum guides and instructional materials prepared by others, and if necessary adapt them to better serve their students' social studies needs.

COMPETING VISIONS OF SOCIAL STUDIES AS CITIZEN EDUCATION

The emergence of social studies as an interdisciplinary school subject is often credited to an influential committee report issued by the National Education Association (1916), although the term "social studies" and the key ideas advocated in the report have been traced to earlier sources (Saxe, 1991). The 1916 report called for establishing a curriculum strand to be called "social studies." Social education would be its primary purpose, its content would be informed by history and several social science disciplines, and selection of this content would be based on its personal meaning and relevance to students and its value in preparing them for citizenship. These same themes are still emphasized today by leading social studies educators and organizations. For example, the National Council for the Social Studies (NCSS) recently defined social studies as "the integrated study of the social sciences and humanities to promote civic competence." It added that "the primary purpose of social studies is to help young people develop the ability to make informed and reasoned decisions for the public good as citizens of a culturally diverse, democratic society in an interdependent world" (NCSS, 1993, p. 3).

Elementary social studies (Grades K–6) did in fact develop along the lines envisioned in the 1916 report. The curriculum drew from history, geography, civics, and economics, and later from sociology, anthropology, and psychology. Furthermore, the content was taught as interdisciplinary social studies organized by topic, rather than as school-subject versions of the academic disciplines taught as separate courses. Gradually, the *expanding communities* approach became the dominant framework for structuring the elementary social studies curriculum. Also known as the expanding horizons or the expanding environments approach, this framework begins with the self and then gradually expands the purview to the family and school, the neighborhood, the community, the state, the nation, and the world.

Secondary social studies courses (Grades 7–12) also are taught within a social studies curriculum strand that includes responsibility for preparing students for citizenship. However, most secondary courses are school-subject versions of history or one of the social sciences, in which content is addressed primarily within the single discipline rather than through interdisciplinary treatment of topics. There have been exceptions to this general trend: Contemporary ones include courses in law-related education, global education, environmental studies, or conflict resolution. Past exceptions have included minicourses on a variety of topics and a twelfth-grade Problems of Democracy course intended as a capstone for K–12 citizenship preparation. For the most part, though, secondary social studies courses have featured titles such as U.S. History, Economics, or American Government.

Most social educators accept the idea that social studies bears a special responsibility for citizen education, but their visions of the ideal curriculum conflict because they differ in their definitions of citizen education and in their assumptions about how to accomplish it (Martorella, 1994). Some of these disagreements are linked to curricular tensions observable in all school subjects, some reflect issues that are especially salient to social studies, and some reflect competition for curriculum space among disciplinary and special interest groups.

Kliebard (1987) noted that curriculum debates in all school subjects reflect continuing struggle among supporters of four competing ideas about what should be the primary basis for K–12 education. The first group believes that schools should equip students with knowledge that is lasting, important, and fundamental to the human experience. This group typically looks to the academic disciplines, both as storehouses of important knowledge and as sources of authority about how this knowledge should be organized and taught. The second group believes that the natural course of child development should be the basis for curriculum planning. This group would key the content taught at each grade level to the interests and learning needs associated with its corresponding ages and stages. The third group works backwards from its perceptions of society's needs, seeking to design schooling to prepare children to fulfill adult roles in the society. Finally, the fourth group seeks to use the schools to combat social injustice and promote social change. Consequently, it favors focusing curriculum and instruction around social policy issues. Many past and present curricular debates in social studies can be understood as aspects of the ongoing competition among these four general approaches to K–12 curriculum development.

In addition to these varied approaches to curriculum development, social studies scholars have identified several competing approaches to teaching social studies. Barr, Barth, and Shermis (1977) identified three main traditions:

1. Teaching social studies as *citizenship transmission*, with emphasis on inculcating traditional values
2. Teaching social studies as *social science*, with emphasis on disciplinary knowledge and data-gathering skills
3. Teaching social studies as *reflective inquiry*, with emphasis on analyzing values and making decisions about social and civic issues

Research using this Three Traditions model indicates that most teachers are eclectics rather than pure types. However, understanding the priorities that teachers favor helps us to understand and predict what they do in the classroom (Stanley, 1985).

Haas (1979) elaborated on the Three Traditions and placed them into historical context. He noted that citizenship transmission has always been the mainstream approach in the elementary grades. It features support for the status quo, emphasis on the development of Western civilization, and uncritical celebration of and inculcation in American political values and traditions.

Periodically, the citizenship transmission approach is challenged by two reform approaches. Calls for one type of reform typically come from academic historians and social scientists who want more organization of curricula around conceptual structures drawn from the disciplines, more and better coverage of disciplinary content, and more preservation of the integrity of the separate disciplines in the form of separate courses. The other recurring reform position calls for an emphasis on the process of thinking reflectively. Rooted in the ideas of John Dewey, this approach is associated with discussions of problems and issues that feature critical thinking, values analysis, and decision making.

Martorella (1994) argued that both the evolution of social studies over time and the differences in current curricula can be understood in terms of differences in emphasis on five approaches (including the Three Traditions already described). All of these approaches agree that citizen education should be the major focus of social studies, but they differ in their perspectives on citizen education and their descriptions of how it should be played out in classrooms.

The contrasting emphases in the Three Traditions and in Martorella's five approaches to social studies indicate that reasonable people will disagree about what is needed to prepare students for current and future citizenship. However, the two lists also contain many commonalities that indicate that most of the diversity observable in social studies is not random or chaotic. Instead, it results from competition among well-understood alternative interpretations of its citizen education mission. To prepare yourself to make good social studies planning decisions, you will need to clarify your own priorities concerning social education purposes and goals and their implications for your social studies teaching.

PERSPECTIVE	DESCRIPTION
Social Studies Should Be Taught as:	**Citizenship Education Should Consist of:**
1. Transmission of the cultural heritage	Transmitting traditional knowledge and values as a framework for making decisions
2. Social science	Mastering social science concepts, generalizations, and processes to build a knowledge base for later learning
3. Reflective inquiry	Employing a process of thinking and learning in which knowledge is derived from what citizens need to know in order to make decisions and solve problems
4. Informed social criticism	Providing opportunities for an examination, critique, and revision of past traditions, existing social practices, and modes of problem solving
5. Personal development	Developing a positive self-concept and a strong sense of personal efficacy

CURRENT SOCIAL STUDIES ISSUES AND DEBATES

In addition to continuing competition among alternative positions on social education purposes and goals, current curricular debates reflect renewed competition among the disciplines for curricular "air time." Recently, organizations representing history and the social sciences have begun to issue policy statements concerning how their respective disciplines should be represented and taught in K–12 social studies. Economics educators produced a framework for teaching economics that outlines basic concepts to emphasize (Saunders et al., 1984) and a set of scope-and-sequence guidelines based on this framework (Gilliard et al., 1988). Associations representing geographers and geographic educators identified five main themes to emphasize in teaching geography (Joint Committee on Geographic Education, 1984) and subsequently published more detailed guidelines and suggested activities for developing these themes (Geographic Education National Implementation Project, 1987, 1989; Stoltman, 1990). The Center for Civic Education (1991) published the *CIVITAS* document suggesting reforms in civic education. It emphasizes knowledge of law and political processes, examination of public issues, and involvement of students in civic participation activities. Finally, the National Center for History in the Schools (1994a, 1994b, 1994c) produced three documents suggesting opportunity-to-learn standards for history teaching: one on history for Grades 1–4, one on U.S. history for Grades 5–12, and one on world history for Grades 5–12.

These statements from disciplinary groups contain helpful summaries of powerful ideas and suggestions about teaching methods and activities. However, they also imply that their disciplines ought to be taught much more extensively than they are now. In building a positive case for their disciplines, the authors of these statements usually do not address the question of what might be reduced in the curriculum if space for their disciplines were to be increased. Sometimes, however, they attack the educational value of rival disciplines, at least as they are currently represented in typical instructional materials.

Advocates of history have been especially prone to attack other disciplines, which they believe have supplanted history as the core of the social studies curriculum. History-oriented reform proposals call for a return to a social studies curriculum centered on history and supported by geography and civics. Social science content would be included within history courses. Advocates argue that history is the naturally integrative focal point for social studies instruction because it allows for comprehensive coverage of each topic— including not only historical aspects but also geographical, civic, cultural, economic, and social aspects. Reform models based on these ideas include the Bradley Commission's (1988) *Historical Literacy: The Case for History in American Education* and the curriculum guidelines for history and social science teaching published by the California State Department of Education (1988).

History-centered reform proposals have not been received warmly by social studies opinion leaders and professional organizations. Part of the conflict involves disciplinary turf protection: The social sciences do not want to cede curricular air time to history. In addition, social scientists argue that their disciplines offer important insights about how the social world functions that all citizens ought to understand and be able to bring to bear in their civic decision making. Some of them also disparage the value of history as a basis for citizen education, arguing that knowledge about the past has limited application to the complexities of the contemporary world (Engle & Ochoa, 1988; Evans, 1989; Thornton, 1990).

Social studies scholars also fault history-centered reform proposals for embodying an overly traditional knowledge- and values-transmission approach to citizen education. These critics would like to see social studies curricula be more global and multicultural in purview, more critical of traditions, and more focused on current and future issues than on the past. Fairly or not, many social studies educators view history-centered proposals as products of a politically conservative philosophy of schooling that emphasizes inculcation over education.

For the most part, the arguments and curriculum ideas advanced in reform proposals issued by discipline-based organizations and special commissions are focused on the secondary grades. They do not say much about elementary social studies, and especially not about the primary grades. However, one important exeception involves opposition to the expanding communities sequencing framework, especially in history-centered reform proposals.

The Expanding Communities Framework

Textbook publishers and elementary teachers traditionally have relied on the expanding communities framework for organizing the social studies curriculum. This framework and the content scope and sequence associated with it have become almost universal in U.S. schools, to the point that Naylor and Diem (1987) called it the de facto national curriculum. The following topics are typically addressed in K–6 social studies programs:

Kindergarten: Self, home, school, community. Discovering myself (Who am I? How am I alike and different from others?), school (my classroom, benefits of school), working together, living at home, community helpers, children in other lands, rules, and celebrating holidays.

Grade One: Families. Family membership, recreation, work, cooperation, traditions, families in other cultures, how my family is alike and different from others, family responsibilities, the family at work, our school and other schools, and national holidays.

Grade Two: Neighborhoods. Workers and services in the neighborhood; food, shelter, and clothing; transportation; communication; living in different neighborhoods; my role within the neighborhood; neighborhoods and communities in other cultures; farm and city life; and protecting our environment.

Grade Three: Communities. Communities past and present, different kinds of communities, changes in communities, community government and services, communities in other countries, cities, careers, urban problems, business and industry, and pioneers and American Indians.

Grade Four: Geographic regions. World regions, people of the world, climatic regions, physical regions, population, food. Also, *state studies.* Our state government, state history, people of our state, state laws, state workers, communities past and present. (Note: K–6 or K–8 social studies series typically cover geographic regions in their fourth-grade texts. However, local districts often omit purchase or minimize use of these texts and instead mandate that fourth grade be devoted to study of the state, using locally produced materials.)

Grade Five: U.S. history and geography. The first Americans, exploration and discovery, colonial life, revolution and independence, westward movement, the American Civil War, immigrants, the Roaring 20s, lifestyles in the United States, values of the American people, and the United States as world power. Some fifth-grade texts also include units on U.S. regions, Canada, and Mexico.

Grade Six: World cultures/hemispheres. Political and economic systems, land and resources, people and their beliefs, comparative cultures. Western hemisphere: Early cultures of South America, the major contemporary South American countries, Central American countries, Canada, Mexico, historical beginnings of the Western world. Eastern hemisphere: Ancient Greece and Rome, Middle Ages, Renaissance, Middle East, Europe, Africa, India, and China.

Content is drawn from various sources and blended to center on each unit's topic rather than organized according to the separate disciplines. The basic framework can accommodate most emerging topics (environmentalism, multicultural education, etc.), and it can be taught with very different mixtures of the five emphases described by Martorella (1994). It also can be taught with different degrees of emphasis on across-subjects integration, causal explanation, life applications, and associated skills and dispositions.

Hanna (1963) rationalized the expanding communities approach as being both *logical* in starting with the family and then moving outward toward progressively wider human communities and *convenient* in allowing for a holistic, coordinated approach to the study of people living in societies. He recommended that students study the ways in which people in each community carry out basic activities such as providing for their physical needs, transporting goods and people, communicating with one another, and governing their societies.

Children begin by studying small, familiar communities and then study the same issues in larger, less familiar communities. If implemented as Hanna envisioned, the expanding communities curriculum would produce systematic social studies instruction structured around powerful ideas. However, elementary social studies texts have been criticized as ill-structured collections of factual expositions and skills exercises that follow the letter but not the spirit of Hanna's recommendations.

Much of this criticism has been directed at the expanding communities framework itself. Some critics claim that primary-grade children are interested in stories about heroes, the exotic, and the "long ago and far away," so that primary curricula should concentrate on these topics rather than on familiar aspects of the family, neighborhood, and community (Egan, 1988; Ravitch, 1987). Others who want students to develop a global rather than a more narrow American purview note that television now brings non-Western lands and cultures into the home early, so that if one waits until the sixth grade to begin teaching world geography and cultures with an emphasis on human commonalities, it may be too late to overcome ethnocentrism that has developed in the meantime (Mitsakos, 1978).

Expanding communities curricula also have been criticized for being too age-grade oriented; being too traditional and middle-class oriented in their treatment of families and communities; being sequenced according to adult rather than child logic (e.g., a state is just as abstract a concept as a nation, so there is no reason why children must study the state before studying the nation); being too fragmented so that students do not get to see relationships that exist across communities; and failing to integrate skills instruction with instruction in content (Joyce & Alleman-Brooks, 1982; Naylor & Diem, 1987). Yet the expanding communities approach remains entrenched. It is familiar to teachers and so far has proven adaptable enough to incorporate new content and respond to common criticisms without changing its basic structure.

SUGGESTIONS FOR REFORM OF ELEMENTARY SOCIAL STUDIES

Whether or not the expanding communities sequence is identified as the culprit, there is widespread dissatisfaction with the curriculum content and instructional materials associated with this framework, especially in the primary grades. Surveys of teaching practices indicate that social studies is taught irregularly in Grades K–3 (Atwood, 1986), and critiques of instructional materials indicate that its content is not driven by coherent social education goals. As we will explain in detail in Chapter 2, there is broad agreement that (1) the content base of K–3 social studies is thin and redundant, and (2) most of this content as presented in the textbooks is trite, uninteresting, and either already known by students or likely to be learned through everyday experience (and thus not worth teaching in school).

A major reason for these problems is that the textbook series fail to articulate K–3 social studies as a coherent subject designed to develop connected sets of fundamental understandings about the social world and to move students toward clearly identified social education goals. As a result, most elementary teachers view (and teach) social studies as a collection of disconnected content and skill clusters, rather than as a coherent goals-driven curriculum composed of connected networks of knowledge, skills, values, and dispositions to action. These concerns have led to calls for more substantive and coherently organized content for elementary social studies. Most of the suggested reforms are variations on three basic types. We will review these briefly before outlining the direction that we advocate pursuing.

Reforms Suggested by Others

E. D. Hirsch Jr. (1987) and others have proposed *cultural literacy* as the basis for developing curricula for social studies (and other subjects). The early grades would be devoted to teaching traditional cultural knowledge and related values and dispositions to equip students with a common base of prior knowledge to inform their social and civic decision making. We agree with the need for a shared common culture, but we also agree with critics of Hirsch who view his lists of ostensibly important knowledge as dubiously extensive and detailed. Furthermore, because they are long lists of specifics, they lead to teaching that emphasizes breadth of coverage of disconnected details over depth of development of networks of connected knowledge structured around powerful ideas. Hirsch's ideas conflict with an emerging consensus (Brophy, 1992) about what is involved in teaching school subjects for understanding, appreciation, and life application (i.e., structuring content around powerful ideas developed in sufficient depth to ensure understanding of their meanings and connections, appreciation of their significance, and the ability to access and use them in appropriate application situations; teacher–student discourse patterns that feature reflective discussion rather than drill and recitation; and activities and assignments that feature authentic applications of what is learned rather simple recall of facts).

A second approach to reform is advocated by proponents of the *academic disciplines* that underlie social studies. These critics favor abandoning social studies as a subject designed to pursue citizen education goals using integrated content. Instead, they would offer separate courses in the academic disciplines, simplified as needed but designed to pursue the goals of history and the social sciences rather than the goals of citizenship education. This was the approach taken by "structures of the disciplines" advocates who developed the "new social studies" programs in the 1960s and 1970s. These programs never caught on in the schools for a variety of reasons, including the perceptions that they were not effective for addressing broad citizenship education goals and that they focused young children on relatively narrow and specialized disciplinary concerns prematurely, before they had acquired a basic social education.

More recently, Kieran Egan (1988), Diane Ravitch (1987), and others have advocated a variation of this approach that calls for replacing the expanding communities content of the early social studies curriculum with a heavy focus on history and related children's literature (not only historical fiction but myths and folk tales). However, although K–3 children can and should learn certain aspects of history, they also need a balanced and integrated social education curriculum that includes sufficient attention to powerful ideas drawn not only from history but from the various social sciences. Consequently, their social education needs are not well served by replacing most social science content with history content.

Certain forms of children's literature (e.g., historical fiction, stories of life in other cultures) are useful social education tools, but little social education value exists in replacing reality-based social studies with myths and folklore. Whatever value the study of myth and folklore may have will be realized primarily within the language arts curriculum. Allocating significant social studies time to myths, folklore, and most other forms of children's literature amounts to an extension of the language arts curriculum at the expense of a coherent social studies curriculum focused on citizen education goals. Furthermore, proponents of this approach have made no attempts to test it empirically, and exemplary elementary teachers whom we have interviewed do not favor it (Brophy & VanSledright, 1993). Finally, analyses of curriculum guidelines (California's History and Social Science Framework) and textbooks (the 1991 Houghton Mifflin elementary social studies series) that are based on the history/literature approach have identified some important problems with it (Alleman & Brophy, 1994).

A third approach to reform has been suggested by Shirley Engle, Anna Ochoa, and others who believe that social studies should deemphasize providing students with information and instead engage them in inquiry and debate about *social policy issues* (Engle & Ochoa, 1988; Evans, 1989). Critical thinking, decision making, and other higher-order applications should be emphasized in teaching social studies at all grade levels, but a heavy concentration on inquiry and debate about social policy issues is premature for K–3 students. They do not yet have systematic knowledge about how and why the social system evolved to function in its present form.

The Approach That We Recommend

Reforms are needed in at least the K–3 portion of the elementary social studies curriculum; much of the content taught in those grades is trite, redundant, and unlikely to help students achieve significant social education goals. However, the problem lies not with the topics addressed within the expanding communities framework, but with the way these topics have been taught. Many of these topics—families, communities, food, clothing, shelter, government, occupations, transportation, and communication, among others—provide a sound basis for developing fundamental understandings about the human condition. They tend to be *cultural universals*—basic human needs and social experiences found in all societies, past and present. If these topics are taught with appropriate focus on powerful ideas, students will develop a basic set of connected understandings of how the social system works, how and why it got to be that way over time, how and why it varies across locations and cultures, and what all of this might mean for personal, social, and civic decision making. Part Two of this book explores these ideas.

First, Chapter 2 illustrates in detail the problems with contemporary social studies textbook series. If you are not already familiar with elementary social studies series, you may find Chapter 2 to be quite surprising. In any case, you certainly will find it to be depressing. You need to understand the scope of the problems with elementary social studies series, however, in order to fully appreciate and be prepared to act upon this book's suggestions for rectifying these problems.

YOUR TURN: WHAT IS SOCIAL STUDIES?

For most people, trying to put together a large jigsaw puzzle without having any idea of what the finished product should look like would be a pretty frustrating experience. For many children, social studies lessons are like puzzle pieces that are examined individually but never connected to a big picture. These children experience years of content and learning opportunities without ever understanding, appreciating, or applying social studies. Students rarely can articulate why social studies is important and how it impacts their lives.

As a teacher, prepare lessons depicting the picture on the puzzle box—your vision of social studies. When planning your lesson(s), consider the following elements drawn from this chapter:

- Social studies is an interdisciplinary subject.
- Social studies bears a special responsibility for citizenship education.
- Social studies tends to be presented using the expanding communities model.

There are many approaches to social studies, including:

1. Teaching social studies as citizenship transmission
2. Teaching social studies as a social science with emphasis on disciplinary knowledge and data-gathering skills
3. Teaching social studies as reflective inquiry with emphasis on analyzing values and making decisions about social and civic issues
4. Teaching social studies as informed social criticism with emphasis on opportunities for examination, critique, and revision of past traditions, existing social practices, and methods of problem solving
5. Teaching social studies as personal development with emphasis on a positive self-concept and a strong sense of personal efficacy

Given your beliefs about the purposes of schooling, select one or more of these approaches and develop life examples that are age- and context-appropriate to illustrate how you will teach your students. Use *specific* content examples and instructional strategies to illustrate your teaching.

One teacher whom we have observed does a remarkable job of helping students see what social studies is all about. Using maps, charts, cultural artifacts, real-life problems, historical documents, and so on, she explains how the class will come to make sense out of these as a part of life's story. Analyzing this information and the values connected to it, the class will make informed decisions about geographic, social, historical, civic, and other issues that impact their lives now and in the future.

Another teacher connects content examples with student projects from the previous grade and spends time reflecting on the content covered and insights acquired, then begins showing how those prior experiences are connected to this year's social studies curriculum. At the end of the year, the students are interviewed by the next-level teacher about what they have learned and the teacher helps them begin to form links with the social studies subject matter that will be addressed next year.

After you have carefully planned your approach on paper, collect visuals to illustrate your key points. Share your plan with a peer and elicit feedback. Remember, to excite students about social studies, engage all five senses, if possible: Use more than just words! Knowing what the picture on the puzzle box will look like—at least in broad terms—will go a long way toward creating a desire to participate in making sense of it. *Special note*: *People*, a book written and illustrated by Peter Spier, published by Delacorte Press (1980), is an excellent resource for planning your "big picture" presentation.

REFERENCES

Alleman, J., & Brophy, J. (1994). Trade-offs embedded in the literary approach to early elementary social studies. *Social Studies and the Young Learner, 6* (3), 6-8.

Atwood, V. (1986). Elementary social studies: Cornerstone or crumbling mortar? In V. Atwood (Ed.), *Elementary school social studies: Research as a guide to practice* (Bulletin No. 79; pp. 1-13). Washington, DC: National Council for the Social Studies.

Barr, R., Barth, J., & Shermis, S. (1977). *Defining the social studies.* Arlington, VA: National Council for the Social Studies.

Bradley Commission on History in Schools. (1988). *Building a history curriculum: Guidelines for teaching history in schools.* Washington, DC: Educational Excellence Network.

Brophy, J. (1992). Probing the subtleties of subject-matter teaching. *Educational Leadership, 49* (7), 4-8.

Brophy, J., McMahon, S., & Prawat, R. (1991). Elementary social studies series: Critique of a representative example by six experts. *Social Education, 55*, 155-160.

Brophy, J., & VanSledright, B. (1993). *Exemplary elementary teachers' beliefs about social studies curriculum and instruction* (Elementary Subjects Center Series No. 93). East Lansing: Michigan State University, Institute for Research on Teaching, Center for the Learning and Teaching of Elementary Subjects.

California State Department of Education. (1988). *History-social science framework for California public schools kindergarten through grade 12.* Sacramento: Author.

Center for Civic Education. (1991). *Civitas: A framework for civic education* (Bulletin No. 86). Washington, DC: National Council for the Social Studies.

Egan, K. (1988). *Primary understanding: Education in early childhood.* New York: Routledge.

Engle, S., & Ochoa, A. (1988). *Education for democratic citizenship: Decision making in the social studies.* New York: Teachers College Press.

Evans, R. (1989). A dream unrealized: A brief look at the history of issue-centered approaches. *The Social Studies, 80,* 178-184.

Geographic Education National Implementation Project. (1987). *K-6 geography: Themes, key ideas, and learning opportunities.* Skokie, IL: Rand McNally.

Gilliard, J., Caldwell, J., Dalgaard, B., Reinke, R., & Watts, M. (1988). *Economics: What and when: Scope and sequence guidelines, K-12.* New York: Joint Council on Economic Education.

Haas, J. (1979). Social studies: Where have we been? Where are we going? *Social Studies, 70,* 147-154.

Hanna, P. (1963). Revising the social studies: What is needed? *Social Education, 27,* 190-196.

Hirsch, Jr., E. D. (1987). *Cultural literacy: What every American needs to know.* New York: Houghton Mifflin.

Joint Committee on Geographic Education. (1984). *Guidelines for geographic education: Elementary and secondary schools.* Washington, DC: Association of American Geographers and National Council for Geographic Education.

Joyce, W., & Alleman-Brooks, J. (1982). The child's world. *Social Education, 46,* 538-541.

Kliebard, H. (1987). *The struggle for the American curriculum 1893-1958.* New York: Routledge and Kegan-Paul.

Lybarger, M. (1991). The historiography of social studies: Retrospect, circumspect, and prospect. In J. Shaver (Ed.), *Handbook of research on social studies teaching and learning* (pp. 3-15). New York: Macmillan

Martorella, P. (1994). *Social studies for elementary school children: Developing young citizens.* New York: Macmillan.

Mitsakos, C. (1978). A global education program can make a difference. *Theory and Research in Social Education, 6* (1), 1-15.

National Center for History in the Schools. (1994a). *National standards for history: Expanding children's world in time and space* (Grades K-4 expanded edition). Los Angeles: University of California, Los Angeles.

National Center for History in the Schools. (1994b). *National standards for United States history: Exploring the American experience* (Grades 5-12 expanded edition). Los Angeles: University of California, Los Angeles.

National Center for History in the Schools. (1994c). *National standards for world history: Exploring paths to the present* (Grades 5-12 expanded edition). Los Angeles: University of California, Los Angeles.

National Council for the Social Studies (NCSS). (1993, Jan-Feb.) *The social studies professional.* Washington, DC: Author.

National Education Association. (1916). *Social studies in secondary education: A six-year program adapted to the 6-3-3 and the 8-4 plans of organization.* (Bulletin No. 28). Washington DC: U.S. Department of the Interior, Bureau of Education.

Naylor, D., & Diem, R. (1987). *Elementary and middle school social studies.* New York: Random House.

Ravitch, D. (1987). Tot sociology or what happened to history in the grade schools. *American Scholar, 56,* 343-353.

Saunders, P., Bach, G., Calderwood, J., & Hansen, W. (1984). *A framework for teaching economics: Basic concepts* (2nd ed.). New York: Joint Council on Economic Education.

Saxe, D. (1991). *Social studies in schools: A history of the early years*. Albany: State University of New York Press.

Stanley, W. (1985). Recent research in the foundations of social education: 1976–1983. In W. Stanley (Ed.), *Review of research in social studies education: 1976–1983* (pp. 309–399). Washington, DC: National Council for the Social Studies.

Stodolsky, S., Salk, S., & Glaessner, B. (1991). Student views about learning math and social studies. *American Educational Research Journal, 28*, 89–116.

Stoltman, J. (1990). *Geography education for citizenship*. Bloomington, IN: ERIC Clearinghouse for Social Studies/Social Science Education.

Thornton, S. (1991). Teacher as curricular-instructional gatekeeper in social studies. In J. Shaver (Ed.), *Handbook of research on social studies teaching and learning* (pp. 237–248). New York: Macmillan.

Chapter 2

LIMITATIONS OF TEXTBOOK SERIES AS PRIMARY BASES FOR SOCIAL STUDIES CURRICULA

In Chapter 1, we noted that few elementary teachers have developed well-articulated positions on social studies purposes and goals that they can use to guide their curriculum planning. Instead, they tend to rely on local tradition and the curriculum materials supplied by the major publishers (Mehlinger, 1981; Shaver, 1987; Thornton, 1991). Local tradition may be quite helpful to teachers who work in districts that have developed detailed social studies curriculum guides, especially if these are supplemented by collections of specialized instructional materials (such as kits containing children's literature selections and historical artifacts for use in units on Native Americans or frontier life). Unfortunately, very few elementary teachers have access to such rich resources.

This leaves most of them heavily dependent on the publishers of instructional materials, especially the major market-share textbook series. New teachers often have high expectations for these textbook series, which are attractively packaged and presented so as to suggest that they have been carefully developed and revised to meet the needs of students at each grade level. Even experienced teachers may suppress their misgivings about these textbook series because they think, "These texts are written by experts who know what they are doing; who am I to question their work?"

Teachers' misgivings are well founded, however, for at least three reasons. First, these instructional materials are not written by the kinds of experts that teachers envision. A "writing team" composed of social studies professors and teachers develops outlines for the materials and provides feedback after writers have developed drafts. Most of the actual writing, however, is done by employees of the publishing company who are not recognized experts either in child development or in social studies.

Second, notwithstanding the hype featured in advertisements for the series and in the front matter of the teachers' editions, these textbook series are not painstakingly developed and revised through successive field testings. Usually there is no systematic classroom testing at all—just revision in response to the comments of reviewers.

Third, although publishers are interested in feedback from teachers, their efforts are driven primarily by the textbook adoption guidelines established by state departments of education and major school districts. Unfortunately, state and district guidelines tend to feature long lists of disconnected knowledge and skill objectives. This creates coverage pressures, and publishers have responded by producing texts that say less and less about more and more. Instead of networks of connected knowledge structured around important ideas, these texts offer disconnected facts, seemingly random questions, and isolated skills exercises. Heavy reliance on such texts creates a dreary routine of reading the text, answering questions during recitations and on assignments, taking tests, and then forgetting most of what was "learned."

Students become discouraged. Even though social studies is about people and therefore should be highly interesting, students consistently rate it as their least favorite among the major school subjects. Heavy emphasis on memorization and regurgitation of miscellaneous facts is usually given as the reason (Atwood, 1986; Shaughnessy & Haladyna, 1985).

Some of the problems with elementary social studies series are merely special cases of generic problems rooted in the economics and politics of the textbook industry (Elliott & Woodward, 1990; Tyson-Bernstein, 1988). Among these generic problems are the following:

1. The texts attempt to cover more topics than they can treat respectfully within the page limits.
2. Even important topics are treated superficially, requiring that readers know a great deal about the topic already in order to make sense of the material.
3. Writing is dry and wooden, consisting of simple declarative sentences all about the same length. There are few adjectives or vignettes to enliven the text, few examples or counterexamples to give roundness to ideas, and too many paragraphs that are unclear because the material is too compressed or sketchy. These problems have resulted partially from misguided attempts to produce lower scores on "readability" indexes.
4. Authors frequently do not provide readers with a context that makes the facts presented meaningful for them.
5. Information about minorities and women is often conspicuously tacked on rather than integrated into the content flow.
6. Excessive space is allocated to pictures and graphics that are unrelated to the text.

CRITICISMS OF ELEMENTARY SOCIAL STUDIES SERIES

Along with these generic concerns, several additional criticisms focus specifically on elementary social studies series. One common criticism is that not enough content is included in the texts for the primary grades, and much of what is included does not need to be taught. Ravitch (1987) dismissed much of K–3 social studies content as "tot sociology." She viewed it as a collection of boring information in which students have little interest and which does not need to be taught anyway because children learn it through normal experiences outside of school. Similarly, Larkins, Hawkins, and Gilmore (1987) argued that much of the K–3 curriculum is "hopelessly noninformative": Children already know that families contain parents and children and that people live in houses, wear clothes, and eat food. These authors added that much of the content of K–3 texts is needlessly redundant (children already possess the knowledge), superfluous (children will acquire it without instruction), text-inappropriate (it should be taught more directly than through reading about it in texts), sanitized (purged of anything that might offend anyone), biased (presented from a single viewpoint when multiple viewpoints are appropriate), or aimless (not clearly related to important social education goals or to any other content in the text).

Whereas critics of K–3 texts find them thin and redundant, critics of social studies texts for Grades 4–6 complain that they are too thick and not redundant enough. These texts emphasize breadth of coverage over depth of development of ideas; they contain disconnected facts rather than networks of connected content structured around powerful ideas. Beck and McKeown (1988) argued that, in order to promote student understanding, texts must be high in *coherence*—the extent to which the sequence of ideas or events makes sense and the relationships among them are made apparent. These authors found that commonly used fifth-grade U.S. history texts are difficult for students to understand because they lack coherence. Historical accounts need to be built around causal chains indicating that events have causes and consequences, including people's reactions to them. To learn history with understanding, students need to learn not only the elements in a chain, but also how these elements are related—why a certain action caused some event and why that event led to subsequent events.

Beck and McKeown stressed that clarity about content goals is needed to avoid addressing too much breadth in not enough depth. Content needs to be selected in a principled way, guided by ideas about what students should gain from studying the topic. Failure to do this leads to three problems that they observed in fifth-grade history texts:

1. Lack of evidence that clear content goals were used to guide text writing (the texts read as chronicles of miscellaneous facts rather than as narratives built around connecting themes)
2. Unrealistic assumptions about students' prior knowledge (key elements needed to understand a sequence often were merely alluded to rather than explained sufficiently)

3. Inadequate explanations that failed to clarify connections between actions and events (in particular, causal relationships)

Beck, McKeown, and Gromoll (1989) found similar coherence problems in fourth-grade geography texts. Subsequent work by McKeown and Beck (1994) showed that texts rewritten to make them more coherent and engaging to students produced better recall, and especially more connected learning of key ideas, than the original texts.

A final set of criticisms of elementary social studies series focuses on their skills components. Woodward (1987) identified three primary problems in the way that skills are handled in these series. First, more is promised in the front matter and the scope-and-sequence charts than is actually delivered in the lessons. Mere mention of a skill is often treated as sufficient for it to be cited in the charts, while inspection of the lesson reveals that it does not develop the skill at all. Second, the skills given the most emphasis tend to be those that are most easily measured, such as map and globe skills. These skills are repeated unnecessarily throughout the series, whereas inadequate attention is given to information gathering, report writing, critical thinking, decision making, value analysis, and other higher-order application skills. Third, despite publishers' claims to have integrated knowledge and skills teaching, the skills content is typically separated from the knowledge content.

DETAILED CRITIQUE OF A REPRESENTATIVE TEXTBOOK SERIES

To illustrate the problems with elementary social studies series in more detail, we will highlight findings and examples from a critique of the 1988 Silver Burdett and Ginn (SBG) series (Brophy, 1992; Brophy, McMahon, & Prawat, 1991). This series was selected for analysis because it was representative of late 1980s series and one of the most popular. Sewell (1987) estimated that the SBG fifth-grade U.S. history and geography text controlled 70 percent of the market in the mid-1980s. This text and others like it continue to dominate the market in the 1990s. Our critique considers the curriculum that would result if a teacher not only used the textbook but followed all of the suggestions in the teacher's edition concerning questions to ask the students, activities and assignments, and assessment devices. The critique is organized into eight sections:

1. Goals
2. Content selection
3. Content organization and sequencing
4. Content explication in the text
5. Teacher–student relationships and classroom discourse
6. Activities and assignments
7. Assessment and evaluation
8. Directions to the teacher

Goals

The materials contained no statement of goals as such, but a single page of program rationale made the following claims:

> *Built on a solid factual foundation.* Developed to help students understand themselves and the world around them and to instill in them the knowledge and skills necessary for responsible citizenship. Built on a solid factual foundation, using the expanding environments design.

> *Instills knowledge and skills.* Reflects the belief that students need to *know*, *appreciate*, and *do*. A grasp of basic facts is essential in gaining understanding of social studies, so a wealth of material is provided. Each lesson begins with a Directed Study Question to make students aware of the main idea. Lesson check-ups, chapter and unit reviews, and chapter tests ensure students' understanding of text material. Opportunities to develop language, reading, higher-level thinking, and social studies skills are provided through exercises and activities.

> *Encourages active learning.* Involves the students in *doing* by working with photos, maps, charts, graphs, tables, and time lines as a vital part of the learning process. Students build models, conduct interviews, hold debates, and take part in a variety of other activities. In short, students are active participants.

> *Fosters responsible citizenship.* Enables students to appreciate themselves, the world around them, and their roles as citizens of the United States. Students learn important links between themselves and their families, communities, states, regions, nation, and world. In doing so, they develop an appreciation of historic and geographic factors and economic and political relationships that have shaped their world. Students are given specific suggestions for assuming a responsible role—in capacities commensurate with age and ability—in their community, state, region, nation, and world. The program helps them to function meaningfully in the present and prepares them for their future role as good citizens.

This is the entire statement of the SBG series rationale, and it sounds terrific if we take it at face value. It identifies selective, if not clear and specific, goals. It focuses on citizen education rather than disciplinary knowledge or personal development, doing so with an emphasis on teaching factual knowledge and inculcating values and dispositions. The primary intended outcome is responsible citizenship, which appears to mean knowing and doing one's duty as a citizen. Other outcomes include developing students' knowledge and appreciation of themselves, the world around them, and the historic, geographic, economic, and political factors that have shaped that world. There is little mention of goals associated with values analysis or decision making.

Throughout the series there is frequent lip service to the goals of fostering conceptual understanding and higher-order applications of content, but little evidence of follow through. The term "understanding" is used frequently, but the materials suggest that the term means the ability to repeat factual explanations, to define or recognize examples of concepts, or to execute skills correctly. Similarly, "applications" tend to call for mere exercise of skills rather than life applications of content, and "critical thinking" questions are mostly broad questions about students' preferences rather than questions calling for critical assessment of the validity of claims or the advisability of courses of action. Nothing is said about requiring students to take positions on issues and defend them by citing relevant evidence.

Lessons are structured around key ideas stressed in the introductions and in the review material. However, the identified key ideas tend to be low-level facts, concept definitions, or trite generalizations, rather than causal explanations or other powerful generalizations that might anchor networks of knowledge organized for life applications. For example, a lesson on shelter is built around the key idea that people in different places live in many different kinds of houses. This is a much less powerful key idea than the one that might have been developed—that people in different places live in different kinds of houses in part because of the climate and natural resources of the region.

Along with knowledge and skill goals, three sets of attitudinal or dispositional goals are mentioned. First is the disposition to act as a responsible citizen. The authors kept this goal in mind in writing the textbooks, consistently attempting to inculcate citizenship values and dispositions. A second attitudinal goal is appreciation, presumably of how and why the social world works as it does. This goal is neither defined on the rationale page nor mentioned later, although much of the content could be seen as fostering appreciation (of the local community, the state, the nation, and the American way generally). The third attitudinal goal is student interest in the content. Several features of the program are designed to build student interest, and each lesson begins with an ostensibly motivational activity.

Taken together, the goals of the SBG series might be seen as appropriate by those who favor an inculcation approach. However, except for the consistent attempt to install values and beliefs supporting responsible citizenship and to generate student interest, there is little evidence that the goals implied in the series rationale really drove curriculum development. Content selection appears to respond to cultural literacy concerns, and the exercises and activities selection appears to respond to skills lists commonly found in state and district curriculum guides.

Content Selection

Given goals that emphasize facts and citizen education via inculcation, the content can be seen as appropriate (although limited in effectiveness by clutter and poor development of key ideas). The content also might be seen as coherent across grade levels; there is a great deal of spiraling and repetition in Grades K-3. However, coherence at the unit and lesson levels is poor because the content is not structured around powerful ideas developed in depth.

The history content is inconsistent. Much of it is presented as facts chronicled with relatively little explanation or even identification of major trends occurring over time. There is little sense of history as interpretation and little use of original source material, despite the claims in the front matter of the teachers' manuals.

The fifth-grade text does tell the story of the development of the United States as a nation. It includes several themes that lend coherence to individual chapters (e.g., growth of the nation as a world power, expansion of democracy to a broader range of citizens). This text has good material on everyday life in most of the periods covered. Finally, it does a reasonably good job in the text (although not in the inserts) of developing the main themes without getting lost in personalities, battle dates, or other trivia. Still, this is primarily a cultural literacy, chronicle-of-facts treatment of history with emphasis on inculcation of traditional American values, and not a critical historical interpretation.

The geography sections are moderately interesting, easy to read, and supported by outstanding maps, photos, and other graphics. Enough useful raw material is provided for a good treatment of basic geographical principles by a teacher who is familiar with these key ideas, but the key ideas themselves are not spelled out either for teachers or for students. The emphasis is on place geography rather than human–environment relationships. Much of the geographical content is reminiscent of travel agency brochures, although it does have some emphasis on natural resources and products and on things of special interest to children.

The social science content is poor, offering some useful basic facts and concepts but minimal treatment of powerful generalizations. Basic economics concepts (needs, wants) are introduced in the primary grades, and later coverage includes such topics as recessions, cash crops, inflation, extension of markets, and interdependence. However, there is no place in the series where economics concepts and principles are pulled together and treated as a network.

Sociology is introduced in the primary grades (especially the third-grade text on communities), then integrated into later coverage of history and geography. Good sections cover the economic and social aspects of sociology, but coverage of the political aspects is distorted by the U.S.-centered, rather than global, perspective adopted throughout the series. This same perspective makes the series weak on anthropology. Few cross-cultural examples are included in the material on families, neighborhoods, and communities, and the world geography covered in Grades 4 and 6 focuses on places more than on cultures. When the text does cover cultures, it is respectful but relatively uninformative. For example, students learn that many Muslims resented and resisted forced Westernization in countries where this occurred, but few examples are given to provide concrete details about the kinds of conflict that arose.

Civics material is limited by an almost exclusive focus on the United States. It includes a simplified version of the U.S. Constitution and several charts and graphs relating to the workings of the federal government, but it never provides a coherent explanation of how governments function. What comes through is vague patriotism rather than more detailed and balanced information.

Few life applications are developed, except for recreation-oriented preference questions ("Would you rather live in a small town or a big city?"). Weak and often irrelevant activities are part of this problem, as are poor explanations. Examples of generalizations often are not identified as such, and seldom are compared directly. Processes seldom are described even at the level of their major steps. In general, there is not enough emphasis on understanding to provide a basis for life applications, let alone follow through in the form of activities calling for such applications.

There is a large jump from a primarily picture-based curriculum requiring minimal reading in second grade to much lengthier text in third grade. However, neither the reading level nor the nature of the content should present problems to typical students at any grade level. Problems with coherence of understanding, along the lines identified by Beck and McKeown (1988) and Beck et al. (1989), may be due in part to unjustified assumptions about prior knowledge, but most are due to inadequate explanations of the topics treated.

The content selection reflects consideration for students' interests: The graphics are good, each lesson begins with a motivational starter, and many suggested questions concern students' opinions or prior experiences. To the extent that the series has problems motivating students to learn, these are rooted in its failure to include more critical thinking and decision making in lieu of inculcation.

Content Organization and Sequencing

The series follows the *expanding communities* sequence. It is organized more by topic than by discipline, except for its primarily geographical treatment of regions in fourth grade and its chronological treatment of U.S. history in fifth grade. Teachers who are knowledgeable about social studies curricula and organizational schemes could identify SBG's scheme if they conducted a careful analysis of its scope and sequence. However, its organization is not likely to be recognized as coherent by most students or even teachers, due to its failure to provide a clear explanation of the organizing frameworks within which the content has been embedded.

Along with the expanding communities framework, the sequencing includes elements of the *spiral curriculum*—basic ideas are introduced at one grade and then revisited at deeper levels or in different aspects at later grades. Also evident is *gradual differentiation*—ideas introduced earlier in global fashion are treated later in more differentiated fashion.

Content Explication in the Texts

As an ill-organized parade of facts, the content is not very appropriate except in readability level. It provides students with miscellaneous facts but does not equip them with enough systematic knowledge about how and why the social world works as it does or with concepts and principles that they can apply to their lives outside of school.

Clarity is often a problem because of vague, global language used to cover even the most basic of content. In the early grades, the text is skimpy and vague. Students learn, for example, that different levels of government have "leaders" (presidents, governors, mayors) who work in special buildings and make laws "to keep us safe." However, they do not learn much about the functions that various levels of government perform, or how they do so. Much of the primary curriculum is "happy talk"—celebration of the benign, supportive world that we all supposedly live in. First graders learn that we all live in families where we love and help one another; families are proud of their neighborhoods and work to keep them clean and safe; workers in factories work together. The photos suggest that everyone lives in bright and attractive surroundings, free of crowding, litter, and danger. These themes continue in Grade 2, where the text teaches that neighbors come together to help one another, and this makes the work more fun; cities are full of places to have fun; governmental leaders work together to solve problems for our benefit; and all Americans help to make the U.S. a great country. The Grade 3 text extends these themes: People in small communities take pride in their town and its past; there are many dedicated people who do good for the environment and the animals; the ever-changing world gets better all the time and is full of people eager to make things better for all of us.

The texts for Grades 4–6 are sanitized and avoid controversy. They are no longer laced with happy talk and other empty generalities, but their lack of structuring around key ideas makes it difficult for students to learn the information as organized bodies of knowledge. There are too many pronouns in lieu of nouns, too many generalizations stated without elaboration of specifics or examples, and not enough explanations of why things are the way they are.

The content of the series is not treated in enough depth to promote understanding of key ideas. In Grades 1 and 2, the content lacks clarity and detail. Many sections are confusing because the illustrations show a great variety of examples, many of them atypical rather than prototypical. Grade 1 students learn that there are many different kinds of communities, homes, and clothing styles, but very little about why there are differences. In Grade 2, there is good material about the lifestyles of different Native American tribes, but little structuring around basic geographical and anthropological concepts that would help students to understand reasons for the similarities and differences described.

In Grade 3, a chapter on cities confusingly begins with Tenochtitlan, a city that no longer exists as such and was a very unusual example when it did exist. A better introduction to this section might be accomplished by elaborating on division of labor, specialization, and trade to help students understand how cities got started. The remaining examples of cities are better chosen, but the principles that they are meant to exemplify are lost in the details presented about the cities themselves.

In Grade 4, the introduction to the unit on plains regions fails to provide a clear definition of plains and misleadingly suggests that large cities are located on coastal plains but not central plains. The coverage of states within regions brings up a great range of historical, economic, and other issues that require digressions to explain. Often these explanations are too brief to be helpful to students who are not already familiar with the term or event.

The content in Grades 5 and 6 is choppy: long on miscellaneous details, but short on coherent coverage of important political, economic, or historical trends in Grade 5 and geographical relationships in Grade 6. There are many unexplained statements and loose ends.

The series is mixed in its use of nonverbal representations. It makes good use of time lines, maps, photos, and occasional diagrams, but it is weak in its use of charts and related tools for comparing and contrasting cases or examples. Many of the photos of life in particular cultures depict children or children's activities. However, caption questions and suggested lesson development questions often address trite or irrelevant issues instead of key ideas. Many of the illustrations focus on trivial aspects of the topic rather than main ideas, portray a sanitized version of the world, or emphasize unusual or exotic examples rather than prototypical ones.

It is clear that the skills portion of this series was developed essentially separately from the knowledge portion. Four general types of skills are addressed, separately both from the knowledge content and from one another.

Social studies tool skills (maps, globes, graphs, gathering and communicating or depicting information) are developed in separate units that appear at the beginning of each grade level. These units are generally well done, notable for good illustrations and nice development of skills across grade levels. Tool skills often are reinforced in exercises included in later units, but these exercises (1) tend to provide only isolated part-skills practice rather than capitalizing on naturally occurring opportunities to use the skills in applying the content of the unit, and (2) are often unrelated to the knowledge taught during the unit, except in the most trivial ways. In the most ironic example, a lesson describing four different Native American tribes virtually cries out for a charting exercise comparing and contrasting their cultures and customs. Yet, the unit lacks this key component even though the skill emphasized in the exercise attached to it is charting—applied to content having nothing to do with Native Americans!

Critical-thinking skills are not taught as such but presumably developed through the "critical thinking" questions. However, these questions typically call only for student expression of opinion or preference rather than for articulation and defense of positions.

Language arts skills are exercised through "language arts tie-in" activities and various skill sheets. Many of these have little or nothing to do with social education goals, and many others distort or trivialize the social education aspects in order to accommodate the language arts aspects.

Finally, there are boxed "visual skills" questions to develop students' abilities to interpret photos. These questions often address issues that have little or no relevance to the main themes of the chapters.

Teacher–Student Relationships and Classroom Discourse

The majority of suggested questions focus on facts. There is little evidence that the authors view discourse, let alone sustained, critical, reflective dialogue, as crucial to the development of understanding or higher order applications. The suggested discourse amounts to recitation of miscellaneous facts. Little sustained discussion of key ideas is suggested and practically no student–student discourse.

Activities and Assignments

At first glance, the activities component of this series is impressive. Large projects are suggested at the beginnings of units, each lesson begins with a motivational activity, workbook pages and practice masters provide vocabulary and geography exercises, and "thinking" activities include "what if" questions, creative writing, interviewing, mapmaking, analyzing information, sequencing, outlining, making charts or tables, and role-playing. Many activities are presented as providing content-area tie-ins to language arts, science, mathematics, music, or art.

However, most of these activities have the same problems noted in the content and the questions: They focus on reproducing miscellaneous facts rather than on concepts, generalizations, or applications. The worksheets and practice masters are predominantly matching and fill-in-the-blank activities that reinforce but do not extend or apply the content. There are no tie-ins to current events and few invitations to apply content to life outside of school. Many suggested projects, especially those calling for artistic construction, are quite time-consuming and yet not of much use in furthering students' understanding of or ability to apply key ideas.

GOOD ACTIVITIES

The manuals do suggest some good activities. A first-grade lesson on school helpers calls for inviting a school helper to come to the class, bringing tools used on the job, to talk about the job, answer questions, and tell students how they can be helpful. The class follows up by preparing a thank-you card. In an early activity used to introduce maps, students make a simplified map of the classroom by drawing in symbols for the clock, bookshelf, wastebasket, door, table, and teacher's desk in appropriate places. This concrete experience in constructing a map of a familiar and observable environment is useful for helping students develop an understanding of maps as two-dimensional schematic representations of three-dimensional places.

A second-grade activity extends a lesson on the federal government by asking students to do research and make presentations to the class on topics such as national parks or the postal service, to underscore the fact that the government not only makes laws but also provides services. If properly scaffolded by the teacher, this activity should promote understanding and help students learn about doing research and about organizing and communicating their findings to others. (Instructional *scaffolding* is a general term for the task assistance or simplification strategies that teachers might use to bridge the gap between what students are able to do on their own and what they are capable of doing with help. Like the scaffolds used by house painters, the support provided through scaffolding is temporary, adjustable, and removed when no longer needed. Examples include demonstrating how to do a task, offering prompts or cues when students are "stuck," or providing them with a list of the steps involved in working through a complex assignment.)

Students in fifth-grade classes locate England and the American colonies on a map, use the scale to determine the distances involved, speculate how England and the colonies communicated, and discuss the difficulties that can arise when people cannot communicate easily. This activity helps students understand the events leading up to the American Revolution and sensitizes them to factors such as the state of development of transportation and communication at the time.

A "thinking" activity that successfully ties in art asks students to develop a poster or pamphlet advertising colonial Pennsylvania to Europeans, bearing in mind that their product should function as propaganda designed to motivate immigration rather than as a well-balanced and accurate source of information. This activity promotes critical thinking and allows for integration of ideas and skills developed elsewhere in the curriculum (concerning propaganda techniques and construction of persuasive arguments). One of the few debating activities calls for students to debate whether or not the colonists were right to disobey the laws imposed on them by Great Britain. In a creative writing activity students imagine that they were among the Native Americans forced to endure the "Trail of Tears" and write diaries describing their experiences.

MISSING ACTIVITIES

Many activities that would have added substantially to the value of the curriculum are missing. In many places, students would have benefited from structured discussions, chart construction, or other activities that would encourage them to organize information or to compare and contrast examples. The same is true of small-group and cooperative activities, field trips, visits by resource people, simulations, extended writing, citizen action projects, and "concluding" activities calling for integration and communication of what had been learned.

POOR ACTIVITIES

Many activities are sound in conception but flawed in design. For example, the idea of beginning lessons with a motivational activity is a good one, but many of the activities suggested as motivation devices do not seem likely to serve that function. Others seem unduly time-consuming, troublesome, or irrelevant to ideas developed in the lesson. Similarly, the idea of placing questions under pictures to stimulate student study and interpretation of the pictures is a good one, but many of the caption questions focus on trivial or irrelevant details.

At many places in the series, certain activities seem to be included because the authors saw opportunities to introduce dichotomies and use them as the basis for questioning students. This root problem is often compounded by ambiguities in the illustrations. For example, one worksheet calls for students to distinguish producers of goods from producers of services. However, a man shown picking apples is classified as a service worker when he could just as well be the owner of the farm and classified as a producer of goods, and a man at a workbench is described as a producer of goods when he could just as well be doing repairs as a service.

Many activities match learning processes with content to which they are not well suited. There are activities calling for charting material that does not lend itself to charting, diagramming material that does not lend itself to diagramming, and so on. Such mismatches occur when curriculum developers insert skills exercises arbitrarily instead of calling for students to use skills that are naturally suited to authentic applications of the content taught in the unit.

Certain activities are fundamentally unsound in their conception. Many workbook activities are little more than busywork: word searches, cutting and pasting, coloring, connecting dots, and so on. Many others are artificial exercises included to provide practice, often on skills that are of dubious value in the first place: alphabetizing state capitals, recognizing states from the outlines of their shapes, retrieving miscellaneous and undiscussed information from time lines, tracing maps, graphing miscellaneous and undiscussed factual data, finding the geographical coordinates for battle sites, and finding information about state symbols (flags, flowers, etc.).

Problems are especially evident in activities intended as integration with other subjects. Many of the suggested tie-ins are language arts activities that do not belong in a social studies curriculum at all (alphabetizing, pluralizing, finding the main idea in a paragraph, using the dictionary, matching synonyms). Much unnecessary counting and sequencing is inserted as a way to incorporate mathematics skills. One activity calls for reading statements about various constitutional amendments and identifying the amendments by number. This dubious activity is complicated by further directions calling for the amendment numbers to be put into a three-by-three matrix which, if filled out correctly, will yield the same "magic number" as the sum for each row and column. As if this were not convoluted enough, the instructions call for the student to "put the number of the amendment in the box with the same letter as the sentence that describes it."

In general, the separation of the skills curriculum from the knowledge curriculum and the consistent insertions of language arts and other skills exercises are major detractors from the coherence of this social studies series. The problem is not just poor implementation of a fundamentally sound idea; its root lies in the very notion of using the social studies curriculum as a place to locate skills-practice exercises. It will not be truly rectified until curriculum developers abandon this approach completely and instead select activities because they are well suited to accomplishing the social education goals that are supposed to provide the rationale for the curriculum in the first place. The resulting curriculum would still include selections from literature and the arts as input and would frequently incorporate skills developed in other school subjects, but in ways that were natural and likely to promote student understanding of the social education content.

Assessment and Evaluation

The evaluation component of SBG focuses on memory for miscellaneous facts rather than on key ideas or applications. In fact, test items often are less demanding than related items on the worksheets used in teaching the units. Even the essay questions included at the higher grade levels typically call only for retrieving information given in the text, not for applying it or developing and defending a personal response to it. The content tests are basically vocabulary tests. The skills tests are self-contained exercises comparable to those found on standardized achievement tests. That is, they present a paragraph, a chart, a table, or some other form of input and then require students to answer questions about it. Usually there is little or no connection between the content of these skills tests and the content of the unit. Many of the skills tested are language arts skills (e.g., matching pictures of food items whose names begin with the same letter).

Directions to the Teacher

The only general instructions to the teacher are that the units can be taught in any order, the skills material that begins each text can be taught as a separate unit or integrated into later content units, and the material can be adapted in any way that seems necessary to fit state guidelines or local needs. Essentially, then, SBG supplies tools but leaves it up to the teacher to decide which ones to use and how to use them. However, many implied expectations are built into the three-step lesson plan used throughout the series:

1. A motivational activity
2. Lesson development to be accomplished through questions about the text and illustrations
3. Reinforcement/evaluation, which begins with re-asking the "directed study question" that opened the lesson and then proceeds to practice masters, workbook pages, suggested activities, and unit tests

The rationale statement takes up less than a page and is not even included in some of the manuals. Instead of a scope-and-sequence chart, there is only a skills index that gives "representative pages" where activities calling for the skill (but usually not lessons teaching the skill) can be found. Some of the manuals also contain content outlines organized by units within grade levels or by the six general content categories of geography, history, economics, government/citizenship, sociology/anthropology, and humanities. These informational components for teachers provide little explanation of the intended outcomes, rationale, or features of the program.

At the unit and lesson level, the teachers' manuals contain suggested questions and activities and occasional inserts elaborating on the text or mentioning relevant children's literature. However, there is little guidance about main ideas to develop in introducing topics, common misconceptions to address, ways to structure productive discussions of content, or ways to structure activities and assignments.

To use this series effectively, teachers would need to make good decisions about how to focus and elaborate on the content in the text, and how to cull and supplement the suggested activities, in order to transform the program's emphasis on memorizing facts and practicing skills to an emphasis on learning the content within the context of life applications. This requires teachers to have both good knowledge of the subject matter and well-articulated ideas about the nature and purposes of elementary social studies.

THE NEED FOR TEACHER DECISION MAKING IN USING INSTRUCTIONAL MATERIALS

We have presented a detailed critique of a single elementary social studies series because the problems we have described are common ones, not at all unique to the 1988 SBG series. We conducted similar critiques of the 1986 Holt series, the 1987 Ginn series, and the 1987 Macmillan series as well. Each series had a unique pattern of strengths and weaknesses, but all were much more similar to the 1988 SBG series than different from it. Problems like those seen in SBG will continue to plague elementary social studies series until three major shifts occur in the ways that these series are developed:

1. A shift of focus from lists of topics and skills to be covered to more general social education purposes and goals as the major force driving selection and organization of content
2. A shift from broad but shallow coverage to deeper development of limited networks of connected information structured around powerful ideas
3. A shift from separation of the skills curriculum from the knowledge curriculum to development and use of skills as strategies for applying the knowledge

Our analyses of more recent elementary social studies series indicate that many of the problems seen in the 1986–1988 series continue. Some of the series published in the 1990s feature inserted literature selections and more emphasis on extended writing assignments and cooperative learning activities. They are less likely to call for practice of language arts skills such as alphabetizing, but they still reveal a lack of goal-oriented integration of knowledge and skill components. Many of the inserted literature selections and the questions and activities associated with them have little connection to major social education goals, and suggestions for cooperative learning sometimes are applied to activities that do not lend themselves well to the cooperative format. Thus, the publishers are still making piecemeal responses to miscellaneous coverage pressures rather than offering coherent social education curricula (Brophy & Alleman, 1992-1993; Alleman & Brophy, 1994).

A few states and districts have begun to replace their long lists of content coverage requirements with shorter and more coherent statements of major social education goals and intended outcomes. We hope that this trend continues and creates market conditions that will encourage publishers to develop series that are more coherent and effective as tools for teaching social studies for understanding, appreciation, and life application. In the meantime, if you want to overcome some of the limitations of currently available materials, you will have to examine your instructional materials in light of your major social education goals. You will need to identify what content to ignore or downplay and what content to emphasize. You may need to augment the latter content if major ideas or themes are not well developed in the texts. Identify pointless questions and activities to skip, and develop other questions and activities that will support progress toward major goals.

Do not junk textbooks altogether, despite the problems with them. It is unrealistic to expect novice teachers to operate without texts, and unnecessary to ask veteran teachers to do so (although some may prefer this option). However, view the textbook as just one among many resources to draw upon in planning and implementing a curriculum designed to accomplish social studies goals—do not view the textbook as "the" curriculum. In the remainder of this book, we offer guidelines and examples designed to help you adapt and supplement your instructional materials and to develop more powerful social studies curriculum and instruction.

YOUR TURN: TEXTBOOK LIMITATIONS

Select a social studies textbook with an accompanying teacher's guide that is recommended by the district with which you are affiliated. Use the following checklist, based on ideas developed in this chapter, to examine the textbook and guide to determine its level of usefulness in your classroom. Share the results with a peer. Then, together, develop a plan for offsetting the limitations that you have uncovered in your analysis.

TEXTBOOK ASSESSMENT

Circle your responses

Goals-Driven Approach

Yes	No	Are the goals clearly stated?
Yes	No	Do they represent understanding, appreciation, and life application?
Yes	No	Do they focus on the big ideas?

Content Selection

Yes	No	Is the content adequate?
Yes	No	Where appropriate, are multiple perspectives provided in order to alleviate bias?
Yes	No	Does the content promote important social education goals?

Coverage

Yes	No	Does the sequence of ideas or events make sense?
Yes	No	Are relationships between the big ideas apparent?
Yes	No	Are prior knowledge and/or experience issues recognized?

Skills

Yes	No	Is what is promised in the front matter of the teacher's guide delivered in the student text?
Yes	No	Are the skills linked to the knowledge content?
Yes	No	Is a range of skills included (i.e., map and globe skills, information gathering, report writing, critical thinking, decision making, value analysis, etc.)?

Teacher–Student Relationships and Classroom Discourse

Yes	No	Are there planned discussions of key ideas?
Yes	No	Will the plans yield sustained, critical, and reflective dialogue?
Yes	No	Are there opportunities for student–student discourse?

Activities and Assignments

Yes	No	Are the activities and assignments goals driven?
Yes	No	Are they at the appropriate level of difficulty?
Yes	No	Do they focus on concepts, generalizations, and applications?
Yes	No	Do they tie in to current events?
Yes	No	Do they apply to life outside of school?
Yes	No	Are the activities and assignments properly scaffolded?
Yes	No	Are the suggested learning processes well suited to the content?
Yes	No	Are integration activities clearly social studies driven?
Yes	No	Are the activities and assignments cost effective?

Assessment and Evaluation

Yes	No	Do assessment items and activities clearly reflect the social education goals?
Yes	No	Do they focus on major social studies understandings instead of miscellaneous facts?
Yes	No	Do they incorporate skills that mesh with the content?
Yes	No	Is there an absence of memorization and regurgitation of miscellaneous facts?
Yes	No	Do the assessment and evaluation measures, as a whole, reflect the big picture of the unit?

REFERENCES

Alleman, J., & Brophy, J. (1994). Trade-offs embedded in the literary approach to early elementary social studies. *Social Studies and the Young Learner, 6* (3), 6–8.

Atwood, V. (1986). Elementary social studies: Cornerstone or crumbling mortar? In V. Atwood (Ed.), *Elementary school social studies: Research as a guide to practice* (Bulletin No. 79, pp. 1–13). Washington, DC: National Council for the Social Studies.

Beck, I., & McKeown, M. (1988). Toward meaningful accounts in history texts for young learners. *Educational Researcher, 17* (6), 31–39.

Beck, I., McKeown, M., & Gromoll, E. (1989). Learning from social studies texts. *Cognition and Instruction, 6,* 99–158.

Brophy, J. (1992). The de facto national curriculum in U.S. elementary social studies: Critique of a representative example. *Journal of Curriculum Studies, 24,* 401–447.

Brophy, J., & Alleman, J. (1992–1993). Elementary social studies textbooks. *Publishing Research Quarterly, 8* (4), 12–22.

Brophy, J., McMahon, S., & Prawat, R. (1991). Elementary social studies series: Critique of a representative example by six experts. *Social Education, 55,* 155–160.

Elliott, D., & Woodward, A. (Eds.). (1990). *Textbooks and schooling in the United States* (Eighty-ninth yearbook of the National Society for the Study of Education, Part I). Chicago: University of Chicago Press.

Larkins, A., Hawkins, M., & Gilmore, A. (1987). Trivial and noninformative content of elementary social studies: A review of primary texts in four series. *Theory and Research in Social Education, 15,* 299–311.

McKeown, M., & Beck, I. (1994). Making sense of accounts of history: Why young students don't and how they might. In G. Leinhardt, I. Beck, & C. Stainton (Eds.), *Teaching and learning in history* (pp. 1–26). Hillsdale, NJ: Erlbaum.

Mehlinger, H. (1981). Social studies: Some gulfs and priorities. In H. Mehlinger & O. Davis (Eds.), *The social studies* (Eightieth yearbook of the National Society for the Study of Education, Part II; pp. 244–269). Chicago: University of Chicago Press.

Ravitch, D. (1987). Tot sociology or what happened to history in the grade schools. *American Scholar, 56,* 343–353.

Sewall, G. (1987). *American history textbooks: An assessment of quality.* New York: Education Excellence Network.

Shaughnessy, J., & Haladyna, T. (1985). Research on student attitude toward social studies. *Social Education, 49,* 692–695.

Shaver, J. (1987). What should be taught in social studies? In V. Richardson-Koehler (Ed.), *Educators' handbook: A research perspective* (pp. 112–138). New York: Longman.

Thornton, S. (1991). Teacher as curricular-instructional gatekeeper in social studies. In J. Shaver (Ed.), *Handbook of research on social studies teaching and learning* (pp. 237–248). New York: Macmillan.

Tyson-Bernstein, H. (1988). *A conspiracy of good intentions: America's textbook fiasco.* Washington, DC: Council for Basic Education.

Woodward, A. (1987). Textbooks: Less than meets the eye. *Journal of Curriculum Studies, 19,* 511–526.

PART TWO

Planning Powerful Social Studies Teaching

The chapters in Part One described issues and problems with contemporary elementary social studies and emphasized the need for teachers to clarify and prioritize their social studies goals and plan their teaching accordingly. The chapters in Part Two have been written to help you accomplish this by presenting a vision of powerful social studies curriculum, instruction, and assessment. Guided by recent position statements published by the National Council for the Social Studies and by organizations concerned about teaching history, geography, and the social sciences, these chapters address key issues involved in and offer principles and criteria useful for decision making about social studies content selection and representation, questions and classroom discourse, learning activities and assignments, and assessment methods. The chapters also address key issues and offer principles and criteria concerning integration of school subjects across the curriculum and teaching your students how to function as a learning community in which members actively collaborate to construct knowledge.

Chapter 3

GOAL-ORIENTED CURRICULUM PLANNING

A curriculum is not an end in itself but a means, a tool for accomplishing educational goals. These goals are learner outcomes—the knowledge, skills, attitudes, values, and dispositions to action that one wishes to develop in students. Ideally, curriculum planning and implementation decisions will be driven by these goals, so that each element—the basic content, the ways that this content is represented and explicated to students, the questions that will be asked, the types of teacher–student and student–student discourse that will occur, the activities and assignments, and the methods that will be used to assess progress and grade performance—will be included because it is believed to be needed as a means for moving students toward accomplishment of the major goals. The goals are the reason for the existence of the curriculum, and beliefs about what is needed to accomplish them should guide each step in curriculum planning and implementation.

Today's social studies textbook series feature broad but shallow coverage of a great range of topics and skills. Lacking both coherence of flow and structuring around key ideas developed in depth, textbooks are experienced as parades of disconnected facts and isolated skills exercises. These problems have evolved as unintended consequences of publishers' efforts to satisfy state and district curricular guidelines that feature long lists of topics and skills to be covered rather than succinct statements of major goals to be accomplished. If teachers use the textbooks and provided ancillary materials and follow the manuals' lesson development instructions, the result will be a reading/recitation/seatwork curriculum focused on memorizing disconnected knowledge and practicing isolated skills. Nevertheless, this is what many teachers do, because most elementary teachers and many secondary teachers who are assigned to teach social studies courses have not had enough social studies preparation to allow them to develop a coherent view of what social education is all about, let alone a rich base of social education knowledge and an associated repertoire of pedagogical techniques. Acting on the assumption that the series has been developed by experts far more knowledgeable about social education purposes and goals than they are, such teachers tend to concentrate on the procedural mechanics of implementation when planning lessons and activities, without giving much thought to their purposes or how they might fit into the larger social education program.

The first of these two italicized paragraphs summarizes the classical view of curriculum development as a goal-oriented process. The second paragraph summarizes findings of recent research on the status of social studies, as we detailed in previous chapters. The contrasts between the two paragraphs reflect the major problems in contemporary social education.

An important reason for these problems is that publishers of social studies textbooks and the teachers who depend on them have lost the forest for the trees—they have lost sight of the major, long-term goals that reflect the purposes of social education and that *should* drive the development and enactment of social studies curricula. Consequently, we are calling for a return to the notion of developing curricula as a means to accomplish major goals. To be most valuable for curriculum planning, these goals will need to be phrased in terms of intended student outcomes—capabilities and dispositions to be developed in students and used in their lives inside and outside of school, both now and in the future.

We recommend two connected sets of goals as guides for planning curriculum and instruction in elementary social studies. The first set is generic to powerful teaching in any school subject; the second set is specific to social studies.

GENERIC SUBJECT-MATTER GOALS: UNDERSTANDING, APPRECIATION, AND LIFE APPLICATION

The *academic disciplines* are means of generating and systematizing knowledge. The *school subjects* that draw from them are means of preparing students for life in our society by equipping them with essential knowledge, skills, values, and dispositions. We want students not just to learn what we teach them in school, but to access and use it in appropriate application situations. These goals will not be met if students merely memorize disconnected bits of information long enough to pass tests and then forget most of what they "learned."

Consequently, in planning curriculum and instruction in any school subject, it is important to emphasize goals of understanding, appreciation, and life application. *Understanding* means that students learn both the individual elements in a network of related content and the connections among them, so that they can explain the content in their own words. True understanding goes beyond the ability to define concepts or supply facts. It involves making connections between new learning and prior knowledge, subsuming the new learning within larger networks of knowledge, and recognizing at least some of its potential applications.

Appreciation means that students value what they are learning because they understand that there are good reasons for learning it. Along with potential practical applications, these reasons include the roles that the learning might play in enhancing the quality of the learners' lives. In the case of social studies, students might appreciate the value of their learning for helping them to understand how the world as we know it came to be and what is occurring in it now, as well as for helping them to make personal and civic decisions. They also might come to appreciate their own developing understandings—to take pride in seeing how what they have learned applies to their own lives, to appreciate their attainment of new insights, or to enjoy interpreting or predicting current events or enhancing their knowledge by reading or watching programs on social issues.

Life application goals are accomplished to the extent that students retain their learning in a form that makes it usable when needed in other contexts. Connections between social studies learning and its potential life applications are less direct than they are in the basic skills subjects. With just a few exceptions such as information about maps and globes, the knowledge taught in social studies is not linked directly to particular applications. For example, we do not teach about history or world cultures to provide specific preparation for particular kinds of problem solving or decision making. Instead, we teach this information as part of a general knowledge base that people will need to enable them to interpret and respond to events in their lives and in the world at large. Ultimately, however, social studies learning should inform one's personal, social, and civic thinking and decision making.

Research on Teaching for Understanding

Throughout the rest of the book, we will use the term "teaching for understanding" as shorthand for "teaching for understanding, appreciation, and life application of subject-matter knowledge." Recently, there has been a confluence of theorizing, research, and publication of guidelines by professional organizations, all focusing on what is involved in teaching for understanding. Analyses of these efforts have identified a set of principles that are common to most if not all of them (Anderson, 1989; Brophy, 1989, 1992; Prawat, 1989). These common elements, which might be considered components in a model of good subject-matter teaching, include the following:

1. The curriculum is designed to equip students with knowledge, skills, values, and dispositions that they will find useful both inside and outside of school.
2. Instructional goals focus on developing student expertise within an application context, emphasizing conceptual understanding of knowledge and self-regulated application of skills.
3. The curriculum balances breadth with depth by addressing limited content but developing this content sufficiently to foster conceptual understanding.

4. The content is organized around a limited set of powerful ideas (basic understandings and principles).
5. The teacher's role is not just to present information but also to scaffold and respond to students' learning efforts.
6. The students' role is not just to absorb or copy input but also to actively make sense and construct meaning.
7. Students' prior knowledge about the topic is elicited and used as a starting place for instruction, which builds on accurate prior knowledge but also stimulates conceptual change if necessary.
8. Activities and assignments feature tasks that call for problem solving or critical thinking, not just memory or reproduction.
9. Higher-order thinking skills are not taught as a separate skills curriculum. Instead, they are developed in the process of teaching subject-matter knowledge within application contexts that call for students to relate what they are learning to their lives outside of school.
10. The teacher creates a social environment in the classroom that could be described as a learning community featuring discourse or dialogue designed to promote understanding.

These generic goals and key features involved in teaching school subjects for understanding are implied in what we say about good teaching in the rest of this book. In addition, we emphasize the goals of powerful social studies teaching as identified in a position statement published by the National Council for the Social Studies (NCSS) (1993).

SOCIAL STUDIES GOALS: SOCIAL UNDERSTANDING AND CIVIC EFFICACY

Powerful social studies teaching helps students develop social understanding and civic efficacy. *Social understanding* is integrated knowledge of the social aspects of the human condition: how they have evolved over time, the variations that occur in different physical environments and cultural settings, and emerging trends that appear likely to shape the future. *Civic efficacy* is readiness and willingness to assume citizenship responsibilities. It is rooted in social studies knowledge and skills, along with related values (such as concern for the common good) and dispositions (such as an orientation toward confident participation in civic affairs).

The NCSS position statement goes on to identify *five key features* that must be in place if social studies teaching and learning is to be powerful enough to accomplish its social understanding and civic efficacy goals: *Social studies teaching and learning is powerful when it is meaningful, integrative, value-based, challenging, and active.* The implications of these key features follow.

Meaningful

The content selected for emphasis is worth learning because it promotes progress toward important social understanding and civic efficacy goals, and teaching methods help students to see how the content relates to those goals. As a result, students' learning efforts are motivated by appreciation and interest, not just by accountability and grading systems. Students acquire dispositions to care about what is happening in the world around them and to use the thinking frameworks and research skills of social science professionals to gather and interpret information. As a result, social learning becomes a lifelong interest and a basis for informed social action.

Instruction emphasizes depth of development of important ideas within appropriate breadth of topic coverage. Rather than cover too many topics superficially, the teacher covers limited topics and focuses this coverage around the most important content.

The significance of the content is emphasized in presenting it to students and developing it through activities. New topics are framed with reference to where they fit within the big picture, and students are alerted to the citizenship implications of the topics. Students are asked to relate new knowledge to prior knowledge, to think critically about it, and to use it to construct arguments or make informed decisions.

Teachers' questions promote understanding of important ideas and stimulate thinking about the potential implications of these ideas. Teacher–student interactions emphasize thoughtful discussion of connected major themes, not rapid-fire recitation of miscellaneous bits of information. Meaningful learning activities and assessment strategies focus students' attention on the most important ideas embedded in what they are learning. The teaching emphasizes authentic activities and assessment tasks—opportunities for students to engage in the sorts of applications of content that justify the inclusion of that content in the curriculum in the first place. For example, instead of labeling a map, students might plan a travel route and sketch landscapes that a traveler might see on the route. Instead of copying the Bill of Rights, students might discuss or write about its implications for particular court cases. Instead of filling in a blank to complete a statement of a principle, students might use the principle to make predictions about a case example or to guide their strategies in a simulation game.

The teacher is reflective in planning, implementing, and assessing instruction. Reflective teachers work within state and district guidelines, but they adapt and supplement those guidelines and their instructional materials in ways that support their students' social education needs. In particular, they select and represent content to students in ways that connect it with the students' interests and with local history, cultures, and issues.

Integrative

Powerful social studies teaching crosses disciplinary boundaries to address topics in ways that promote social understanding and civic efficacy. Its content is anchored by themes, generalizations, and concepts drawn from the social studies foundational disciplines and supplemented by ideas drawn from the arts, sciences, and humanities, from current events, from local examples, and from students' experiences.

Powerful social studies teaching also is integrative across time and space, connecting with past experiences and looking ahead to the future. It helps students to appreciate how aspects of the social world function, not only in their local community and in the contemporary United States, but also in the past and in other cultures.

Powerful social studies teaching integrates knowledge, skills, beliefs, values, and dispositions to action. In particular, it teaches skills as tools for applying content in natural ways. The teaching includes effective use of technology when it can add important dimensions to learning. Students may acquire information through films, videotapes, CD-ROMs, and other electronic media, and they may use computers to compose, edit, and illustrate research reports. Live or computer-based simulations allow students to apply important ideas in authentic decision-making contexts.

Finally, powerful social studies teaching integrates across the school curriculum. It provides opportunities for students to read and study text materials, appreciate art and literature, communicate orally and in writing, observe and take measurements, develop and display data, and in other ways to conduct inquiry and synthesize findings using knowledge and skills taught in other school subjects. It is important, however, to see that these integrative activities support progress toward social understanding and civic efficacy goals.

Value-Based

Powerful social studies teaching considers the ethical dimensions of topics, so it provides an arena for reflective development of concern for the common good and application of social values. Students are made aware of potential social policy implications and taught to think critically and make value-based decisions about related social issues.

Such teaching encourages recognition of opposing points of view, respect for well-supported positions, sensitivity to cultural similarities and differences, and a commitment to social responsibility and action. It recognizes the reality and persistence of tensions but promotes positive human relationships built on understanding and willingness to search for the common good.

Challenging

Students are expected to strive to accomplish the instructional goals through thoughtful participation in lessons and activities and careful work on assignments. The teacher encourages the class to function as a learning community, using reflective discussion to work collaboratively to deepen understandings of the meanings and implications of the content.

The teacher stimulates and challenges students' thinking by exposing them to many information sources that include varying perspectives on topics and offer conflicting opinions on controversial issues. Students learn to listen carefully and respond thoughtfully, citing relevant evidence and arguments. They are challenged to come to grips with controversial issues, to participate assertively but respectfully in group discussions, and to work productively with peers in cooperative learning activities.

Active

Powerful social studies teaching and learning is rewarding but it demands a great deal from both teachers and students. It demands thoughtful preparation and instruction by the teacher and sustained effort by the students to make sense of and apply what they are learning.

Rather than mechanically follow instructions in a manual, the teacher adjusts goals and content to students' needs, uses a variety of instructional materials, plans field trips or visits by resource people, develops current or local examples to relate content to students' lives, plans questions to stimulate reflective discussion, plans activities featuring authentic applications, scaffolds students' work in ways that provide them with needed help but also encourage them to assume increasing responsibility for managing their own learning, structures the classroom as a communal learning environment, uses accountability and grading systems that are compatible with these instructional goals and methods, and monitors reflectively and adjusts as necessary. The teacher also adjusts plans to developing circumstances, such as "teachable moments" that arise when students ask questions, make comments, or offer challenges worth pursuing.

Students develop new understandings through a process of active construction. They process content by relating it to what they already know (or think they know) about the topic, striving to make sense of what they are learning. They develop a network of connections that link the new content to pre-existing knowledge and beliefs anchored in their prior experience. Sometimes the learning involves conceptual change, because the students discover that some of their beliefs are inaccurate and need to be modified. The construction of meaning required to develop important social understandings takes time and is facilitated by interactive discourse. Clear explanations and modeling from the teacher are important, but so are opportunities to answer questions, discuss or debate the meanings and implications of the content, or use the content in activities that call for tackling problems or making decisions.

Teacher and student roles shift as learning progresses. Early in a unit, the teacher may need to provide considerable guidance by modeling, explaining, or supplying information that builds on students' existing knowledge. The teacher also may assume much of the responsibility for structuring and managing learning activities at this stage. As students develop expertise, however, they can begin to assume responsibility for regulating their own learning by asking questions and by working on increasingly complex applications with increasing degrees of autonomy.

The teaching emphasizes authentic activities that call for using content for accomplishing life applications. Critical-thinking dispositions and abilities are developed through policy debates or assignments calling for critique of currently or historically important policies, not through artificial exercises in identifying logical or rhetorical flaws. Students engage in cooperative learning, construction of models or plans, dramatic recreations of historical events that shaped democratic values or civic policies, role-play and simulation activities (such as mock trials or simulated legislative activities), interviews of family members, and data collection in the local community. Such activities help them to develop social understandings that they can explain in their own words and can apply in appropriate situations.

PLANNING GOAL-ORIENTED TOPICAL UNITS

We have argued that instructional planning should reflect the generic subject-matter goals of understanding, appreciation, and application as well as the more specific social education goals of social understanding and civic efficacy. In the process, we have identified some key features of curriculum and instruction that reflect such goal-oriented planning. We will now argue that, at least for the elementary grades, these powerful forms of curriculum and instruction are most likely to be accomplished within topically organized units of instruction.

In addressing issues of content scope and sequence, we focus on the knowledge component of the curriculum rather than on its skills, values, or dispositional components. We do not mean to suggest that the knowledge component is more important than the other components or that it should (or even can) be planned and taught separately from them. However, we believe that curriculum development will proceed most smoothly if it begins by asking what knowledge is fundamental to accomplishment of the instructional goals and how this knowledge might be developed in students. Given the goals of elementary social studies, we would emphasize knowledge about how the social system works as it does, how it developed through time, how it varies across cultures, and what all of this might mean for personal, social, and civic decision making.

Most commonly, social studies curricula have been organized around (1) disciplinary concepts, generalizations, or themes; (2) questions or social issues, or (3) interdisciplinary treatment of topics. The first alternative is best suited to courses in the secondary grades that are based on a single academic discipline. Courses in history are typically organized chronologically, with instruction about each era focused around an interpretive theme (such as "movement toward independence" or "the closing of the frontier"). Courses in the social sciences are organized around key concepts (needs and wants, scarcity, production of goods and services, cost, price) and generalizations (unlimited wants chasing limited goods produce scarcity, every economic decision involves foregone opportunities as well as obtained benefits).

These disciplinary course structures are not well suited to elementary social studies because elementary students are not yet ready for systematic instruction in the disciplines. Such instruction presupposes the existence of cognitive developments and prior knowledge attainments that have not yet occurred. Elementary students need concrete and experiential learning opportunities to help them construct and begin to connect initial ideas about the social world. They do not yet possess well-developed bases of knowledge that they are ready to abstract and systematize along disciplinary lines.

Nor do we recommend organizing elementary social studies curricula around questions or social issues. This alternative is popular with those who favor group inquiry or social construction of knowledge as their model of learning, because it routinely engages students in critical thinking and decision-making activities. However, it assumes that students possess sufficient prior knowledge about the question or issue to enable them to engage in reflective dialogue in which they do not merely express opinions but support them by citing relevant arguments and evidence. Elementary students do not yet possess this level of social knowledge, so it is not feasible to organize elementary social studies around questions or social issues. However, the curriculum should include opportunities for reflective dialogue and debate whenever they are appropriate.

Instructional units featuring interdisciplinary treatment of topics provide the best basis for selecting and organizing content for elementary social studies. In comparison to disciplinary structures, topical units offer much more flexibility concerning the nature and sources of content. Guided by the social understanding and civic efficacy goals of social studies, the teacher can include any sources of content that seem appropriate, drawing not only from the social studies foundational disciplines (history and the social sciences), but also from the arts, sciences, and humanities, from current events, and from the students' familial and cultural backgrounds. *The point is to develop a basic network of useful knowledge about the topic,* not to develop knowledge within a particular discipline.

The unit approach also offers flexibility with respect to teaching methods and learning activities. There is no exclusive reliance on inquiry or any other single approach. There will be variation, both across units and across subtopics within units, in the proportion of time spent introducing new information, developing comprehension of key ideas through discourse, and engaging students in inquiry or application activities. The kinds of activities emphasized will vary with the content and learning outcomes to be developed. Thus, students might generate a report or product relating to one subtopic but engage in debate about another. Where subtopics lend themselves to it, activities include hands-on projects, site visits, collection of data in the home or neighborhood, or other experiential learning.

We do not mean to imply that all topical units are effective. Such units will not have much value if they are developed around topics that do not have much potential as vehicles for accomplishing important social studies goals.

Even if the topic is well chosen, it may not be developed in goal-oriented ways. The subtopics selected for emphasis might be trite details rather than powerful ideas, or the treatment might amount to a parade of disconnected facts that leaves students without a network of usable knowledge.

Most of the problems with contemporary instructional materials can be traced to the *development* of topics rather than to the *choice* of the topics themselves. Most of the unit topics are good ones because they are cultural universals that comprise the basic components of all social systems that have been developed in the past or exist currently in various human cultures. These topics are fundamental to social understanding and thus appropriate for introducing students to social studies. However, we see a need to shift from an emphasis on the expanding communities sequential scheme to an emphasis on the notion of cultural universals in rationalizing the choice of these topics to teachers and in introducing them to students.

One reason is that the expanding communities sequential scheme refers more to the contexts within which topics will be addressed (family, community, nation, etc.) than it does to the topics themselves (food, work, transportation, etc.). Consequently, it does not really provide a basis for rationalizing content selection and development. Shifting to the notion of cultural universals provides direction in selecting topics to address, identifying those aspects of each topic that are most fundamental and powerful as basic social knowledge, and representing this content as a network of knowledge structured around powerful ideas.

A second reason for a shift in emphasis is that the expanding communities model tends to yield disconnected parades of facts about each topic. In contrast, a focus on cultural universals as fundamental to the human experience provides a basis for developing elementary social studies programs that are much more goals-oriented, coherent, and authentic. In the next several chapters, we will consider how powerful units on these topics might be developed, beginning in Chapter 4 with principles for content selection and representation.

YOUR TURN: GOAL-ORIENTED CURRICULUM PLANNING

Select a social studies unit you have designed or taught, or one that you have observed being taught or have read about, and examine it according to the guidelines provided in this chapter.

Complete the following planning guide in order to reveal the strengths and limitations of the unit. Share the results with a peer, then return to the unit materials and address the limitations. Share your proposed enhancements with a peer or, if possible, a veteran teacher who has taught the unit. When possible, volunteer to teach the revised unit, this time to another class. Compare the results.

GOAL-ORIENTED PLANNING GUIDE

Title of Unit _____

Provisions for Understanding	Activities and Assignments	Assessment
Goal		
Major Understandings		

Provisions for Appreciation		
Goal		
Major Understandings		

Provisions for Life Application		
Goal		
Major Understandings		

If you have the opportunity to teach the unit again soon after you have made the enhancements, interview students regarding their understandings, appreciations, and life applications. For example, if you selected a unit on food, you might ask the following questions:

- Where does food come from?
- How do people get their food?
- What kinds of choices do people make about food?
- What is involved in these decisions?
- Do people all over the world eat the same foods? Why? Why not?
- How do peoples' backgrounds influence the kinds of foods they eat?
- What kinds of jobs do people have that connect to the food industry?
- If you could work in the food industry, what would you choose to do and why?
- How has the food industry changed over time?
- How did the pioneers get their food? How do you get your food? How have things changed?

REFERENCES

Anderson, L. (1989). Implementing instructional programs to promote meaningful, self-regulated learning. In J. Brophy (Ed.), *Advances in research on teaching: Vol. 1. Teaching for meaningful understanding and self-regulated learning* (pp. 311–343). Greenwich, CT: JAI Press.

Brophy, J. (Ed.). (1989). *Advances in research on teaching: Vol. 1. Teaching for meaningful understanding and self-regulated learning*. Greenwich, CT: JAI Press.

Brophy, J. (1992). Probing the subtleties of subject-matter learning. *Educational Leadership, 49* (7), 4–8.

National Council for the Social Studies (NCSS). (1993). A vision of powerful teaching and learning in the social studies: Building social understanding and civic efficacy. *Social Education, 57,* 213–223.

Prawat, R. (1989). Promoting access to knowledge, strategy, and disposition in students: A research synthesis. *Review of Educational Research, 59,* 1–41.

Chapter 4

Selecting and Representing Content

We do not have time to teach everything worth learning in social studies. Only so many topics can be included in the curriculum, and not all of these can be developed in sufficient depth to promote deep understanding of the topic, appreciation of its significance, and exploration of its applications to life outside of school. This tension between breadth of coverage and depth of topic development is an enduring dilemma that teachers must try to manage as best they can; it is not a problem that they can solve in any permanent or completely satisfactory manner. Still, teachers can develop compromise solutions that reflect the purposes and goals of their social studies instruction.

Recent research indicates that most social studies curriculum and instruction has drifted into an overemphasis on breadth at the expense of depth. As we noted in Chapter 2, critics of textbooks routinely complain that these texts offer seemingly endless parades of disconnected facts, not coherent networks of connected content structured around powerful ideas. Reports of social studies teaching and learning observed in classrooms suggest a similar picture. Although there are exceptions, most of these descriptions portray teachers as hurriedly attempting to cover too much content and students as attempting to memorize as much as they can. Students spend too much time reading, reciting, filling out worksheets, and taking memory tests, and not enough time engaging in sustained discourse about powerful ideas or applying these ideas in authentic activities (Goodlad, 1984; Shaver, 1991; Stodolsky, 1988).

Disconnected factual information is not very meaningful or memorable. Lacking contexts within which to situate their learning and richly connected networks of ideas to enhance its meaningfulness, students are forced to rely on rote memorizing instead of more sophisticated learning and application strategies. They remember as much as they can until the test, but then forget most of it afterwards. Furthermore, most of what they do remember is inert knowledge that they are not able to use in relevant application situations (Prawat, 1989; Resnick, 1989).

Scholars who have studied this problem are in general agreement about what needs to be done to enable students to construct meaningful knowledge that they can access and use in their lives outside of school. First, there needs to be a retreat from breadth of coverage in order to allow time to develop the most important content in greater depth. Second, this important content needs to be taught as networks of connected information structured around powerful ideas. Instruction should focus on explaining these important ideas and the connections among them.

Goal-Oriented Development of Powerful Ideas

It ought to be easy to focus social studies instruction on important topics and develop these topics with emphasis on powerful ideas. Teachers would only need to pose the following questions and then follow through accordingly:

1. What topics are most useful as bases for advancing my students' social understanding and civic efficacy?
2. What are the most important understandings about the topics that my students will need to develop, and how do these connect to one another and to related skills, values, and dispositions?

If major social education goals were used in this way to guide curriculum development and instructional planning, they would yield coherent social studies programs. However, major social understanding and civic efficacy goals tend to get lost as operational plans are developed for implementing state and district curriculum guidelines. Planning gets driven by content coverage *lists* rather than major social education *goals.* As a result, the content of many lessons and even entire units becomes disconnected, often lacking in life-application potential and thus having little social education value. For example, Naylor and Diem (1987, p. 51) cited the following hierarchy of curriculum goals as typical for social studies:

District-wide goal (taken from the NCSS guidelines): to prepare young people to become humane, rational, participating citizens in a world that is becoming increasingly interdependent

Program-area goal for social studies, K–12: to enable students to recognize and appreciate that people living in different cultures are likely to share some common values but also to hold other different values that are rooted in experience and legitimate in terms of their own culture

Grade-level goal for social studies, Grade 1: to understand and appreciate that the roles and values of family members may differ according to the structure of the family, its circumstances, and its cultural setting

Unit-level goal for social studies, Grade 1: to understand that families differ in size and composition

Notice that the last (unit-level) goal is phrased in purely descriptive, knowledge-level language, and that it is trite for a unit goal even at the first-grade level. It makes no reference to the anthropological and sociological concepts (cultures, roles) or to the values and dispositions (multicultural appreciation, citizen participation) referred to in the higher level goals. Unless the teacher has a coherent view of the nature and purposes of social education and thus is aware of how this topic fits within the big picture, the result is likely to be a version of social studies that is long on isolated practice of facts or skills but short on integration and application of social learning. Students will learn a few obvious generalities about families, such as that families differ in size and composition, that they grow and change, and that their members work and play together. However, they will not learn much about variations in family roles across time and culture, the reasons for these variations, or the lifestyle trade-offs that they offer. There will be little to advance the students' knowledge of the human condition, to help them put the familiar into broader perspective, or even to stimulate their thinking about family as a concept.

Several consequences follow from limiting the unit-level goal to developing the understanding that families differ in size and composition. The "composition" part at least has potential: If developed properly, it could lead to informative and thought-provoking lessons on family composition and roles as they have evolved through time and as they exist today in different societies. To have much social education value, however, such lessons would have to emphasize not merely *that* such differences exist, but *why*. For example, the students might learn that a major social effect of industrialization is a reduction of the extended family's role as a functional economic unit, and that this precipitates a shift to the nuclear family as the typical household unit. Instead of living and working together as a large extended family, small nuclear families live in separate households and spend much of their time with nonrelatives. Their members may pursue more varied occupational and lifestyle options than exist in nonindustrialized societies, but they usually must do so without the continuing involvement and support of a large extended family. Teaching such conceptually based content about families (in age-appropriate language) will help students to place the familiar into broader perspective. In this case, it will help them to appreciate the trade-offs involved in various economic systems and associated life-styles, and perhaps to function more effectively as family members within our society.

The "size" part of the unit-level goal statement appears to lack social education value. First graders are already well aware that families differ in size, so what is the point of making this a major goal of the unit? Even worse, what is the point of following up such instruction with exercises requiring students to classify families as either "big" or "small"? Textbook publishers have discovered that a focus on family size provides an entry point for inserting certain generic skills exercises into the social studies curriculum. Thus, students are asked to *count* the members in depicted families or to *compare and contrast* big and small families. Other such exercises call for students to *infer* by indicating whether depicted families are "working" or "playing" or by inspecting drawings of families depicted before and after an addition has occurred and circling the family member who represents the addition.

Similarly, units on shelter usually convey the fact that people live in a great variety of homes, but say very little about the reasons why they live in these different kinds of homes and nothing at all about advances in construction materials and techniques, weatherproofing, insulation, or temperature control that have made possible the features of modern housing that most children in the United States take for granted. Units on government mention a few titles (president, governor, mayor), places (Washington, state capitols), and symbols (flag, ballot box), but say little about the functions and services performed by various levels of government. Thus, students learn that the positions of mayor, governor, and president exist, but not what these people or their governments do. In later grades, students are exposed to reams of geographical and historical facts without enough concentration on major themes and generalizations, cause-and-effect relationships, linkage to local examples and current events, or other instructional framing that might help them appreciate the significance of the information and consider how it might apply to their lives outside of school.

To bring social studies curriculum and instruction into better alignment with the major goals of social understanding and civic efficacy, we need to honor these goals not just in theory but in practice. In particular, we need to use them as the functional bases for curriculum planning. Two brief examples of this are given below.

A Unit on Shelter

Social studies teaching in the primary grades emphasizes universal human characteristics, needs, and experiences (food, clothing, shelter, transportation, communication, occupations, social rules, government and laws) addressed within the contexts of family, neighborhood, and community. An important social education goal for each of these topics is to build initial understandings that will enable students to grasp the basics of how that aspect of the social world functions, not only in the local community and in the contemporary United States generally but also in the past and in other cultures today. The idea is to expand the students' limited purviews on the human condition and especially to help them put the familiar into historical, geographical, and cultural perspective. This will increase their understanding and appreciation of social phenomena that most of them have so far taken for granted without much awareness or appreciation.

Thus, rather than just teach that shelter is a basic human need and that different forms of shelter exist, the instruction will help students to understand and appreciate the reasons for these different forms of shelter. Students learn that people's shelter needs are determined in large part by local climate and geographical features and that most housing is constructed using materials adapted from natural resources that are plentiful in the local area. They learn that certain forms of housing reflect cultural, economic, or geographic conditions (tepees and tents as easily movable shelters used by nomadic societies, stilt houses as adaptation to periodic flooding, highrises as adaptation to land scarcity in urban areas). They learn that inventions, discoveries, and improvements in construction knowledge and materials have enabled many modern people to live in housing that offers better durability, weatherproofing, insulation, and temperature control, with fewer requirements for maintenance and labor (e.g., cutting wood for a fireplace or shoveling coal for a furnace) than anything that was available to even the richest of their ancestors.

They also learn that modern industries and transportation make it possible to construct almost any kind of shelter almost anywhere on earth, so that it is now possible for those who can afford it to live comfortably in very hot or very cold climates. These and related ideas are taught with appeal to the students' sense of imagination and wonder. There is emphasis on values and dispositions (e.g., consciousness-raising through age-suitable activities relating to the energy efficiency of homes or the plight of the homeless). Development and application activities include such things as a tour of the neighborhood (in which different types of housing are identified and discussed) or an assignment calling for students to take home an energy-efficiency inventory to fill out and discuss with their parents. Students begin to see function and significance in elements of their physical and social environment that they were not aware of before, as well as to appreciate their current and future opportunities to make decisions about and exercise some control over aspects of their lives related to their shelter needs. See Chapter 11 for details.

A U.S. History Unit

In teaching a history unit on the American Revolution to fifth graders, our goals emphasize developing understanding and appreciation of the origins of American political values and policies. Consequently, our treatment of the Revolution and its aftermath emphasizes the historical events and political philosophies that shaped the thinking of the writers of the Declaration of Independence and the Constitution. Content coverage, questions, and activities focus on the issues that developed between England and the colonies and the ways that these impacted on various types of people, as well as on the ideals, principles, and compromises that went into the construction of the Constitution (especially the Bill of Rights). Assignments calling for research, critical thinking, or decision making focus on topics such as the various forms of oppression that different colonial groups had experienced (and the influence of this on their thinking about government), as well as the ideas of Jefferson and other key framers of the Constitution. There is less emphasis on Paul Revere or other Revolutionary figures who are not known primarily for their contributions to American political values and policies, and no emphasis at all on the details of particular battles. See Chapter 14 for details.

These examples do not suggest that our preferred goals, content emphases, and instructional approaches are the only or even necessarily the best ones to adopt in addressing these two topics. Instead, the examples are illustrations of how clarity of primary goals encourages the development of units and lessons that are likely to cohere and function as tools for accomplishing those goals, and in the process, likely to result in instruction that students find meaningful, relevant, and applicable to their lives outside of school. The particular goals to emphasize will vary with one's social education philosophy, the ages and needs of the students, and the purposes of the course. Teachers of military history in the service academies, for example, will have very different goals and will approach the unit on the American Revolution with very different content emphases than those in our example.

GOAL-ORIENTED UNITS ON CULTURAL UNIVERSALS

Different teachers might favor contrasting approaches to a particular topic because of differences in their students' prior knowledge or differences in how the instructional unit fits into the larger social studies program at their schools. All approaches, however, should be designed to promote students' progress toward social understanding and civic efficacy goals.

Powerful social studies units display other characteristics as well. Regardless of grade level, all such units include the key features involved in teaching for understanding that were outlined in Chapter 3. In Grades 4–6, units developed around primarily historical or geographic content will reflect the principles presented in Chapter 7. *For Grades K–3, we suggest four principles to emphasize in selecting and developing content* so as to help students understand how and why the social system works as it does, how it came to be that way, how it varies across cultures, and what this might mean for personal, social, and civic decision making.

First, using contemporary and familiar examples, the unit helps students to understand how and why the social system functions as it does with respect to the cultural universal being studied. In the case of shelter, for example, the unit might begin with the forms of shelter commonly found in the contemporary United States, especially in the students' own neighborhoods. Instruction helps students articulate the tacit knowledge that they already possess, as well as expand on and embed it within a knowledge network structured around powerful ideas.

Second, the unit includes a historical dimension illustrating how human responses to the cultural universal have evolved through time due to inventions and other cultural advances. For example, shelters have evolved from caves and simple huts to sturdier and more permanent homes, such as log cabins, to modern weather-proofed homes that feature running water, heat, light, insulation, and so on. Technological advances have enabled us to meet our shelter needs and wants more effectively, yet with less personal effort and time investment, than in the past.

Third, the unit includes a geographical/cultural dimension that exposes students to current variations in human responses to the cultural universal. Different forms of shelter exist in different cultures and geographical locations, in part because of differences in climate and the local availability of construction materials. Along with the historical dimension, this geographical/cultural dimension of the unit extends students' concepts to include examples different from the ones that they view as prototypical. This helps the students to place themselves and their familiar social environments into perspective as parts of the larger human condition as it has evolved through time and as it varies across cultures. In the language of anthropologists, such units "make the strange familiar" and "make the familiar strange" to students.

Fourth, each topic is developed with emphasis on its applications to students' current and future lives. This is accomplished through critical thinking and decision-making activities designed to raise students' consciousness of the fact that they will be making choices (both as individuals and as citizens) about appropriate responses to each of these cultural universals. The emphasis is not on inculcating preferences for particular choices but instead on building knowledge about the trade-offs associated with the major choice options. Shelter, for example, may engender discussions of the trade-offs offered by different housing types and locations (urban, suburban, rural) or the problem of homelessness and what might be done about it.

Although they address many of the same topics taught traditionally as part of the expanding communities curriculum, units on cultural universals that incorporate the principles outlined in Chapter 3 and in this chapter are far more powerful than the units found in contemporary textbooks. They focus on the elementary and familiar in that they address fundamental aspects of the human experience by connecting with experience-based tacit knowledge that students already possess. However, they do not merely reaffirm what students already know. Instead, they raise students' consciousness of and help them to construct articulated knowledge about aspects of the cultural universal that they have only vague and tacit knowledge about now. Such units also introduce students to a great deal of new information, develop connections to help them transform scattered items of information into a network of integrated knowledge, and stimulate them to apply the knowledge to their lives outside of school and to think critically and engage in value-based decision making about the topic.

In this chapter, we have emphasized that the development of powerful social studies units begins with identification of suitable topics. Then, content selection and representation are planned so as to feature networks of integrated knowledge structured around powerful ideas. In the next two chapters, we consider how these powerful ideas might be developed through classroom discourse (Chapter 5) and through work on activities and assignments (Chapter 6).

YOUR TURN: SELECTING AND REPRESENTING CONTENT

Identify the units you have taught—or plan to teach—this year. Examine them first by responding to the following questions:

1. What topics are most useful as bases for advancing my students' social understandings and civic efficacy?

_____

_____

_____

2. What are the most important understandings that my students will need to develop, and how do these connect to one another and to related skills, values, and dispositions?

KEY TOPICS	MAJOR UNDERSTANDINGS
1.	
2.	
3.	
4.	

K–3

Select a unit you have taught or plan to teach. Examine it carefully to determine whether it is reflective of the principles identified in this chapter for selecting and developing content. When it is not, revise your plans accordingly. Share the results with a colleague. As you teach the unit—with the enhancements—be mindful of the changes. In your reflective log, document the results.

PRINCIPLES	EXAMPLES OF APPLICATION
Principle 1: Use contemporary and familiar examples to help students understand how and why the social system functions as it does with respect to the cultural universal under study.	
Principle 2: Include a historical dimension illustrating how human responses to the cultural universal have evolved through time due to inventions and other cultural advances.	
Principle 3: Include a geographical/cultural dimension that exposes students to current variations in human responses to the cultural universal.	
Principle 4: Develop each topic with emphasis on its applications to students' current and future lives.	

Intermediate Grades

In Chapter 7, we provide principles for selecting content related to the history and geography that are traditionally taught at this level. Instead of skipping

FIGURE 4.1
Social Studies Strands

	UNIT ONE	UNIT TWO	UNIT THREE	UNIT FOUR
Culture				
Time, Continuity, Change				
People, Places, Environments				
Individual Development and Identity				
Interactions Among Individuals, Groups, Institutions				
Power, Authority, Governance				
Production, Distribution, Consumption				
Science, Technology, Society				
Global Connections				
Civic Ideals and Practices				

SOURCE: National Council for the Social Studies Task Force. (1994). *Curriculum standards for the social studies: Expectations of excellence* (Bulletin 89). Washington, DC: National Council for the Social Studies.

ahead, assess your units according to the curriculum guidelines published by the National Council for the Social Studies (see Figure 4.1). If one or more of these curricular strands have not been developed sufficiently, add the appropriate content. Share your work with a colleague or with the school principal. This exercise could serve as an extremely valuable activity for members of the social studies curriculum committee.

REFERENCES

Goodlad, J. (1984). *A place called school.* New York: McGraw-Hill.

Naylor, D., & Diem, R. (1987). *Elementary and middle school social studies.* New York: Random House.

Prawat, R. (1989). Promoting access to knowledge, strategy, and disposition in students: A research synthesis. *Review of Educational Research, 59,* 1–41.

Resnick, L. (Ed.). (1989). *Knowing, learning, and instruction.* Hillsdale, NJ: Erlbaum.

Shaver, J. (Ed.). (1991). *Handbook of research on social studies teaching and learning.* New York: Macmillan.

Stodolsky, S. (1988). *The subject matters.* Chicago: University of Chicago Press.

Chapter 5

DEVELOPING CONTENT THROUGH CLASSROOM DISCOURSE

Until recently, most models of effective teaching emphasized the teacher as the dominant actor in the classroom: explaining content to students, checking their understanding, and then supervising their work on practice and application activities. The widely disseminated model of Madeline Hunter (1984), for example, suggested that effective lessons contain the following elements:

1. Anticipatory set (prepare students to learn and to focus on key ideas)
2. Objective and purpose (tell students the purpose of the lesson)
3. Input (provide them with new information)
4. Modeling (demonstrate skills or procedures)
5. Checking for understanding (through questions or requests for performance)
6. Guided practice (under direct teacher supervision)
7. Independent practice (once students know what to do and how to do it)

Hunter's approach typifies what has become known as the *transmission view* of teaching and learning. The following assumptions are implied in this view (Good & Brophy, 1994):

1. Knowledge is treated as a fixed body of information transmitted from teacher or text to students.
2. Teachers and texts are viewed as authoritative sources of expert knowledge to which students defer.
3. Teachers are responsible for managing students' learning by providing information and leading the students through activities and assignments.
4. Teachers explain, check for understanding, and judge the correctness of students' responses.

5. Students memorize or replicate what has been explained or modeled.
6. Classroom discourse emphasizes drill and recitation in response to convergent questions, with a focus on eliciting correct answers.
7. Activities emphasize replication of models or applications that require following step-by-step procedures.
8. Students work mostly alone, practicing what has been transmitted to them in order to prepare themselves to compete for rewards by producing it on demand.

The transmission view embodies some important principles of good teaching, especially in its emphasis on the role of the teacher in stimulating students' motivation and readiness for learning, providing them with needed information and modeling, and structuring and monitoring their learning experiences. However, this view treats students as relatively passive receivers or copiers of knowledge. It does not convey images of students undergoing conceptual change as they construct new understandings, engaging in debate or carrying on sustained discussions rather than just responding to recitation questions, or collaborating in pairs or small groups as they work on cooperative learning activities.

In contrast, contemporary models of effective teaching and learning emphasize the role of the student as well as the role of the teacher. We noted in Chapter 3 that the following principles have emerged from research on teaching for understanding: The students' role is not just to absorb or copy input but also to actively make sense and construct meaning; activities and assignments feature tasks that call for problem solving or critical thinking, not just memory or reproduction; and the teacher creates a social environment in the classroom that could be described as a learning community featuring discourse or dialogue designed to promote understanding. In that chapter we also summarized the implications of the 1993 NCSS position statement that depicts social studies teaching and learning as powerful when it is meaningful, integrative, value-based, challenging, and active. All five of these key features, but especially the latter two, emphasize the need for active student engagement in knowledge construction, particularly through reflective teacher–student and student–student discourse.

These contemporary models of effective teaching reflect the emergence of a constructivist view of learning. *Constructivists* believe that students learn by making connections between new information and existing networks of prior knowledge. They emphasize the importance of relating new content to knowledge that students already possess, as well as providing opportunities for students to process and apply the new learning. Before knowledge becomes truly *generative*—usable for interpreting new situations, thinking or reasoning, or solving problems—students must elaborate and question what they are told, examine the new content in relation to more familiar content, and build new knowledge structures (Resnick & Klopfer, 1989). Otherwise, the knowledge may remain *inert*—recallable when cued by questions or test items like the ones used in practice exercises, but not accessible when it might be useful in everyday living.

ACTIVE CONSTRUCTION OF MEANING

The core idea of constructivism is that *students develop new knowledge through a process of active construction.* They do not merely passively receive or copy input from teachers or textbooks. Instead, they actively mediate it by trying to make sense of it and relate it to what they already know (or think they know) about the topic. Each student builds his or her own unique representation of what was communicated, and this may or may not include a complete and accurate reconstruction of what the teacher or textbook author intended to convey. Sometimes the learning is incomplete or distorted.

Even when the basic message is reconstructed as intended, different learners construct different sets of meanings and implications of "the same" set of ideas. For example, on reading about mountain climbers who overcame potential disasters to scale a peak successfully, one student might remember and think about the text primarily as a story about achievement motivation, another as a story about the value of teamwork, another as a story about how shared adventure seals the bonds of friendship, and yet another as an illustration of the challenges and specialized techniques involved in mountain climbing. The students all read the same story and their reconstructions of it all include the same basic story line, but they emphasize different meanings and potential implications.

Students routinely draw on their prior knowledge as they attempt to make sense of what they are learning. Accurate prior knowledge facilitates learning and provides a natural starting place for instruction, but inaccurate prior knowledge can distort learning. If new content gets connected to existing ideas that are oversimplified, distorted, or otherwise invalid, students may develop misconceptions instead of the target conceptions that the teacher is trying to teach. For example, students learning about U.S. history for the first time often overgeneralize what they learn about Jamestown, so that they come to think of colonies as very small villages surrounded by wooden stockades. Most of these students later elaborate their concept of "colony" as they learn about events that occurred between 1607 and 1776. Some of them do not, however, so that they retain their original "Jamestown" image of a colony even when they begin studying the American Revolution. As a result, these students may emerge from fifth grade with an image of the American Revolution as a spat between King George and a few villages, rather than as a significant war between two large and populous nations.

CONCEPTUAL CHANGE

Besides *adding* new elements to a child's existing cognitive structure, active construction of knowledge may involve *changing* that structure through processes of restructuring and conceptual change. Sometimes the needed restructuring is relatively minor and easily accomplished, but sometimes students need to undergo more radical restructuring that involves simultaneous changes in large networks of connected knowledge (Chinn & Brewer, 1993).

Merely exposing students to correct ideas will not necessarily stimulate needed restructuring, because the students may activate long-standing and firmly believed misconceptions that cause them to ignore, distort, or miss the implications of the new learning that contradict these powerful misconceptions. It may be necessary first to help students to see the contradictions between what they currently believe and what you are trying to teach, and then to appreciate that the target ideas are more valid, powerful, or useful than their existing concepts. Drawing out students' ideas during whole-class lessons or engaging them in pair or small-group discussions are two ways to help students to recognize and correct their misconceptions.

SOCIALLY CONSTRUCTED KNOWLEDGE

Some constructivist accounts of learning, especially those that have been influenced heavily by the developmental psychology of Jean Piaget, depict learning as primarily a solitary activity. They focus on the individual child who develops knowledge through exploration, discovery, and reflection on everyday life experiences. However, most constructivist accounts are variants of social constructivism. In addition to emphasizing that learning is a process of active construction of meaning, *social constructivists* emphasize that the process works best in social settings in which two or more individuals engage in sustained discourse about a topic. Participation in such discussions helps the participants to advance their learning in several ways. New input from others makes them aware of things that they did not know and leads to expansion of their cognitive structures. Exposure to ideas that contradict their beliefs may cause them to examine those beliefs and perhaps restructure them. The need to communicate their ideas to others forces them to articulate those ideas more clearly, which sharpens their conceptions and often leads to recognition of new connections. As a result, cognitive structures become better developed (both better differentiated and better organized).

Social constructivists' ideas have been influenced heavily by the writings of the Russian developmental psychologist Lev Vygotsky (1962, 1978). Vygotsky believed that children's thought and language begin as separate functions but become intimately connected during the preschool years as they learn to use language as a mechanism for thinking. Gradually, more and more of their learning is mediated through language, especially learning of cultural knowledge that is difficult if not impossible to develop through direct experience with the physical environment. Children initially acquire much of their cultural knowledge through *overt speech* (conversations with others, especially parents and teachers). Then they elaborate on this knowledge and connect it to other knowledge through *inner speech* (self-talk, or thinking mediated through language).

Social studies consists mostly of the kinds of cultural knowledge that Vygotsky viewed as socially constructed. He suggested that this learning proceeds most efficiently when children are consistently exposed to teaching in the zone of proximal development. *The zone of proximal development* refers to the range of knowledge and skills that students are not yet ready to learn on their own but could learn with help from teachers. Children already know things that are "below" the zone, or can learn them easily on their own without help. They cannot yet learn things that are "above" the zone, even with help.

Ideas about teaching within the zone of proximal development resemble in some ways the ideas connected with the notion of *readiness* for learning. However, readiness is passive in its implications. It suggests that teachers can do little but wait until children become ready to learn something (presumably due to maturation of needed cognitive structures) before trying to teach it to them. The notion of *teaching within the zone of proximal development* assumes that children's readiness for learning depends much more on their accumulated prior knowledge about the topic than on maturation of cognitive structures. A related notion is that advances in knowledge will be stimulated primarily through the social construction that occurs during sustained discourse, most rapidly with respect to topics currently in the student's zone of proximal development (Moll, 1990; Newman, Griffin, & Cole, 1989; Tharp & Gallimore, 1988).

Social constructivists emphasize teaching that features sustained dialogue or discussion in which participants pursue a topic in depth, exchanging views and negotiating meanings and implications as they explore the topic's ramifications. Along with teacher-structured whole-class discussions, this includes cooperative learning that is constructed as students work in pairs or small groups.

Earlier in this chapter we listed the key features of the transmission view of teaching and learning. Standing in contrast to the transmission view is the *social constructivist view.* Its key features are as follows (Good & Brophy, 1994):

1. Knowledge is treated as a body of developing interpretations co-constructed through discussion.
2. Authority for constructed knowledge is viewed as residing in the arguments and evidence cited in its support (by students as well as by texts or teachers, so that everyone has expertise to contribute).
3. Teachers and students share responsibility for initiating and guiding learning efforts.
4. Teachers act as discussion leaders who pose questions, seek clarifications, promote dialogue, and help the group recognize areas of consensus and of continuing disagreement.
5. Students strive to make sense of new input by relating it to their prior knowledge and by collaborating in dialogue with others to co-construct shared understandings.
6. Discourse emphasizes reflective discussion of networks of knowledge, so that the focus is on eliciting students' thinking through questions that are divergent but designed to develop understanding of the powerful ideas that anchor each network.
7. Activities emphasize applications to authentic issues and problems that require higher-order thinking.
8. Students collaborate by acting as a learning community that constructs shared understandings through sustained dialogue.

TABLE 5.1

Teaching and Learning as Transmission of Information Versus as Social Construction of Knowledge

TRANSMISSION VIEW	SOCIAL CONSTRUCTIVIST VIEW
Knowledge is viewed as fixed body of information transmitted from teacher or text to students.	Knowledge is viewed as developing interpretations constructed through discussion.
Texts and teacher are viewed as authoritative sources of expert knowledge to which students defer.	Authority for constructed knowledge resides in the arguments and evidence cited in its support by students as well as by texts or teacher; everyone has expertise to contribute.
Teacher is responsible for managing students' learning by providing information and leading students through activities and assignments.	Teacher and students share responsibility for initiating and guiding learning efforts.
Teacher explains, checks for understanding, and judges correctness of students' responses.	Teacher acts as discussion leader who poses questions, seeks clarifications, promotes dialogue, helps group recognize areas of consensus and of continuing disagreement.
Students memorize or replicate what has been explained or modeled.	Discourse emphasizes reflective discussion of networks of connected knowledge; questions are more divergent but designed to develop understanding of the powerful ideas that anchor these networks; focus is on eliciting students' thinking.
Activities emphasize replication of models or applications that require following step-by-step algorithms.	Activities emphasize applications to authentic issues and problems that require higher-order thinking.
Students work mostly alone, practicing what has been transmitted to them in order to prepare themselves to compete for rewards by reproducing it on demand.	Students collaborate by acting as a learning community that constructs shared understandings through sustained dialogue.

SOURCE: From *Looking in Classrooms* by J. Brophy and T. Good. Copyright 1994 by HarperCollins Publishers, Inc.

The transmission view and the social constructivist view represent opposite extremes on important dimensions of teaching. In practice, most teaching lies somewhere in between these extremes, incorporating features of both views (with the particular mix depending on the situation). Table 5.1 presents the key features of these two views, with corresponding features arranged side by side. Study these comparisons to develop an appreciation of the contrasting forms of classroom discourse that they create.

RESEARCH ON DISCOURSE IN SOCIAL STUDIES CLASSROOMS

Until recently, most accounts of teaching and learning in social studies painted a dismal picture of overreliance on textbook-based reading and recitation followed by solitary work on fill-in-the-blank assignments (Goodlad, 1984;

Thornton, 1991). However, researchers have begun to describe social studies teaching that reflects social constructivist views and research-based principles for teaching for understanding.

Secondary Grades

A major contribution has been the work of Fred Newmann and his colleagues (Newmann, 1990; Onosko, 1990; Stevenson, 1990), based on Newmann's broad conception of higher-order thinking. Newmann described *higher-order thinking* as challenging students to interpret, analyze, or manipulate information in response to a question or problem that cannot be resolved through routine application of previously acquired knowledge. He argued that this definition of higher-order thinking implies that social studies instruction should both develop and reflect a set of student dispositions that together constitute *thoughtfulness:* a persistent desire that claims be supported by reasons (and that the reasons themselves be scrutinized), a tendency to be reflective by taking time to think through problems rather than acting impulsively or automatically accepting the views of others, a curiosity to explore new questions, and a flexibility to entertain alternative and original solutions to problems.

Newmann and his colleagues identified six key *indicators of thoughtfulness* that have been observed in their studies of high school social studies classes:

1. Classroom discourse focuses on sustained examination of a few topics rather than superficial coverage of many.
2. The discourse is characterized by substantive coherence and continuity.
3. Students are given sufficient time to think before being required to answer questions.
4. The teacher presses students to clarify or justify their assertions, rather than accepting and reinforcing them indiscriminately.
5. The teacher models the characteristics of a thoughtful person (showing interest in students' ideas and their suggestions for solving problems, modeling problem-solving processes rather than just giving answers, and acknowledging the difficulties involved in gaining clear understandings of problematic topics).
6. Students generate original and unconventional ideas in the course of the interaction.

Thoughtfulness scores based on these indicators distinguish classrooms that feature sustained and thoughtful teacher–student discourse about the content from two types of less desirable classrooms: (1) classrooms that feature lecture, recitation, and seatwork focused on low-level aspects of the content, and (2) classrooms that feature discussion and student participation but do not foster much thoughtfulness because the teachers skip from topic to topic too quickly or accept students' contributions uncritically.

Teachers whose classroom observation data yielded high thoughtfulness scores were more likely to mention critical thinking and problem solving as important goals that focused their lesson planning. In talking about the satis-factions of teaching, they tended to cite evidence of good student thinking about the content, whereas low-scoring teachers tended to talk only about student interest or positive response to lessons (without emphasizing good thinking about the content).

All teachers felt pressure to cover more content, but high-scoring teachers experienced this primarily as external pressure and tended to resist it by favoring depth over breadth. In contrast, low-scoring teachers experienced it primarily as internal pressure and thus emphasized breadth of content coverage over depth of topic development. All teachers mentioned that students are likely to resist higher-order thinking tasks, at least initially, but high-scoring teachers nevertheless emphasized these tasks in their classrooms. Students described their classes as more difficult and challenging but also as more engaging and interesting.

Finally, thoughtfulness scores were unrelated to entry levels of student achievement, indicating that teachers can structure thoughtful discourse at all ability levels. Taken together, these findings suggest that thoughtful, in-depth treatment that fosters higher-order thinking about social studies topics is feasible in most classrooms (not just those dominated by high achievers) and that teachers can overcome initial resistance and bring students to the point where they see higher-order thinking activities as more engaging and interesting than lower-order recitation and seatwork.

Fraenkel (1992) drew on case studies of high school social studies classes to identify factors associated with differences in effectiveness. Like Newmann, Fraenkel found that the major factor determining the success of a class was the teacher, not student achievement levels.

Less effective teachers tended to present ready-made ideas rather than to ask students to develop ideas for themselves. They tended to talk *to* students rather than *with* them. Often they did not seem to have a clear sense of where they were heading. They tended to engage students in busywork and to stress memorization and regurgitation of facts rather than understanding of ideas. Many did not seem to like what they were doing, to like their students, or to be having much fun. Unsurprisingly, their students rarely were active learners and often were discipline problems.

In contrast, the more effective teachers often engaged students in discussions. When they did lecture, they combined speech with use of the overhead or showing pictures, maps, or other visuals. Their questions tended to elicit discussion rather than mere recitation and they often asked students to respond to one another's comments. Students often worked in pairs or small groups while the teacher circulated and interacted with them. They were often required to function as active learners by role-playing or giving presentations in class. The teachers made a point of engaging students in activities designed to help them understand and require them to use the ideas they were learning.

These teachers appeared to like what they were doing, like their students, and like their subject matter. They had high expectations for the students, emphasized depth rather than breadth of coverage, were able to explain things clearly using examples that related to the students' lives, had good wait times and were good listeners when students talked, demonstrated patience when students did not understand initially, varied their instructional approaches and types of activities, and displayed considerable command of their subject and ability to relate it to a variety of daily-life examples.

They also were highly attuned to their students. They encouraged students to take public risks by contributing their opinions to discussions and by publicly discussing their mistakes. Yet they were quick to notice indicators of confusion or anxiety and to react by providing additional explanations, alternative assignments, or other scaffolding. They emphasized bringing to light students' thought processes for public examination and discussion. They maintained personal contacts with their students and arranged for frequent interaction among students through cooperative small-group activities.

Elementary Grades

Most of the ideas and methods observed by Newmann and by Fraenkel in high school classes also appear to be applicable in elementary classes. Only limited research relevant to these methods has been done in elementary social studies, but Thornton and Wenger (1990) reported observing lessons that exhibited many of the characteristics of thoughtfulness as described by Newmann, and Stodolsky (1988) reported that the quality of students' task engagement was higher during more cognitively complex activities than during lower level activities. In addition, White (1993) described several case studies in which teachers set up contexts and arranged tasks to allow students to construct meaning interactively instead of relying on a low-level text-book/recitation approach.

Other chapters in the same collection of case studies (Brophy, 1993) provide examples of desirable forms of classroom discourse. Levstik (1993) presented the case of Ruby, whose approach to teaching history to at-risk first graders featured a great deal of inquiry and discussion. Sosniak and Stodolsky (1993) presented the case of Carol Olsen, a teacher who used a conversational approach to teach inner-city fourth graders about geography, history, and world cultures. In both of these cases, the students had limited prior knowledge and thus needed to be provided with bases of information from which to work, but the teachers nevertheless were able to emphasize social construction of knowledge rather than recitation as their primary discourse pattern.

ENGAGING STUDENTS IN REFLECTIVE DISCOURSE ABOUT POWERFUL IDEAS

When preparing your lesson plans, develop sets of questions that will stimulate your students to reflect on what they are learning and engage in thoughtful discussion of its meanings and implications. You may have occasion to use drill activities to reinforce learning that needs to be memorized, as well as recitation activities to check and correct understanding of an initial base of knowledge that must be in place to anchor subsequent learning activities. However, most of your questions should be asked not just to monitor comprehension but to stimulate students to think about the content, connect it to their prior knowledge, and begin to explore its applications.

Thus, questioning ordinarily should not take the form of rapidly paced drills or attempts to elicit "right answers" to miscellaneous factual questions. Instead, questions should be used as means for engaging students with the content they are learning. They should stimulate students to process that content actively and "make it their own" by rephrasing it in their own words and considering its meanings and implications. Furthermore, the questions should focus on the most important elements of the content and guide students' thinking in ways that move them systematically toward key understandings. The idea is to build an integrated network of knowledge structured around powerful ideas, not to stimulate rote memorizing of miscellaneous information.

For each subtopic to be developed, ask questions in sequences designed to help students construct connected understandings. Use different kinds of question sequences to accommodate different instructional goals. To develop an unfamiliar topic, for example, you might begin with questions designed to stimulate interest in the topic or help students connect it to their prior experiences, then move to questions designed to elicit key ideas, then move to questions calling for reflection on or application of these ideas. Where students have more prior knowledge about a topic, you might wish to place them into an application mode immediately, such as by posing a problem, eliciting alternative solution suggestions and rationales, and then engaging the group in reflective discussion of these ideas.

Do not develop complete scripts for question sequences and proceed through them rigidly. This is not possible, because students' responses to teachers' questions are only partially predictable. Nor is it wise, because teachers need to adapt their lesson plans to developing situations and take advantage of "teachable moments" that students create by asking questions or making comments that are worth pursuing. Nevertheless, an important part of goal-oriented planning is the planning of purposeful sequences of questions designed to help students construct key understandings. Such planned question sequences are much more likely to yield thoughtful classroom discourse than the inefficient patterns of questioning that occur when teachers have not thought through their goals in developing a particular topic or subtopic.

Certain aspects of questioning technique can enhance the power of your questions to stimulate student thinking. First, questions ordinarily should be addressed to the entire class or group rather than to a single designated student. This will encourage all students, and not just the designated individual, to think about the question. Second, before calling on anyone to respond, allow sufficient wait time to enable students to process and formulate responses to the question. You may need to emphasize to students that you are more interested in thoughtfulness and quality than in speed of response, as well as to discourage overly eager students from blurting out answers, distracting their peers by saying "I know!", or pleading with you to call on them. Finally, it is a good idea to distribute response opportunities widely rather than allow a few students to answer most of your questions. Students learn more if they are actively involved in discussions than if they sit passively without participating, and distributing response opportunities helps keep all students attentive and accountable.

Even if a discussion begins in a question-and-answer format, it should evolve into an exchange of views in which students respond to one another as well as to you, and in which they respond to statements as well as to questions. To conduct effective discussions, you will need to establish a focus, set boundaries, and facilitate interaction, but in other respects to assume a less dominant and judgmental role than you assume in recitation activities.

If you are collecting ideas, record them (list them on the board or on an overhead projector), but do not evaluate them immediately. Once the discussion is established, continue to participate in it periodically in order to point out connections between ideas, identify similarities or contrasts, request clarification or elaboration, invite students to respond to one another, summarize progress achieved so far, or suggest and test for possible consensus as it develops. However, do not push the students toward some previously determined conclusion (this would make the activity a guided discovery lesson rather than a discussion).

The pace of discussions is slower than that of recitations, with longer periods of silence between bursts of speech. These silent periods provide participants with opportunities to consider what has been said and to formulate responses to it.

Dillon (1988, 1990) has shown that teachers' statements can be just as effective as their questions for producing lengthy and insightful responses during discussions. Questions even may impede discussions at times, especially if they are perceived as attempts to test students rather than to solicit their ideas. Instead of continuing to ask questions, you sometimes can sustain discussions nicely by simply remaining silent; by asking students to respond to what their peers have said; by probing for elaboration ("Tell us more about that" or "Perhaps you could give some examples"); by asking indirect questions ("I wonder what makes you think that" or "I was just thinking about whether that would make any difference"); by summarizing or restating what a student has said; or simply by making some declarative statement that adds to the discussion and indirectly invites further comment from students.

To encourage your students to participate optimally in discussions and get the most from them, you will need to socialize them to function as a learning community. Students will need to understand that the purpose of reflective discussion is to work collaboratively to deepen their understandings of the meanings and implications of content. They will be expected to listen carefully, respond thoughtfully, and participate assertively but respectfully in group discussions. Both in advancing their own ideas and in responding critically to their peers, they should build a case based on relevant evidence and arguments but avoid divisive or other inappropriate behavior.

In summary, recent theory and research suggest that, even in the elementary grades, teacher questioning of students should be designed to emphasize sustained interactive discourse, not mere recitation. To the extent necessary, students should be taught to participate in such discourse in ways that support the development of the class as a collaborative learning community.

YOUR TURN: DEVELOPING CONTENT THROUGH CLASSROOM DISCOURSE

While you may not want to plan every lesson in your social studies curriculum to the level of specificity called for in the following activity, it will give you an opportunity to test your level of understanding of the content in Chapter 5 and to apply our guidelines for using discourse. Questions need to be selected and scaffolded so as to elicit the desired social construction of knowledge among members of the class.

Unit topic: _____

Specific lesson topic: _____

Specific goal(s) for the lesson: _____

Major understandings to be developed: _____

Identify questions you will use to assess existing networks of prior knowledge.

_____

_____

Identify questions you will use to detect misconceptions.

_____

_____

Identify questions you will use to encourage students to connect prior knowledge with new information.

_____

_____

Identify the considerations you will entertain for teaching within the zone of proximal development.

_____

_____

Identify specific question sequences you will use to focus students in depth on key ideas.

_____

_____

Identify specific questions you will use to stimulate students to think about the content and how it is connected to prior knowledge, and begin to share its applications.

_____

_____

Identify specific questions and/or summary comments you will use to bring closure to the lesson.

_____

_____

After you have carefully structured your lesson using classroom discourse as the major modality for developing content, prepare to tape-record it. Select several of the following criteria to serve as your focus for assessing your lesson. You can monitor your progress toward becoming an effective user of classroom discourse by continuing to tape your lessons and expanding the criteria for your reviews. This activity can also be effective for peer coaching and collaboration. Share the results with your principal. Listen for:

Coherence

Continuity

Wait time

Students' work habits

- Do they give auditory evidence of working collaboratively to deepen their understandings of meanings and implications of the content?

- Do they clarify or justify their assertions?
- Do they generate original ideas?
- Do they show evidence of respect for each other's ideas?
- Do they make content their own by rephrasing it and considering its meanings and implications?

Teacher's behaviors

- Do I show interest in students' ideas?
- Do I model problem-solving processes?
- Do I acknowledge the difficulties involved in gaining clear understandings of problematic topics?
- Do I emphasize higher-order thinking?
- Do I distribute response opportunities widely?
- Do I combine lectures and discussions with illustrative materials and minds-on/hands-on learning activities?
- Do I encourage students to interact among themselves and respond to each other's comments?
- Do I demonstrate good listening skills?
- Do I encourage students to share in large- and small-group settings?
- Do I emphasize questions that move students systematically toward the key social education understandings?
- Is my pacing appropriate, giving students time to reflect, question, and formulate responses?
- Do I summarize and refocus when necessary?

REFERENCES

Brophy, J. (Ed.). (1993). *Advances in research on teaching: Vol. 4. Case studies of teaching and learning in social studies.* Greenwich, CT: JAI Press.

Chinn, C., & Brewer, W. (1993). The role of anomolous data in knowledge acquisition: A theoretical framework and implications for science instruction. *Review of Educational Research, 63,* 1–49.

Dillon, J. (Ed.). (1988). *Questioning and teaching: A manual of practice.* London: Croom Helm.

Dillon, J. (Ed.). (1990). *The practice of questioning.* New York: Routledge.

Fraenkel, J. (1992, November). *A comparison of elite and non-elite social studies classrooms.* Paper presented at the annual meeting of the National Council for the Social Studies, Detroit.

Good, T., & Brophy, J. (1994). *Looking in classrooms* (6th ed.). New York: HarperCollins.

Goodlad, J. (1984). *A place called school.* New York: McGraw-Hill.

Hunter, M. (1984). Knowing, teaching and supervising. In P. Hosford (Ed.), *Using what we know about reading.* Alexandria, VA: Association for Supervision and Curriculum Development.

Levstik, L. (1993). Building a sense of history in a first-grade classroom. In J. Brophy (Ed.), *Advances in research on teaching: Vol. 4. Case studies of teaching and learning in social studies* (pp. 1–31). Greenwich, CT: JAI Press.

Moll, L. (Ed.). (1990). *Vygotsky and education: Instructional implications and applications of socio-historical psychology.* Cambridge: Cambridge University Press.

Newman, D., Griffin, P., & Cole, M. (1989). *The construction zone: Working for cognitive change in school.* Cambridge: Cambridge University Press.

Newmann, F. (1990). Qualities of thoughtful social studies classes: An empirical profile. *Journal of Curriculum Studies, 22,* 253–275.

Onosko, J. (1990). Comparing teachers' instruction to promote students' thinking. *Journal of Curriculum Studies, 22,* 443–461.

Resnick, L., & Klopfer, L. (Eds.). (1989). *Toward the thinking curriculum: Current cognitive research: 1989 Yearbook of the Association for Supervision and Curriculum Development.* Alexandria, VA: Association for Supervision and Curriculum Development.

Sosniak, L., & Stodolsky, S. (1993). Making connections: Social studies education in an urban fourth-grade classroom. In J. Brophy (Ed.), *Advances in research on teaching: Vol. 4. Case studies of teaching and learning in social studies* (pp. 71–100). Greenwich, CT: JAI Press.

Stevenson, R. (1990). Engagement and cognitive challenge in thoughtful social studies classes: A study of student perspectives. *Journal of Curriculum Studies, 22,* 329–341.

Stodolsky, S. (1988). *The subject matters.* Chicago: University of Chicago Press.

Tharp, R., & Gallimore, R. (1988). *Rousing minds to life: Teaching, learning, and schooling in social context.* Cambridge: Cambridge University Press.

Thornton, S. (1991). Teacher as curricular-instructional gatekeeper in social studies. In J. Shaver (Ed.), *Handbook of research on social studies teaching and learning* (pp. 237–248). New York: Macmillan.

Thornton, S., & Wenger, R. (1990). Geography curriculum and instruction in three fourth-grade classrooms. *Elementary School Journal, 90,* 515–531.

Vygotsky, L. (1962). *Thought and language.* Cambridge, MA: MIT Press.

Vygotsky, L. (1978). *Mind in society: The development of higher psychological processes* (edited by M. Cole, V. John-Steiner, S. Scribner, & E. Souberman). Cambridge: Harvard University Press.

White, J. (1993). Teaching for understanding in a third-grade geography lesson. In J. Brophy (Ed.), *Advances in research on teaching: Vol. 4. Case studies of teaching and learning in social studies* (pp. 33–69). Greenwich, CT: JAI Press.

Chapter 6

PLANNING AND IMPLEMENTING LEARNING ACTIVITIES

In one of our studies (Alleman & Brophy, 1993–1994), we asked preservice teachers in senior-level social studies methods classes to reflect on their elementary-school social studies experiences. For each of three grade ranges (K–3, 4–6, and 7–8), we asked them to identify at least one activity that they remembered clearly and to explain what they learned from it. Here is what was written by a student who apparently experienced a relatively barren social studies curriculum:

POWERFUL/MEMORABLE ACTIVITY	EXPLANATION OF WHAT YOU LEARNED
Grades K–3	
(No memory)	(No statement of learning)
Fourth Grade	
We wrote letters to a specific state (Texas) and requested information about that state. When we got the information we wrote reports and drew the flag, flower, and so on.	I learned how to write a formal letter, learned a great many facts about Texas, and learned from other students' posters and reports.
Seventh Grade	
We used maps and grease pencils to learn geography, latitude, and longitude. For every chapter we had to read and outline it.	I learned how to locate places by reading maps and using lines of latitude and longitude. I learned to outline.
Eighth Grade	
We had to research a particular subject and write a report on it. My topic was the Holocaust.	I learned how to use the library and to find research materials and I learned a great deal about the Holocaust.

The next student's memories were typical in most respects, except that she reported a cultural unit rather than a First Thanksgiving activity at the K-3 level:

POWERFUL/MEMORABLE ACTIVITY	EXPLANATION OF WHAT YOU LEARNED

First Grade

We did a unit on the Hopi Indians. I remember that we did a little program for the parents because I got to be the narrator and had the most lines. I thought this was because I was the best reader.	I don't remember anything about the play or what I read. All I remember is that the Hopi did not live in tepees like I thought all Indians did at that time.

Grades 4–6

I can faintly remember doing a report on a European country. Each person chose a country and researched it, then turned in a written report and presented an oral report to the class.	I studied Belgium. I learned what flax was and that it was one of Belgium's main resources.

Seventh Grade

By seventh grade I had a strong dislike for social studies and my teacher did not help one bit. All we did in his class was worksheets that were multiple choice.	(No statement of learning)

Eighth Grade

At one point we did a report on a president. I chose Andrew Jackson just because I liked the name. We had to research the president and then write a research report.	I found out that Jackson wasn't that great of a guy after all. I didn't find out about any of the other presidents, though, because no one shared with the class the information we gathered.

Our third example is from a student who reported unusually rich activities and learning outcomes:

POWERFUL/MEMORABLE ACTIVITY	EXPLANATION OF WHAT YOU LEARNED

Third Grade

We learned about economics by dividing into groups and "selling" supplies. Each group of sellers were also purchasers. Each buyer was given a different amount of money to simulate different income levels. Groups would set prices based on the competition. In the end, results were recorded and the class discovered how high and low prices and purchasing power had affected obtaining supplies.	Through this activity I learned how prices are set (competition), how high and low prices affect the supply of the seller and the demand of the buyer, and how income level affects what and how much a person can buy.

Grades 4–6

Create a country: We were required (at year end) to integrate what we had learned about government, monetary systems, cultures, and	This project taught me how interrelated and complex the components of society are. For example, geography determines climate and

Grades 4–6 *(continued)*

geography to create our own country with currency, government, and so on. All had to be workable but could be unique.	growing conditions. This in turn affects imports and exports, which then affect the economy.

Eighth Grade

We viewed several movies on Nazi Germany and their treatment of Jews. Each movie was very graphic, portraying the true horrors. We then had to write about the impact we thought these atrocities had on history and the Jewish community.	I learned that history is not just past events' determiners and predictors of the future. I remember experiencing social studies emotionally and not just intellectually. This made learning history a completely different experience.

Before reading further, try this exercise yourself. What activities do you remember from elementary social studies? What do you think these activities were intended to teach you? What did you actually learn from them? What do your responses imply concerning your own ideas about good versus poor learning activities?

We will return to these examples and summarize the findings from our study at the end of this chapter. First, however, we will offer our principles and suggestions for selecting and implementing learning activities.

Previous chapters have underscored the importance of using major social education purposes and goals to guide the planning of curriculum and instruction. Review of research indicates that such goals-oriented planning is not often evident in the content selection and development found in textbooks or in the recitation-dominant discourse patterns observed in classrooms. The way to improvement lies in focusing content development more clearly around powerful ideas associated with social understanding and civic efficacy goals.

We continue with these themes in the present chapter on learning activities. The term "activities" refers to the full range of classroom tasks, activities, and assignments—anything that students are expected to do in order to learn, apply, practice, evaluate, or in any other way respond to curricular content. Activities may call for speech (answer questions; participate in discussion, debate, or role-play), writing (short answers, longer compositions, research reports), or goal-directed action (conduct inquiry, solve problems, construct models or displays). Activities may be done either in or out of the classroom (i.e., as homework); in whole-class, small-group, or individual settings; and under close and continuing teacher supervision or largely independently (on one's own or in collaboration with peers).

Our research on elementary social studies has addressed certain fundamental questions about the nature and roles of learning activities: What are the intended functions of various types of activities? What is known about the mechanisms through which they perform these functions (*if* they do)? What is it about ideal activities that makes them so good? What faults limit the value of less ideal activities? What principles might guide teachers' planning and implementation of activities?

Our work on activities began with the critique of the 1988 Silver Burdett and Ginn elementary series described in Chapter 2. This work reaffirmed frequently voiced complaints about the activities components of elementary textbook series, such as that too many of the activities were fill-in-the-blank worksheets or that they involved practicing skills independently of the content developed in a unit (instead of using the skills to apply that content in natural ways). Our analyses also pointed to several additional problems that had not yet received much scholarly attention: activities that did not promote progress toward significant goals because they were built around peripheral content rather than key ideas; activities that were built around false dichotomies or other misrepresentations of content; cumbersome or time-consuming activities that did not offer significant enough learning experiences to justify the trouble it would take to implement them; and activities that ostensibly provided for integration across subjects but in reality did not promote progress toward significant goals in either subject.

In subsequent work, we have developed a systematic framework for thinking about learning activities (Brophy & Alleman, 1991). We have applied this framework to analyses of instructional materials and of reports of activities remembered from elementary social studies classes.

The Nature and Functions of Learning Activities

Our position on learning activities has been influenced by the general ideas about teaching for understanding and the more specific ideas about teaching social studies for social understanding and civic efficacy that have been outlined in earlier chapters. Other major influences have been the works of John Dewey, Hilda Taba, Ralph Tyler, and other curriculum theorists, as represented both in their own writings and in the work of more recent authors who have been influenced by them. Zais (1976), for example, emphasized the distinction between learning *activities* as specified in curriculum plans and the actual learning *experiences* that occur when students confront the response demands built into the activities. Students' experiences influence what is actually learned. Curriculum planners can prescribe activities but cannot guarantee that those activities will produce the desired learning experiences (e.g., requiring students to answer questions about events leading to the American Revolution will not guarantee that students think critically about the issues involved).

Zais also offered criteria for the selection of learning activities. He stated that the primary standard should be how well the activities contribute to students' attainment of curricular goals. Other criteria for good activities were that they provide for the attainment of multiple goals, engage students in active forms of learning, help them to develop values and critical thinking capacities, be built around important content, and be well matched to students' abilities and interests.

Fraenkel (1980) offered similar criteria. He suggested that good activities feature justifiability (serve goal-related purposes); multiple focus (further progress toward multiple objectives such as knowledge, thinking, skills, and attitudes); open-endedness (encourage a variety of responses rather than just retrieval of answers to closed questions); potential for increasing self-confidence in ability to learn (encourage students to inquire, think for themselves, or solve problems); sequential structure (build on what came before and prepare for what will come later); transferability of acquired knowledge (enable students to apply what they have learned to new or different situations); and variety (suitable mixture of intake, organization, demonstration, and expression/creation activities).

Raths (1971) suggested that activities should provide opportunities for students to make informed choices about how to carry out tasks and to reflect on the consequences of their choices later; play active rather than passive roles as learners; engage in inquiry into key ideas, apply important intellectual processes, or address personal or social policy problems rather than just learn factual information; work with actual objects rather than just read about them or view pictures of them; examine or apply a previously learned idea in a new setting; examine topics or issues that citizens in our society do not normally examine; take intellectual risks; rewrite, rehearse, or polish initial efforts; share the planning or carrying out of an activity with peers; address their own expressed purposes; and assess their work using criteria drawn from relevant disciplines. He also suggested that an activity is more worthwhile to the extent that it can be accomplished successfully by children operating at different levels of ability.

We have built on these lists and other writings on activities in four ways: (1) expanded them to include additional principles; (2) grouped the principles according to priority levels; (3) distinguished principles that apply to each individual activity from principles that apply only to groups of activities considered as sets; and (4) identified principles describing how teachers might structure and scaffold activities for their students in addition to principles describing features of the activities themselves.

To do so, we have bootstrapped back and forth between top-down and bottom-up analyses. The *top-down analyses* involved applying theoretical and logical tests to *principles* drawn from the scholarly literature. We assessed the validity, breadth of applicability, and level of importance of each of these principles, both by discussing them as abstract generalities and by applying them to particular social studies activities to see if what they implied about the value of these activities matched the assessments that we or others had developed by considering the activities themselves. These top-down analyses led to the recognition that certain suggested principles appear to be more fundamental or broader in applicability than others, and also that certain principles appear to be valid if applied to groups of activities considered as sets but not if treated as necessary features of every individual activity.

For the *bottom-up analyses,* we identified *activities* (suggested in textbook manuals or by teachers) that we agreed were particularly useful, as well as others that we agreed were flawed in various ways. Then we analyzed these activities to articulate more clearly what it was that made the good activities good and the other activities undesirable or ineffective. Where possible, we rephrased our insights into more general principles and then subjected these principles to top-down analyses. Bootstrapping back and forth between these two types of analyses, we gradually developed the theoretical position and set of principles described in the next sections.

BASIC ASSUMPTIONS ABOUT IDEAL CURRICULA

Our position is rooted in certain assumptions about key features of ideal curricula. Most of these assumptions reflect basic principles that are commonly stated in curriculum and instruction texts but that nevertheless are seldom reflected in the instructional materials used in today's schools.

Curriculum development should be driven by major long-term goals, not content coverage lists. Thus, activities should be included because they are viewed as means for helping students to acquire important dispositions and capabilities, not just to acquire cultural literacy construed in a narrow, "trivial pursuit" sense.

Content should be organized into networks structured around important ideas, and these ideas should be taught for understanding and for application to life outside of school. These assumptions about curricular goals and content are fundamental to the planning of activities because content (as represented to students) provides the cognitive base for activities. If goal-oriented planning has produced a curriculum featuring coherent content structured around powerful ideas, it will be natural and easy to use such content as a basis for activities that call for students to think critically and creatively about what they are learning and to use it in applications involving inquiry, invention, problem solving, or decision making. However, if planning is guided by coverage lists and produces a parade-of-facts curriculum, the effect will be to restrict teachers to a reading, recitation, and seatwork approach to pedagogy. Activities will be mostly low-level ones calling for retrieval of definitions or facts (matching, fill in the blanks) or isolated practice of part-skills. There will not be many opportunities for authentic applications to life outside of school.

Teaching social studies for understanding and application requires concentrating on key concepts and generalizations that help students understand and appreciate how the social world works, how and why it has evolved as it has, how these understandings can be used to predict or control social outcomes, and what the implications may be for personal values or social policies. Such content provides a natural base for activities in which students conduct inquiry, think critically, and make decisions about things that matter.

Activities are not self-justifying ends in themselves but instead are means for helping students to accomplish major curricular goals. They are designed to fulfill this function by providing structured opportunities for students to interact with content, preferably by processing it actively, developing personal ownership and appreciation of it, and applying it to their lives outside of school.

We assume that the knowledge and skills component of the curriculum has been integrated in ways that are consistent with the previous assump-

tions. Thus, the skills included in a unit would be the ones most naturally suited to important applications of the knowledge taught in that unit. Critical thinking skills and dispositions can be developed most naturally through assignments calling for addressing value or policy issues that come up in the process of studying particular content. There is no need to manufacture artificial exercises to develop these skills. For example, instead of engaging students in artificial exercises in identifying logical or rhetorical flaws, you would engage them in policy debates or assignments calling for critique of currently or historically important policy arguments or decisions. To the extent necessary, you would model and provide instruction in the skills required for these tasks, but the skills would be developed through authentic applications rather than artificial exercises.

We assume that sets of activities will be embedded within curriculum units, that different types of activities will serve different functions, and that these functions will evolve as the units develop. When *introducing* new content, you might emphasize activities designed to stimulate interest, establish an anticipatory learning set, or link the new learning to prior learning (such as by providing students with opportunities to compare/ contrast or make predictions from the old to the new). When *developing* content, you might stress activities that allow students to extend and apply their learning. When *concluding* subparts or the unit as a whole, you might plan activities that help students to appreciate the connections among learning elements and provide them with opportunities to synthesize their learning.

Activities should be assessed with an eye toward their costs as well as their benefits. To be worthy of inclusion in the curriculum at all, activities should be effective as means of accomplishing significant social education goals. However, a given purpose often can be accomplished through a variety of activities, so cost-effectiveness becomes an important additional criterion. Typically, the most relevant costs to consider are the time and trouble that the activities will require of both teacher and students. Some activities entail other kinds of costs as well, such as financial expense or emotional turmoil.

In combination, the assumptions stated so far imply that *sets of activities* embedded within units should be assessed with reference to their cost-effectiveness as methods for accomplishing major goals, and that *particular activities* should be assessed within this larger context. Given the major goals of a unit, an activity under consideration for inclusion in that unit might be considered (1) essential, (2) directly relevant and useful, although not essential, (3) directly relevant but not as useful as another activity that serves the same functions more effectively, (4) tangentially relevant but not very useful because it does not promote progress toward major goals, or (5) irrelevant or inappropriate to the goals. For example, we noted in Chapter 4 that we emphasize the development of American political values and policies in teaching U.S. history to fifth graders. With this primary goal, units on the colonies, the Revolution, and the founding of a new nation emphasize the historical events and political philosophies that shaped the thinking of the writers of the Declaration of Independence and the Constitution. Certain activities might be considered essential for such a unit: activities calling for research, debate, or critical thinking and decision making about the issues that developed between England and the colonies and about the ideals, principles, and compromises that went into the construction of the Constitution. Other activities might be considered less essential but still relevant and perhaps useful: studying more about the thinking of key framers of the Constitution or about the various forms of oppression that different colonial groups had experienced. Still other activities, even if similar in form to more useful ones, might be rejected because of their focus on peripheral content: studying the lives of Paul Revere or other revolutionary figures who are not known primarily for their contributions to American political values and policies, or studying the details of each of the economic restrictions that England imposed on the colonies. Finally, certain activities would be irrelevant to the unit's goals: studying the details of particular Revolutionary War battles or constructing dioramas depicting these battles.

The key to the effectiveness of an activity is its cognitive engagement potential—the degree to which it gets students thinking actively about and applying content, preferably with conscious awareness of their goals and control of their strategies. If the desired learning experiences are to occur, student involvement must include cognitive engagement with important ideas, not just physical activity or time on task.

The success of an activity in producing thoughtful student engagement with important ideas depends not only on the activity itself but on the teacher structuring and teacher-student discourse that occur before, during, and after the time period in which students respond to the activity's demands. Activities are likely to have maximum impact when the teacher (1) introduces them in ways that clarify their purposes and engage students in seeking to accomplish those purposes; (2) scaffolds, monitors, and provides appropriate feedback concerning students' work on the activity; and (3) leads the students through appropriate postactivity reflection on and sharing of the insights that have been developed.

PRINCIPLES FOR DESIGNING OR SELECTING ACTIVITIES

Consistent with the above assumptions and based on our curricular analyses and research, we suggest the following principles for designing or selecting activities. For more details, see Alleman and Brophy (1992) or Brophy and Alleman (1991, 1992).

Primary Principles That Apply to Each Individual Activity

This first set of principles identifies *necessary criteria that should be met by each individual activity* considered for inclusion in a unit. Failure to meet any of these criteria constitutes a fatal flaw that would disqualify the activity from further consideration.

GOAL RELEVANCE

Activities must be useful as means of accomplishing worthwhile curricular goals (phrased in terms of target capabilities or dispositions to be developed in students). Activities may serve many goals, but each activity should have a *primary goal* that is an important one, worth stressing and spending time on. Activities that amount to mere busywork do not meet this criterion, nor do games and pastimes, no matter how enjoyable, that lack a significant curricular purpose, nor do activities that are limited to reinforcement of vocabulary or skills that are never used in authentic applications.

The content base for activities should have enduring value and life-application potential, not just cultural literacy status as a term that students might encounter in general reading or social discourse. Even if a word, person, or event is currently a common term of reference, you should ask why this is so and whether there are good reasons for it to continue to be so indefinitely. If so, the reference is probably useful as a way to remember some important principle. Thus, it might be worth including Franklin's quote about hanging separately if we do not hang together or Lincoln's quote about not fooling all of the people all of the time in a history curriculum, and perhaps even building activities around them (discussion of their meanings or debate of their validity or application). There would be much less justification, however, for including quotes such as "Don't shoot until you see the whites of their eyes," or "Shoot if you must this old gray head . . . ," let alone for making them the focus of activities.

There must be at least logical (preferably research-based) reasons for believing that an activity will be effective in accomplishing its primary goal. This seemingly obvious principle is violated with surprising frequency. Many supposedly motivational activities appear unlikely to develop desirable student motivation relating to the content (i.e., such as introducing a unit on rules and laws by having students teach classmates some of their favorite games and spending time playing those games). It is true that one can make connections between game rules and rules governing life in the home, the school, and society at large, but it is also true that important differences exist between game rules and social rules. Using the former as an analogy to the latter may create misconceptions; time-consuming play is not needed to introduce the concept of social rules; and there is no reason to believe that playing games will motivate students to want to learn about social rules (if anything, they may resent this intrusion into their fun). Remember, an activity suggested in a teacher's manual will not necessarily fulfill its stated functions. In fact, it may have no significant pedagogical value at all.

Activities should be built around powerful ideas that are basic to the accomplishment of social understanding and civic efficacy goals, not around isolated facts or other peripheral content that lacks life-application potential. The content and associated activities of the geography components of current social studies curricula frequently fail to meet this criterion because they engage students in memorizing miscellaneous facts about a country instead of developing understanding and appreciation of how and why the country developed as it did, creating its current trends and issues.

Be sure that key ideas that provide the content bases for activities are represented accurately, so that the activities do not induce or reinforce misconceptions. Activities can be misleading if they are based on vague or somewhat incorrect definitions (e.g., products are things that we use) or misleading examples (i.e., emphasizing the exotic rather than the prototypical). Some cultural studies units focus on exotic practices in ways that encourage students to develop chauvinistic stereotypes rather than well-informed understandings of the cultural groups they are studying (e.g., singing slaves' spirituals or participating in "Indian pow-wows").

APPROPRIATE LEVEL OF DIFFICULTY

Each activity must be pitched within the optimal range of difficulty (i.e., the students' zones of proximal development). It must be difficult enough to provide some challenge and extend learning, but not so difficult as to leave many students confused or frustrated. You can adjust difficulty levels either by adjusting the complexity of activities themselves or by adjusting the degree to which you structure and scaffold those activities for your students.

Structuring and scaffolding of an activity are sufficient when students can accomplish its primary goal if they invest reasonable effort. If an activity is to function as a vehicle for assisting students to accomplish a goal, the students must undergo certain experiences in the process of engaging in that activity. If they cannot engage in the activity with enough understanding to perform the required tasks, or if (in effect) these tasks are performed for them by the teacher or by the structuring built into the materials, the activity's value will be nullified.

Ordinarily, activities should not combine difficult new processes with difficult new content. Difficult new processes should be introduced by using easy or familiar content. When the main purpose is to get students to process and apply new content, activities should employ easy or familiar formats and processes. Violations of this principle can cause students to become so concerned about the procedural requirements of activities that they fail to attend sufficiently to their content-related purposes (Blumenfeld, Mergendoller, & Swarthout, 1987).

FEASIBILITY

Each activity must be feasible for implementation within the constraints under which the teacher must work (space and equipment, time, types of students, etc.). Reflective thinking about powerful ideas usually can be stimulated through activities that do not involve expensive equipment or procedures that are inappropriate at school. However, certain activities are difficult to implement because they require more noisy commotion than is feasible in most classrooms, and others are difficult to justify because they involve significant risk to students' emotional security or would be offensive (with good reason) to significant elements in the community.

COST-EFFECTIVENESS

The educational benefits expected to be derived from an activity must justify its anticipated costs (for both teacher and students) in time and trouble. Some activities are not worth the time and trouble it would take to implement them. Often this is the case for activities suggested as ways to motivate student interest in a new topic or to culminate curriculum units. Other examples include time-consuming construction of murals or dioramas and overly ambitious pageant-like simulations and games.

Activities should not be burdened with needless complications that may distract students from their primary goals. Simple worksheet activities that should only require circling, underlining, or writing in answers often call for coloring, cutting and pasting, or other modes of response that take up time and distract students from content-related purposes. Many activities are complicated in counterproductive ways by converting them into games that place more emphasis on speed of response than on thoughtful understanding or that focus students' attention on winning a competition rather than on learning or applying content.

Secondary Principles That Apply to Each Individual Activity

The principles in this section identify additional criteria that apply to each individual activity. However, unlike the primary principles described above, these principles refer to features of activities that are *desirable but not strictly necessary.* Each individual activity in a curriculum should embody all of the primary principles listed above and as many of the following secondary principles as can be incorporated in ways that are consistent with the primary principles.

MULTIPLE GOALS

An activity that simultaneously accomplishes many goals is preferable to one that accomplishes fewer goals (so long as it is just as effective in accomplishing the primary goal). In social studies, the best activities are built around powerful ideas, involve using key skills (critical thinking, values analysis, decision making) to process those ideas, and allow students to do so in ways that engage them personally with the content and encourage them to apply it to their lives outside of school. These activities tend to address clusters of knowledge, skill, value, and dispositional goals, and to do so within authentic application contexts.

Activities that allow for integration across subjects or inclusion of special topics (e.g., career education) or skills (e.g., debate) may be desirable. However, such integration should not interfere with accomplishment of the primary social education goal. We view integration across multiple goals as a desirable feature of activities when it works, but it does not always work. Consequently, we classify integration as a secondary rather than a primary principle. It should not be treated as an end in itself.

We believe that most successful integrations will occur, not as a result of deliberate attempts to inject integration into the curriculum, but as natural by-products of goal-oriented attempts to provide opportunities for authentic applications of the content that students are learning. Potential activities should be considered first with reference to major social education goals. This process will identify numerous activities that incorporate various generic inquiry and thinking skills, as well as knowledge or skills associated with language arts or other school subjects, and integration will occur as a natural by-product of good goal-oriented planning. If a potential activity does not provide sufficient integration, you might adapt or substitute some of its elements in order to incorporate more knowledge or skills from other areas. You also might want to convert some activities from individual to cooperative formats. Be sure, however, that any such changes are consistent with the overall goals of your social education program and with the primary goal of each activity. See Chapter 9 for more about curricular integration.

MOTIVATIONAL VALUE

Other things being equal, activities that students enjoy (or at least find meaningful and worthwhile) are preferable to activities that students do not enjoy. Authentic, holistic, life-application activities are not only of greater pedagogical value but also more enjoyable to students than information recognition or retrieval worksheets, isolated skills practice exercises, or boring, repetitive seatwork.

Like integration, motivation is an important but nevertheless secondary principle. Too often, curriculum developers or teachers treat it as primary by planning "fun" activities that lack goal relevance. No matter how much students may enjoy an activity, it has no curricular value unless it promotes progress toward some worthwhile goal.

TOPIC CURRENCY

Activities that are constructed around currently or recently taught powerful ideas and that cohere as a set that builds toward major goals are preferable to "orphan" activities that are constructed around isolated content. Inserted skills exercises or other activities that are built around inserted special topics tend to disrupt the continuity and thrust of the students' progress through curriculum units. Furthermore, the isolated nature of these intrusions minimizes their value as learning experiences.

WHOLE-TASK COMPLETION

Opportunities to complete whole tasks are preferable to the isolated practice of part-skills, matching of words to definitions, or other work that does not cohere and does not result in closure as completion of a meaningful task. This is another principle that will take care of itself if activities are planned with emphasis on major goals and authentic life applications. Such activities tend to be holistic ones that result in accomplishment of some authentic purpose, and thus to be valuable for both cognitive reasons (applying knowledge and using skills within authentic contexts makes it more likely that students will generalize their learning to related life applications) and affective reasons (students find such activities to be meaningful and thus are motivated to engage thoughtfully in them).

HIGHER-ORDER THINKING

The best activities challenge students not just to locate and reproduce information but to interpret, analyze, or manipulate information in response to a question or problem that cannot be resolved through routine application of previously learned knowledge. This principle incorporates Newmann's ideas about thoughtfulness in academic activities. It implies that good activities will engage students in sustained and thoughtful discourse or writing about content in ways that cause them to think critically and creatively about it as they attempt to conduct inquiry, solve problems, make decisions, or engage in citizen action projects. The most desirable discourse activities involve discussion or debate rather than just recitation, and the most desirable writing assignments involve sustained writing rather than just filling in blanks.

ADAPTABILITY

Activities that can be adapted to accommodate students' individual differences in interests or abilities are preferable to activities that cannot. Other things being equal, activities that offer students some opportunity for choice in deciding what to do or autonomy in deciding how to do it are preferable to activities that lack these features. Similarly, activities that students of differing ability levels can address at differing levels of difficulty or sophistication are preferable to activities that require all students to use the same process in order to produce the same outcome.

Principles That Apply to Sets of Activities

The principles in the previous two sections apply to each activity considered individually. In contrast, the principles in this section apply to *sets* of activities developed as part of the plan for accomplishing the goals of a unit. Each of these principles might not apply to each separate activity in the set, but *the set as a whole should reflect these principles* (insofar as it is possible to do so while still meeting the primary goals).

VARIETY

The set should contain a variety of activity formats and student response modes. Within the range of activities suited to the unit's goals, variety is desirable as a way to accommodate individual differences in students' learning styles and activity preferences. There might be both individual and cooperative activities, for example, as well as variety in communication modes (reading, writing, speaking, listening) and information-processing requirements and task forms (communicating understanding, responding critically, conducting inquiry, solving problems, making decisions).

PROGRESSIVE LEVELS OF DIFFICULTY OR COMPLEXITY

Activities should progressively increase in levels of challenge as student expertise develops. As students become more accomplished in meeting the demands of various activity formats, they can take on more complex assignments, assume greater autonomy in deciding how to organize their responses, gather data from a broader range of sources, and so on.

LIFE APPLICATIONS

Students should apply what they are learning to current events or other aspects of their lives outside of school (in ways that make sense given their levels of development). Even if they do not involve taking action, such applications should at least include opportunities to develop understanding and appreciation of how the ideas currently studied in school apply to issues that call for personal and civic decision making. Much current instruction fails to include such applications, and when it does, many of the so-called applications are confined to decontextualized "academic" examples or cases that do not apply to students' lives outside of school. For example, students sometimes are asked to make predictions about a fictional country based on what they are told about its geographical features. If students are to develop appreciation for the value of geographical principles, however, they will need authentic opportunities to see how the principles can help them to understand actual past and current developments in our country and elsewhere in the world.

FULL RANGE OF GOALS ADDRESSED

As a set, the activities should reflect the full range of goals identified for the unit. In particular, to the extent that values or citizen-action goals are included along with knowledge and skill goals, the set should include activities designed to develop values or citizen-action dispositions. Whenever a goal implies doing, activities should include actual doing, not just reading or talking about it.

CONCRETE EXPERIENCES

Where students lack sufficient experiential knowledge to support understanding, sets of activities should include opportunities for them to view demon-

strations, inspect artifacts or photos, visit sites, or in other ways to experience concrete examples of the content. Concrete experiences are especially important in connection with knowledge that children ordinarily do not get much opportunity to develop through their everyday experiences. To learn about conditions of life in past times or in different cultures, for example, children may need to handle artifacts, view photos or films, or read or listen to factually based children's literature in addition to reading textbooks. Resources of this kind are increasingly available in video and CD-ROM formats.

CONNECTING DECLARATIVE KNOWLEDGE WITH PROCEDURAL KNOWLEDGE

Students should learn relevant processes and procedural knowledge, not just declarative or factual knowledge, to the extent that doing so is important as part of developing basic understanding of a topic. In the case of facts or conditions that reflect the end results of series of understood processes, students should not only learn *that* a thing exists but also *how* it is produced and *why*. For example, sets of activities in government and civics units should go beyond teaching facts about government (capitols, names of office holders) to include activities designed to develop understanding of governmental processes (what different levels of government do and how they do it) and citizen participation dispositions and skills (voting, lobbying). Similarly, in learning about different forms of maps, graphs, and other data display formats, students should learn not just *that* the different forms exist, but *why* they exist and *how* they can be used as tools to accomplish particular purposes.

"NATURAL" APPLICATIONS

Activities that are "naturals" for developing understanding of a unit's content should be included in the set for the unit. For example, retrieval charts and related comparison/contrast methods should be used whenever the content has focused on different examples of concepts (Indian tribes, geographic regions, governmental forms) or generalizations (population development tended to follow water transportation routes prior to the invention of motorized vehicles). Activities designed to develop understanding of sequences of causes, effects, and subsequent implications are "naturals" in teaching history. So are activities built around comparisons of historical events with contemporary events that appear to be following similar patterns.

PRINCIPLES FOR IMPLEMENTING ACTIVITIES WITH STUDENTS

The principles discussed in previous sections refer to the features of activities themselves. They are suggested for use in designing or selecting sets of activities to be included in curriculum units. The following principles refer to the ways that such activities might be implemented. In particular, they identify ways that teachers might structure and scaffold the activities for their students.

COMPLETENESS

A complete activity ordinarily would include the following stages:

1. *Introduction* (the teacher communicates the goals of the activity and cues relevant prior knowledge and response strategies)
2. *Initial scaffolding* (the teacher explains and demonstrates procedures if necessary, then asks questions to make sure that students understand what to do before releasing them to work on their own)
3. *Independent work* (students work mostly on their own but with teacher monitoring and intervention as needed)
4. *Debriefing/reflection/assessment* (teacher and students revisit the activity's primary goals and assess the degree to which they have been accomplished)

This principle operationalizes the point made earlier that effective activities require not just physical actions or time on task but cognitive engagement with important ideas. In turn, this depends in part on the teacher structuring and teacher–student discourse that occur before, during, and after students' responses to the activity's demands. Even for an inductive or discovery learning activity, an optimal type and amount of teacher structuring and teacher–student discourse will be needed to maximize the activity's impact.

INTRODUCTION

Students will need to understand the intended purposes of the activity and what these imply about how they should respond to it. These understandings are not self-evident, so you will need to develop them in the process of introducing the activity to the students. Good introductions to activities fulfill at least four purposes or functions:

1. Motivating students' interest in or recognition of the value of the activity
2. Communicating its purposes and goals
3. Cueing relevant prior knowledge and response strategies
4. Establishing a learning set by helping students to understand what they will be doing, what they will have accomplished when they are finished, and how their accomplishments will be communicated or evaluated

Be sure to make the goals and purposes of activities clear when introducing them. Students should understand that activities call for cognitive and affective engagement with important ideas to accomplish curricular goals, not just completion of a series of steps to fulfill a requirement.

Also, cue any relevant prior knowledge. This might include comparison or contrast with previous activities, asking students to use their prior knowledge to make predictions about the upcoming activity, explaining where the activity fits in a sequence or bigger picture, or helping students to make connections between its content and their personal knowledge or experiences.

INITIAL SCAFFOLDING

Before releasing students to work mostly on their own, provide whatever explicit explanation and modeling that students may need in order to understand what to do, how to do it, and why it is important. To the extent that the activity calls for skills that need to be taught rather than merely cued, your introduction should include explicit explanation and modeling of strategic use of the skills for accomplishing the tasks that are embedded in the activity.

INDEPENDENT WORK

Once students have been released to work mostly on their own, monitor their efforts and provide any additional scaffolding or responsive elaboration on the instructions that may be needed to structure or simplify the task, clear up confusion or misconceptions, or help students to diagnose and develop repair strategies when they have made a mistake or used an inappropriate strategy. These interventions should not involve doing tasks for students or simplifying the tasks to the point that they no longer can be expected to engage students in the cognitive processes needed to accomplish the activity's goals. Instead, interventions should involve scaffolding within the students' zones of proximal development in ways that allow them to handle as much of the task as they can at the moment but also to progress toward fully independent and successful performance.

Students will need feedback about their performance—not only information about correctness of responses but also diagnosis of the reasons for errors and explanation of how their performance might be improved. To the extent possible, provide immediate feedback as you circulate to monitor performance while students are engaged in an activity, not just delayed feedback in the form of grades or comments provided at some future time.

DEBRIEFING/REFLECTION/ASSESSMENT

Bring activities to closure in ways that link them back to their intended goals and purposes. Provide students with opportunities to assess their performance and to correct and learn from their mistakes. Ordinarily there should be a teacher-led *postactivity debriefing or reflection* that reemphasizes the activity's purposes and goals, reflects on how (and how well) they have been accomplished, and reminds students about where the activity fits within the big picture defined by the larger unit or curriculum strand.

For teachers, postactivity reflection also includes evaluating the effectiveness of the activity for enabling students to accomplish the goals. Depending on the relative success of the activity and the apparent reasons for it, you may need to take remedial actions now or adjust your plans for next year.

OPTIMAL FORMAT

Where alternatives are possible, implement an activity in whatever format will maximize the time that students spend in active and thoughtful cognitive engagement (and thus minimize the time that they spend being passive, confused, or engaged in busywork). Many activities that involve communicating about or debating content, for example, are better done in pairs or small groups than as whole-class activities that offer active roles to just a few students and require the others only to listen.

OPTIMAL USE OF INSTRUCTIONAL TIME

If the independent work phase of an activity calls for forms of work that are time-consuming but do not require close teacher monitoring, these aspects of the work can be done outside of the time allocated for social studies instruction. Ordinarily, students should do activities such as reading and taking notes for a research assignment, editing initial drafts for grammar and spelling, or working on elaborate illustrations or constructions during general study periods or at home.

EXTENDING THE CURRICULUM THROUGH OUT-OF-SCHOOL LEARNING EXPERIENCES

Learning opportunities in classrooms are necessarily limited and somewhat artificial compared to what is possible under more natural and unconstrained conditions. One way to compensate for this is to use the community as a living laboratory for social studies learning, and in the process, use the diversity of student backgrounds represented in the class as a resource for promoting social studies understandings (Alleman & Brophy, 1994). By "out-of-school learning opportunities," we do not mean mere homework, which traditionally has focused on practice exercises designed to reinforce in-class teaching (Cooper, 1989). Instead, we refer to learning opportunities that expand and enrich the curriculum by causing students to think and collect information about how social studies concepts learned at school apply to family and community situations, then feed their findings back into subsequent class discussions.

The principles outlined above for selecting and implementing in-school activities also apply to out-of-school activities, with some minor modifications. First, out-of-school opportunities for social studies learning can use the students' total environment to provide data or learning resources. This makes certain activities feasible that would not be feasible in the classroom. Also, you do not have to assign as high a priority to cost-effectiveness. Once students are clear about what they need to do, they can work at home on individually negotiated or time-consuming projects that complement the group lessons and activities done in the classroom.

One obvious function of out-of-school learning activities is to provide opportunities for students to apply what they are learning in school to their lives outside of school. In connection with the topic of conservation of natural resources, for example, students might interview appropriate local informants to learn about such matters as why there is no mass transit commuter transportation to a nearby city, why there are designated commuter lots, why packets of recycled paper cost more than others, or why there are or are not restrictions on watering lawns. Better yet, encourage students to get involved in appropriate conservation and renewal activities sponsored by community organizations. Students studying food or consumer aspects of economics might accompany an adult on the next household shopping trip to address a class-generated set of questions (e.g., Where are the most nutritious cereals placed relative to children's sweet favorites? How are sale items positioned? Are there differences in the packaging of the sweetened cereals versus the more healthful ones? How do special offers figure into a cereal's cost?). These questions would set the stage for observations and serve as guidelines for later discussions in class.

Social studies is rich with options for involving the family and community in nonthreatening out-of-school learning opportunities that call for collaboration in ways that can be mutually satisfying and stimulating. Students studying states or regions can talk with their families about connections they have with these states or regions through business contacts, family use of goods from there, or vacations proposed or taken there. Students studying U.S., state, or local history could solicit help from adults in the community in order to gather information about the history of their locale—how it came to be, why, who explored and settled the place, when it became recognized as a settlement, and so on. Local newspapers, graveyards, history buffs, historical societies, and retirement facilities are invaluable resources for bringing history to life in this way.

The collaborative learning that occurs outside the classroom has the potential for improving in-class participation among students. It also tends to create a more informed cadre of human resources sprinkled throughout the community whose informal involvement should enhance their regard for you as a teacher and for social studies as an important school subject. Finally, students will have opportunities to become involved with their parents and other adults in positive and productive relationships, and these adults will have opportunities to enjoy rewarding involvement in the students' education.

If your students represent a diversity of social and cultural backgrounds, you can take advantage of this diversity by using it as a learning resource. For example, in studying families or cultures, ask your students to spend out-of-school time talking with family members about daily rituals or special customs that they enjoy based on their cultural heritage (ethnic foods, special holiday celebrations, etc.). The students can follow up by making drawings or montages, collecting artifacts or other memorabilia for classroom display, or preparing videotapes or other representations of cultural contributions. Similarly, students studying the family might interview family members about their roles at home and at work and about rules and expectations that affect the children. These data can then be "harvested" during follow-up in-class discussions designed to develop knowledge about various family roles and membership configurations, appreciation of the reasons for those diverse patterns, and an inquisitiveness about the similarities and differences across cultures both within the United States and throughout the world.

Data gathered from family members also can enhance students' appreciation of the fact that social studies content can be approached from diverse perspectives. For example, one goal of a geographical unit might be for students to develop appreciation of the connections between their own community and Asia. Typically, students would read text material, discuss it in class, and list connections on the board. Such a lesson would have more impact if the students first interviewed adults in their homes or neighborhoods regarding their views of global connections with Asia. A parent or neighbor who has been laid off from an American automobile plant might feel quite differently than a parent or neighbor who sells Asian-made audio/video equipment at a local appliance store. Such interviewing can be coupled with investigation of the home to determine the number and nature of goods from Asia that are found there.

You also can use out-of-school activities to exploit learning opportunities that are not cost-efficient if done during school time. For example, due to the complications involved in making travel arrangements and rescheduling classes, it might not be feasible to take your whole class to attend a city council meeting or a trial in a local courtroom. However, you might arrange for a few student volunteers to go with their parents to a city council meeting or a court session and serve as observers, data gatherers, and primary resources for a follow-up in-class discussion.

Other examples of outside learning opportunities that can be useful when structured appropriately and tied to in-school goals include watching a television program about a place or group of people (e.g., the Amish); studying commercials over a span of time in an effort to detect patterns; visiting a local pharmacy to compare the costs of generic brands versus popularly labeled ones advertised on television; or studying the marketing strategies used by local supermarkets. Such activities serve as validity checks on "book learning" and provide connections that stretch beyond the scope of the school day.

In theory, much of what is in the social studies curriculum is there because it is thought to be important as preparation for students to cope with the demands of modern living and function as responsible citizens in our society. Unless students are encouraged and given opportunities to apply what they are learning to their lives outside of school, however, they may not see the connections and thus may not get the intended "citizen preparation" benefits. At the same time, out-of-school learning activities provide opportunities to involve parents and other community members in the school's agenda in rewarding ways. Most people are likely to be pleased to be asked to serve as a resource by answering children's questions about what life was like when they were younger, how they reacted to a major news event in the past, the details of what they do at work, or the trade-offs involved in their jobs as lifetime occupations. When children carry on such conversations with their parents, one likely result is reinforcement of familial bonds and an increase in the students' appreciation of and respect for their parents as individuals.

Of course, such activities will need to be planned and implemented with clear goals in mind and followed up with sharing and discussion in subsequent class sessions. You will need to include instructions that clarify the goals of the assignment for students, and perhaps also to supply data collection sheets or other scaffolds to help students carry out the activities as intended. Where assignments are sensitive or demanding, it is advisable to send home explanations for parents or alert them to this aspect of the curriculum when meeting with them.

COLLEGE STUDENTS' REPORTS OF LEARNING ACTIVITIES EXPERIENCED IN ELEMENTARY SOCIAL STUDIES

As an application and indirect test of the principles presented in this chapter, we asked senior education majors to tell us about the social studies activities they remembered from their elementary years and to state what they believed they learned from engaging in those activities. Responses from three students who had experienced contrasting social studies programs were quoted at the beginning of the chapter.

As we began the study, we wondered what activities students would remember and what kinds of learning they would report. Would they just remember the details of the activities, or would they also report powerful understandings as learning outcomes? Would the kinds of activities that we consider powerful be remembered more vividly and be associated with more powerful learning outcomes than the kinds of activities that we consider less valuable? Would certain activities yield noteworthy affective responses?

It was important to ask what the students remembered *learning* because curriculum developers and teachers often cite salience in students' memories as justification for their activity selections ("Students may not remember the everyday stuff, but they all remember our reenactment of the First Thanksgiving"). Such justifications are incomplete. They retain their power if students report learnings that reflect major social education goals, but they become questionable if the students remember the activities only because they were fun or if they report undesirable learning outcomes (e.g., stereotyped perceptions of Native Americans acquired through participation in First Thanksgiving reenactments).

We coded the responses along several dimensions that yielded several variables, but the most important were the following:

High cognitive learning: Student specifies particular aspects of what was learned, or better yet specifies a significant conclusion or insight that reflects social studies purposes and goals (versus producing only a vague statement or being unable to report any cognitive learnings at all).

TABLE 6.1
Activity Types Reported by Grade Level

ACTIVITY	ACTUAL NUMBERS			PERCENTAGES		
Types	K–3	4–6	7–8	K–3	4–6	7–8
Thematic units	9	8	1	6	4	<1
Lecture/Presentation	13	22	23	9	12	14
Seatwork	12	28	37	8	16	23
Research	11	37	30	8	21	19
Model/Construction	23	38	18	16	21	11
Field trip	23	15	13	16	8	8
Discussion/Debate	1	2	9	1	1	6
Pageant/Role Enactment	28	8	8	20	4	5
Simulation	8	14	15	6	8	9
Other	14	8	5	10	4	3
Total	142	180	159	100	99	99

Desirable affective outcomes: Student reports that the learning produced through the activity was very interesting or that the activity enabled him or her to empathize with the people being studied or to see things from their point of view.

Negative assessments: Student disparages the activity as pointless (e.g., learning about state birds) or characterized by boring, repetitive tasks (typically seatwork).

Table 6.1 shows the frequencies with which various types of activities were reported and Table 6.2 shows the percentages of these reports that were coded for high cognitive outcomes, desirable affect, or negative assessments. We expected students to have the fewest memories from Grades K–3 and the most from Grades 7–8 (because they would not have to reach so far back in memory), but they had the most from Grades 4–6. Only four of them could not remember any activities from Grades 4–6, but 13 could not remember any from Grades 7–8 and 20 could not remember any from Grades K–3.

The high frequency of memories from Grades 4–6 appeared to be due in part to use of the unit approach in these grades, in which students engaged in sustained study of a topic over several days or weeks. Also, for many respondents, social studies in Grades 7–8 involved little or nothing more than reading the text, answering end-of-chapter questions, and filling out worksheets.

The trends shown in Table 6.1 generally reflect traditional wisdom about the needs of students at different grade levels. Hands-on activities are commonly remembered from Grades K–3, especially pageants/role enactments, field trips, and construction of models. Research and construction activities are remembered most frequently from Grades 4–6, followed by seatwork and lectures/presentations. The construction activities tended to be maps, photo montages, or

TABLE 6.2

Percentages of Activity Type Codes That Coincided with High Cognitive Learning Codes, Desirable Affective Outcomes, and Negative Assessments

ACTIVITY TYPES	% HIGH COGNITIVE OUTCOMES	% DESIRABLE AFFECT	% NEGATIVE ASSESSMENTS
Thematic Units	89	44	0
Lecture/Presentation	80	23	7
Seatwork	26	1	31
Research	69	14	4
Construction	76	11	4
Field Trip	80	24	0
Discussion/Debate	92	42	0
Pageant/Role Enactment	77	32	0
Simulation	81	22	3
Other	56	11	7

other illustrations to accompany reports on states or nations, whereas constructions in Grades K–3 were more likely to be papier-mâché globes or dioramas of neighborhoods or villages. Seatwork was the most frequently remembered activity in Grades 7–8, followed by research and lectures/presentations.

As expected, students tended to remember special events (field trips, elaborate construction projects, pageants, simulations) more clearly than everyday lecture/presentation or seatwork activities. Many students who did report lecture/presentation or seatwork activities noted that these were the only kinds of activities that they experienced at certain grade levels, so there was nothing else that they could have reported.

The data in Table 6.2 indicate that discussions and debates, which occurred infrequently, yielded the highest ratings of cognitive learnings. These were followed by curriculum units that included multiple activities and by realistic simulations and applications. Seatwork produced by far the lowest cognitive learning scores and the highest percentages of negative assessments.

Activities coded as research, construction, or both were associated with only modest learning outcome ratings. In part, this was because many students concentrated on what they learned about the mechanics of doing research or about working in a group, rather than on cognitive learnings, when they described what they learned from research projects (e.g., "I learned how to use the library and to prepare a research report"). Also, most responses suggested that the data sources used in research activities were limited to encyclopedias and texts.

Desirable affective outcomes generally were coded in conjunction with 20 to 30 percent of the activities reported. However, this percentage reached or approached 50 percent for thematic units, discussions/debates, and pageants/role enactments, but fell to only about 6 percent for seatwork. We were surprised that affective outcomes were not mentioned more frequently for field trips and for simulations.

Characteristics of "Best" Activities

To focus more closely on activities that yielded the most positive outcome ratings, we inventoried activities that either (1) were coded for the highest level of cognitive learning (stating a significant conclusion or insight that reflected social studies purposes and goals, whether or not this was accompanied by coding of desirable affective outcomes), or (2) coding of the next highest cognitive outcome (specifying particular aspects of what was learned) in combination with coding for desirable affective outcomes (interest or empathy). Of the 138 reported activities that met these "best" activity criteria, 24 involved simulations: 8 minisociety or other economics simulations; 5 mock conventions or legislative debates; 2 mock trials; 2 mock elections; 2 "create your own nation" exercises; and 1 simulation each involving family budget planning, pretending to be a child coal miner writing a letter to a relative, forming an assembly line to make sandwiches, acting as anthropologists by figuring out how artifacts (tools made from rocks) were used, and using information about countries' populations and resources to make decisions about where to live.

Twenty-one of these "best" activities involved field trips: 10 to historical museums and restorations; 3 to local sites (stores, police and fire stations, post office); 2 to Washington, D.C.; and 1 each to Mexico, Philadelphia, the state capital, an outdoor education center, a cider mill, and a train station. Seventeen of the "best" codes were for curriculum units: 9 on other nations or Hawaii; 3 on archaeology; and 1 each on the Eskimos, the Cherokee, consumer education, Thanksgiving, and Hanukkah. Fifteen were research reports: 8 on nations or regions; 4 on historical topics; and 1 each on a state, on explorers, and on election-year voting blocs. Eleven involved reenactments or pageants: 4 of the First Thanksgiving; and 1 each of the Civil War, Columbus, the Salem Witch Trials, the Boston Tea Party, a slave auction, a slave ship, and a pageant of nations.

Other "best" activities included: 6 class visits by resource people (3 fire and safety, 3 cultural); 6 construction projects (2 detailed maps of the neighborhood or town, 1 model of the town, 1 diorama of an Indian village, 1 clay volcano, and 1 log cabin constructed from tongue depressors); 6 media experiences (3 World War II videos, 1 World War II radio play, and viewings of *Roots* and *Fiddler on the Roof* for cultural studies); 5 career days; and 5 reports of spending the day in a restored one-room school house recreating nineteenth-century schooling. "Best" activities that appeared infrequently but more than once included 4 self and family activities (student-of-the-week display and presentation, show-and-tell about one's family, writing an autobiography, putting together an "all about me" book); 3 current events discussions; and 2 each for debates, map and globe activities, experiences in acting as classroom helpers, and teacher presentations. Finally, there were single instances of reading the text and answering questions, taking notes, burying a time capsule, singing "This Land Is Your Land," tasting cultural foods, interviewing a relative about experiences in Vietnam, and doing Chinese brush paintings.

Given the relative frequencies among the total memories reported, high percentages of thematic units, simulations, discussions/debates, and field trips emerged as "best" activities. Moderately high percentages were seen for lectures/presentations, mostly due to memorable media presentations or visits by resource people. Low percentages of reported seatwork activities and construction projects emerged as "best" activities.

Qualitative Observations on the Responses

Several qualitative aspects of the responses are worth noting. Given commonly reported research findings, we were not surprised at the frequent reports of seatwork assignments that did not appear to be closely connected to important social studies goals. However, we expected to see more frequent reports of activity types such as research, discussion, and simulation, especially in the middle and upper grades.

Some students' responses indicated that they were more caught up in "doing school" than in goal-oriented learning. Such indications were especially prevalent for seatwork activities such as memorizing the state capitals, learning the states in alphabetical order, writing out definitions, answering questions about the text, coloring maps, doing ditto sheets, or memorizing the locations of states and nations. Although many students who reported such activities criticized them as boring or pointless, a few appeared to be satisfied with them even though they were unable to say much about what they had learned from them. "Reaching" to find meaning in these repetitive, low-level seatwork activities, these students focused on their own strategies for memorizing or getting good grades rather than on the content that the activities were ostensibly designed to develop. They made outcome statements such as "I learned that this was an easy way to get an A"; or "I don't remember any of the flowers or birds, but this was the first time that I learned to use a specific memory strategy."

Many students had salient memories of visits by resource people that included statements of substantive cognitive learning as well as noteworthy affective outcomes. For example, in recalling a visit by a local woman who had come dressed in Japanese ceremonial attire to demonstrate a tea ceremony, one student not only remembered much of what the woman had said but stated that the experience "helped me gain an appreciation for their culture."

Memories of field trips frequently yielded positive learning outcome codes, and we suspect that this percentage would have been even higher if more trips had been accompanied by preliminary structuring to set the stage and by debriefing upon return to the classroom. This might have reduced the frequency of responses such as "I don't remember very much. I do remember it rained."

Role enactments accompanied by the wearing of costumes were not mentioned frequently but often included positive affective outcomes when they were. One student described delivering a report on a president: "Each person in the class picked a president, researched him, and gave an oral report on him.

Everybody dressed up as their chosen president. I learned a great deal about Thomas Jefferson—where he was born, raised, and his accomplishments." Another student described spending a day in a one-room school: "We dressed up like children would have dressed in the nineteenth century and we had our lessons there as children would have learned back then. I learned that school back then was very different than school was for me."

Although they were seldom reported, discussions and debates yielded impressive patterns of outcome ratings (especially current events discussions, as opposed to discussions of events in the past). So did activities that were embedded within thematic units that allowed for sustained study of a substantial topic. However, many reports on states or nations produced little substantive learning. Apparently, these reports focused on activities such as looking up and listing the state birds and flowers or the nation's exports and imports (without learning much about the reasons for these economic characteristics). Social studies goals are better served if report assignments are structured with emphasis on learning the more important aspects of states or nations and the geographical, historical, and economic reasons why the states or nations have the characteristics that they do.

Many students reported constructing products. Often these were maps, photo montages, or other illustrations to accompany reports on states or nations, but many were time-consuming construction activities such as building a pyramid, making a papier-mâché globe, making flags, creating a puzzle of the United States, or building a bridge. The time involved in some of these construction activities raises cost-effectiveness concerns, especially because the learning outcome codes associated with most of them were not impressive.

Certain activities were missing or underrepresented among the memories reported, given their emphasis in social studies textbooks for teachers and students. Relatively few memories, even from K–3, focused on self, family, neighborhood, or community. Also, except for Thanksgiving, there was little mention of activities done in connection with national or religious holidays. Biographies and other activities focusing on famous Americans also seemed underrepresented, as did career studies. Only a few of the reported field trips were to local historical sites or community business and service settings, suggesting either that such trips are not very memorable to students or that schools are not very active in exploiting the local community as a living laboratory for social studies observations and applications. Finally, no student reported any activity involving work with computers.

We have noted that low-level repetitive seatwork was mentioned frequently and often disparaged as boring or counterproductive. Two other negatively assessed activities are worth noting because, although they did not appear frequently, they were singled out for particular criticism when they were reported. The first of these was memorizing and reciting (the Gettysburg Address, the states in alphabetical order, etc.). Students who mentioned such memorizing activities usually did so contemptuously, pointing out that they no longer remembered much of what they had memorized. The other disparaged activity was taking turns reading aloud from the textbook in class. Rather than mere contempt, students who reported this activity usually described it with accompanying expressions of anger and resentment. In addition to sheer boredom, they mentioned the humiliation that this activity caused poor readers (either themselves or peers whom they had to watch agonizing their way through the task). The students sometimes added that such activities made them "hate" social studies and/or the teacher.

CONCLUSION

The findings from this study provided indirect support for the principles put forth in this chapter, in that the ratings of cognitive and affective learning outcomes of reported activities generally corresponded to what our principles would predict. Overall, we are encouraged by the many positive aspects of the students' responses. However, we are concerned by the apparent frequency of a barren social studies curriculum in Grades 7–8, doubly so because students in these grades are now ready to benefit from even more complex and diverse learning experiences than younger students are.

We are also concerned by the relative dearth of major social studies understandings articulated and by the heavy time investments involved in activities that yield limited learning outcomes (especially time-consuming construction projects). After all, what makes an activity worthwhile in the long run is not just that it is memorable but that it has led to important learnings. There is a great deal of room for improvement here and it can be accomplished primarily by placing more emphasis on selecting learning activities with major social education goals in mind, emphasizing these goals when structuring and scaffolding the activities for students, and re-emphasizing them in postactivity debriefing exercises.

YOUR TURN: LEARNING ACTIVITIES

In order to assess your level of understanding regarding the principles contained in this chapter for designing and selecting instructional activities, we have provided an exercise focusing on a third-grade land-use unit. Study the goals of the unit carefully, then read each of the activities. Using the guiding principles, label each activity "good," "bad," or "conditional." Be prepared to give reasons for your decisions.

The content for this exercise was drawn from the third-grade Houghton Mifflin textbook, Unit 4, chapters 9 and 10 (pp. 167A–215). The focus is the United States today. Chapter 9 addresses our current use of the land to meet our needs. Specifically the chapter deals with agriculture, industry, and transportation. Chapter 10 focuses on some of the consequences of our use of natural resources, emphasizing the need for us to work together to solve environmental problems.

Unit Goals

- Develop an understanding and appreciation for how we use the land to meet our needs and wants. (The San Joaquin Valley is described to demonstrate how modern technology is used to produce huge amounts of food. Pittsburgh is used as the example of an industrial city because it occupied an important place in the industrial history of our country, its geographical location influenced its growth as an industrial giant, and its economic history reflects various periods in the economic development of our nation. Another theme woven into the chapter is the role of transportation, especially railroads, in carrying goods and people from coast to coast.

- Develop an understanding and appreciation for the earth as our shared home, the importance of conserving our natural resources, and the consequences of our misuse of these resources.

- Develop understanding, appreciation, and life applications for solving environmental problems.

Possible Activity Selections

ACTIVITY	GOOD	BAD	CONDITIONAL	REASONS
1. Bring in five bunches of grapes and five empty tissue boxes without tops. Form five groups of students and have each group select one member to compete in a fruit-picking contest. Have students pretend that the bunches are fruit trees. The pickers are to neatly fill the boxes without damaging or bruising the fruit.				
2. Tell students that people have figured out how much each acre of farmland in the United States produces, on the average. The number is based on the total amounts of all types of farm products. Have students graph the following data on the overall increase in production, labeling the axes "Year" and "Amount": 1900—146, 1925—143, 1950—213, and 1975—440.				
3. Have students work in small groups to investigate different types of farms, such as crop farms;				

ACTIVITY	GOOD	BAD	CONDITIONAL	REASONS
flower farms; beef cattle, hog, and sheep farms; dairy farms; and poultry farms. Allow time for groups to present their findings in class, and encourage the use of visuals.				
4. Arrange field trips to local farms of different types to give students first-hand knowledge of their operation.				
5. Have each student make a chart of the produce grown in the San Joaquin Valley and indicate with a symbol which products could be harvested by machine and which by hand.				
6. Assign groups of students to interview produce managers at local supermarkets. Have students find out where the store's fruits and vegetables are grown and how they were transported to the store. Ask each group to report its findings to the class.				
7. Focus attention on the Benton painting on page 178, explaining that the year is 1930. Ask students what this steel mill would have smelled, sounded, looked, and felt like. Explain that steel workers form huge bars, sheets, and strips of steel from molten steel which they must hammer, press, roll, and shape under very high heat.				
8. Conduct a class discussion. Focus questions should include: "How might very fast freight trains be helpful to the farmers in the San Joaquin Valley?" "What do you think would happen to the transportation industry if someone invented a faster and cheaper way of moving goods?"				
9. Work with a group. Make a model freight train out of shoeboxes. Draw on a shoebox to make it look like a certain type of train car. Load your train with freight. Decide where it is going and then tell the class.				
10. Many tall-tale characters are heroes to certain industries. For				

ACTIVITY	GOOD	BAD	CONDITIONAL	REASONS
example, Joe Magarec is a hero to the steelmakers, John Henry is a hero to railroaders, and Paul Bunyan is a hero to lumberjacks. Make up your own classroom tall-tale hero. Brainstorm the kinds of things your hero would do. Work in groups to write stories. Put all the stories together to make a classroom book. Vote on a title for your book. Choose someone to draw a cover.				
11. Discuss wasteful practices with students, such as overwatering lawns, lengthy showers, and so on. Have students brainstorm others. Then have each student draw a picture of a wasteful practice that he or she might help eliminate.				
12. Draw attention to the picture of Mt. McKinley on page 201. Tell students to pretend that this is not a protected national park and that they will determine its future. Divide the class into two groups. Have one group represent an environmental protectionist point of view and the other group represent ski resort developers. Provide time for students to prepare their arguments and to present their debate. Explain to students that ideally we need to balance our use of resources and our protection of them. We cannot preserve all places as they are.				
13. Create a large outline shape of a tree from used paper grocery bags. Attach it to the bulletin board and title it "Save This Tree." Then have students brainstorm a list of things they can do to save paper and trees. Have students write their ideas on pieces of paper bags, which they can color and cut into the shape of leaves to attach to the tree shape.				
14. Have students work in small groups to create "Save Our Water" checklists. Their lists should include				

ACTIVITY	GOOD	BAD	CONDITIONAL	REASONS
tightly turning off the faucets; fixing drips and leaks; never letting water continue to run while brushing one's teeth; and using less water for showers and baths. Have the groups share lists and then compile a composite class list.				
15. Have small groups compose letters to the Environmental Protection Agency, Waterside Mall, 401 M Street, S.W., Washington, D.C. 20406. Each group can request different information, such as a list of EPA agencies and their locations; information about what the EPA does; pamphlets about air pollution; brochures about how to start a recycling center; or information about a specific problem in the students' own community. Have students share the information they get.				
16. Conduct a class discussion. Focus it on the question "How does farming in the San Joaquin Valley depend on natural resources?"				
17. Have students draw a factory polluting the air, water, and soil. Suggest that students include billowing smoke stacks, a pipe dumping waste into a nearby river, and huge containers of waste in back of the factory. Then have the students make a second drawing of the same factory showing the pollution reduced through the use of filters, sealed containers, and so on.				
18. Have students predict what would happen to a town in which no one stopped air, soil, or water pollution. Have each student write a paragraph describing the town after 10 years of unchecked pollution.				
19. Have students work in small groups. Use waste materials such as plastics, packaging, newspaper, and string to make a model of a national park.				

ACTIVITY	GOOD	BAD	CONDITIONAL	REASONS
20. Have the students participate in a class trial for someone who is accused of throwing trash in the park. Choose a judge, 12 jury members, witnesses, and the person who is accused of the crime. Have the witnesses tell the judge why they think the person is innocent or guilty. If the accused is guilty, the jury should decide what the punishment will be.				

REFERENCES

Alleman, J., & Brophy, J. (1992). Analysis of the activities in a social studies curriculum. In J. Brophy (Ed.), *Advances in research on teaching: Vol. 3. Planning and managing learning tasks and activities* (pp. 47–80). Greenwich, CT: JAI Press.

Alleman, J., & Brophy, J. (1993–1994). Teaching that lasts: College students' reports of learning activities experienced in elementary school social studies. *Social Science Record, 30* (2), 36–48; *31* (1), 42–46.

Alleman, J., & Brophy, J. (1994). Taking advantage of out-of-school opportunities for meaningful social studies learning. *The Social Studies, 6,* 262–267.

Blumenfeld, P., Mergendoller, J., & Swarthout, D. (1987). Task as a heuristic for understanding student learning and motivation. *Journal of Curriculum Studies, 19,* 135–148.

Brophy, J., & Alleman, J. (1991). Activities as instructional tools: A framework for instructional analysis and evaluation. *Educational Researcher, 20,* 9–23.

Brophy, J., & Alleman, J. (1992). Planning and managing learning activities: Basic principles. In J. Brophy (Ed.), *Advances in research on teaching: Vol. 3. Planning and managing learning tasks and activities* (pp. 1–45). Greenwich, CT: JAI Press.

Cooper, H. (1989). *Homework.* White Plains, NY: Longman.

Fraenkel, J. (1980). *Helping students think and value: Strategies for teaching the social studies* (2nd ed.). Englewood Cliffs, NJ: Prentice-Hall.

Raths, J. (1971). Teaching without specific objectives. *Educational Leadership, 28,* 714–720.

Zais, R. (1976). *Curriculum: Principles and foundations.* New York: Harper & Row.

Chapter 7

SOCIAL STUDIES IN THE INTERMEDIATE GRADES

Problems with social studies in Grades K–3 are so serious as to require fundamental changes in the selection and representation of the content taught. In Grades 4–6, the problems are not so fundamental. There is concern about an emphasis on breadth over depth, but this is a problem with content development rather than content selection. That is, critics accept the potential social education value of the content strands typically emphasized in these grades, but they argue that this potential is not realized because of parade-of-facts texts, classroom discourse patterns that emphasize recitation over discussion, and assignments and tests that emphasize filling in blanks over inquiry, critical thinking, and decision making.

Beginning in Grade 4, there is a shift in the nature and organization of the topics addressed in social studies. The subject remains interdisciplinary, but courses become based more clearly on a single primary discipline. Studies of U.S. and world regions in Grades 4 and 6 draw primarily from geography (including its cultural aspects), and the study of the development of the United States in Grade 5 draws primarily from history. State studies in Grade 4 and studies of ancient civilizations in Grade 6 are more multidisciplinary, although still emphasizing history, geography, and cultural studies.

Compared to younger students, students in Grades 4–6 are able to read with better comprehension and thus to take in content by studying textbooks. As a result, their texts are packed with much more information than primary texts, and their instruction is usually based heavily on textbooks and other print media. More time is allocated for social studies in Grades 4–6 (typically 30–45 minutes per day), but even so, the lengthy texts create content coverage pressures for teachers, especially if social studies is included in their school districts' high-stakes testing programs.

In Grades K–2, social studies texts are generally so lacking in substantive content as to be unsuitable as primary bases for a powerful social studies curriculum. Beginning in Grade 3, however, and increasingly through Grades 4–6, the textbooks, when properly adapted and supplemented, become more usable as primary information sources. This does not mean that they must be used (knowledgeable teachers with access to good resources can put together excellent curricula using combinations of specialized materials instead of textbooks). Nor does it mean that texts should be the only information sources made available to students (even a good text should be supplemented with topic-related children's literature selections, maps, videos, CD-ROMs, artifacts, etc.). What it does mean is that teachers in the intermediate grades can plan in terms of adapting their texts for continuous use rather than in terms of eliminating the texts entirely or using them for only a small portion of their social studies lessons.

Two primary adaptations are needed for most units in most textbooks. First, you will need to shift emphasis from broad but shallow coverage to development of key ideas in depth. In making reading assignments and planning class discussions, emphasize chapters or sections that develop key ideas and skip or downplay the rest. Also, provide your students with advance organizers, outlines, concept maps, story diagrams, or other scaffolds that will help them to structure their learning around powerful ideas.

Second, you will need to both cull and supplement the questions and activities suggested in the teacher's manual. Use the ones that are worth using, but omit the rest and, to the extent necessary, replace them with better ones.

As always, these unit- and lesson-planning decisions should be guided by the principles for teaching for understanding, appreciation, and application, and by the goals of social understanding and civic efficacy. Along with these principles and goals, planning for Grades 4–6 should reflect the guidelines that have been developed by organizations concerned with the teaching of geography and history, especially guidelines that pertain specifically to the elementary grades.

GUIDELINES FOR TEACHING GEOGRAPHY

Reflecting recent publications by organizations concerned with geographical education, we define *geography* as the study of people, places, and environments from a spatial perspective. This is a broad definition that includes cultural studies and various topics that might also be classified as anthropology, economics, or sociology. However, the latter disciplines are not taught as such in elementary social studies, where units are designed as studies of states, nations, regions, or cultures. This content is generally classified as geography (broadly defined), so we follow that practice here.

If viewed as a *science,* geography can be seen as partly a natural science (the study and mapping of land forms, weather patterns, natural resources, etc.) and partly a social science (the study of the ways that people adapt to and change their physical environments). Viewed as a *field of study,* geography is not so much a subject as a point of view that draws on and integrates other subjects (Knight, 1993). Viewed as a *discipline,* geography is whatever geographers do, which subsumes quite a range of activities and fields of knowledge (Demko, 1992; Marshall, 1991).

What geographers have in common is the *spatial point of view* that they bring to bear on the topics they study. However, as Knight (1993, p. 48) noted, "Geography is necessarily concerned with location, much as history is necessarily concerned with time, but geography is no more *about* location than history is about time." Libbee and Stoltman (1988) also compared historians and geographers. They noted that *historians* approach issues or events as developments in *time* and ask what happened, why it happened at that time, what preceded and perhaps caused it, what else was happening at the same time, and what the consequences were for the future. In contrast, *geographers* approach the issues or events as developments in *space* and focus on where the event happened, why it happened where it did, how things at that place and perhaps at other places helped to cause it, and what the consequences were for the place and for other places. Both historians and geographers seek to understand and explain why phenomena occur, not just to locate them on timelines or maps.

Problems with Geography Texts and Teaching

Unfortunately, research on elementary geography textbooks and teaching typically reveals an emphasis on miscellaneous facts rather than on understanding and using powerful geographical knowledge. Textbooks typically stress the physical aspects of geography over its human aspects and feature parades of facts presented without sufficient attention to connections, explanations, or critical thinking (Beck, McKeown, & Gromoll, 1989; Brophy, 1992; Haas, 1991). Similarly, studies involving interviewing teachers and observing in classrooms indicate that teachers' planning, instruction, and assignments relating to geography focus on map work and factual details about capital cities and major exports without much emphasis on understanding why places are where they are and have the characteristics that they do (Farrell & Cirrincione, 1989; Muessig, 1987; Stoltman, 1991; Thornton & Wenger, 1990; Winston, 1986).

A major reason for this is that teachers usually possess only limited knowledge of geographical information and of geography as a discipline, which is not surprising given their limited and somewhat distorted exposure to the subject as students. Along with confusion about the nature of geography and about what geography to teach, problems noted by various investigators include instruction in incorrect or out-of-date facts or concepts (such as an oversimplified environmental determinism as an explanation for human behavior in a particular place), a need to balance an emphasis on regions with a global perspective stressing our interdependent world, and tendencies toward ethnocentrism or stereotyping in treatments of other cultures.

The Five Fundamental Themes

Professional associations concerned with geography and geography education have cooperated in recent years to help teachers understand geography as a discipline and to suggest powerful ideas to emphasize in teaching geography to their students. The first major step was publication of the *Guidelines for Geographic Education: Elementary and Secondary Schools* (Joint Committee on Geographic Education, 1984). These guidelines provide a clear content and skills framework for K–12 geography that is structured around the five fundamental themes outlined below (Petersen, Natoli, & Boehm, 1994). They include a scope and sequence for Grades K–6 that outlines concepts and learning outcomes for each grade level.

The sponsoring organizations later created the Geographic Education National Implementation Project (GENIP) to advance the spirit of the guidelines by developing teaching materials, reviewing teacher certification standards, sponsoring workshops for teachers, and advising groups who prepare diagnostic and competency tests in geography. GENIP's work has included publication of a key document for elementary teachers: *K–6 Geography: Themes, Key Ideas, and Learning Outcomes* (GENIP, 1987). In addition, one of the GENIP authors has written a book on how teachers can connect their theme-based geography teaching to the social understanding and civic efficacy goals of social studies (Stoltman, 1990).

The efforts of GENIP have been assisted by the National Geographic Society, which established its Geography Education Program to develop statewide alliances for geographic education in each state. These alliances are partnerships between teachers and university geographers. They circulate materials and sponsor summer workshops and other geographic education programs for teachers. You can contact your state's geographic alliance for information and resources to help you with your geography teaching. The National Geographic Society also has produced a map of the United States that demonstrates the five fundamental themes (GENIP/NGS, 1986) and has circulated a teacher's handbook based on the themes (Ludwig et al., 1991).

Finally, Boehm and Petersen (1994) developed an elaboration of the five fundamental themes based on experience in using them with teachers. They noted that the themes were not intended to be a definitive or complete explanation of geography, but merely a way to organize its content in a convenient and widely adaptable format and to provide an alternative to the practice of teaching geography through rote memorization. The five themes follow.

LOCATION: POSITION ON THE EARTH'S SURFACE

Absolute and relative location are two ways of describing the positions of people and places. Location is the most basic of the fundamental themes. Every geographic feature has a unique location or global address, both in absolute terms and in reference to other locations.

Absolute location   We can identify locations as precise points on the earth's surface using reference grid systems, such as the system of latitude and longitude. Maps of smaller segments of the earth (such as cities or states) often use alpha-numeric grids. Different types of maps show locations of population centers, climate zones, political entities, or various geographic features. Map projections are needed to transfer information from a spherical earth to a two-dimensional map sheet. This process often leads to distortions in distance (size), direction, or shape. The grids used in location systems allow us to measure distances and find directions between places.

Relative location   Relative location is a way of expressing a location in relation to another site (Peoria is 125 miles southwest of Chicago, Australia is in the southern hemisphere, etc.). Both absolute and relative locations have geographical explanations (e.g., of why places are located where they are or why they have certain economic or social characteristics). As history progresses, certain aspects of relative location may change even though absolute location does not (e.g., as transportation routes in North America shifted from inland waterways to railroads to highways, cities at various locations saw shifts in their relative importance in the transportation system and in the nature of their links to other cities).

PLACE: PHYSICAL AND HUMAN CHARACTERISTICS

Location tells us where, and place tells us what is there (in particular, what makes the place special). All places have distinctive characteristics that give them meaning and character and distinguish them from other places. Geographers generally describe places by their physical or human characteristics.

Physical characteristics   These include the place's land forms (mountains, plains, natural harbors, etc.) and the processes that shape them, its climate (reasons for it and implications for human and animal life), its soils, its vegetation and animal life, and the nature and distribution of its fresh water sources. These physical characteristics are studied with emphasis on how they affect one another and support or challenge human occupation of the place.

Human characteristics   These include the racial and ethnic characteristics of the people who live in the place, their settlement patterns and population factors, and their religions, languages, economic activities, and other cultural characteristics. Also included are the perceived characteristics of places, which may vary across individuals or time periods (Central America might be viewed as a place of political turmoil, an attractive vacation site, an interesting blend of Hispanic and Indian cultures, etc.).

HUMAN–ENVIRONMENTAL RELATIONS (RELATIONSHIPS WITHIN PLACES)

All environments offer geographical advantages and disadvantages as habitats for humans. For example, high population densities tend to accumulate on flood plains, and low densities in deserts. Yet, some flood plains are periodically subjected to severe damage, and some desert areas, such as those around Tel Aviv or Phoenix, have been modified to support large population concentrations. People continually modify or adapt to natural settings in ways that reveal their cultural values, economic and political circumstances, and technological abilities. Centuries ago the Pueblo tribes developed agricultural villages that still endure in the desert southwest. Later, Hispanic and Anglo settlers established mines and mineral industries, cattle ranches, and farms in these deserts, relying on manipulation of water resources. Today, contemporary Americans look to the desert Southwest for resort and retirement developments, military training and research, and high technology industries.

Geography focuses on understanding how such human–environment relationships develop and what their consequences are for people and the environment. Subthemes include the role of technology in modifying environments (with attention to pollution and other costs as well as to benefits), environmental hazards (earthquakes, floods, etc., as well as human-induced disasters), the availability of land and natural resources and the limits this places on human possibilities, the purposes pursued and methods used by people to adapt to environments, and the ethical values and cultural attitudes that affect their behavior.

MOVEMENT: HUMANS INTERACTING ON THE EARTH (RELATIONSHIPS BETWEEN PLACES)

Places and regions are connected by movement. Over time, humans have increased their levels of interaction through communication, travel, and foreign exchange. Technology has shrunk space and distance. People travel out of curiosity, and they migrate because of economic or social need, environmental change, or other reasons. Movement can also be traced in physical forces—traveling weather patterns, ocean and wind currents, flowing water, or plate tectonics.

Several subthemes surround the reasons for movement and the forms that it takes: transportation modes, everyday travel, historical developments, economic reasons, mass movements of physical systems. Other subthemes surround global interdependence: the movement of goods, services, and ideas across national and regional borders; the development of trade and common markets. Still other subthemes surround models of human interaction: the reasons why people move (e.g., from rural areas to cities) and issues relating to the size and spacing of urban areas and the relationships between cities and their surrounding regions.

REGIONS: HOW THEY FORM AND CHANGE

The basic unit of geographic study is the region, an area that displays unity in terms of selected criteria (types of agriculture, climate, land forms, vegetation, political boundaries, soils, religions, languages, cultures, or economic characteristics). Regions may be larger than a continent or smaller than your neighborhood. They may have sharp, well-defined boundaries such as a state or city, or may have indistinct boundaries, such as the Great Plains or the Kalahari Desert.

Subthemes include uniform regions, functional regions, and cultural diversity. Uniform regions are defined by a uniform cultural or physical characteristic (the wheat belt, Latin America, the Bible Belt). Functional regions are organized around a focal point (the San Francisco Bay area, a local school district). Understanding regions sharpens appreciation of the diversity that exists in human activities and cultures, and of the ways in which different groups of people interact with one another within regional contexts.

Using the Five Themes in Your Teaching

Consistent emphasis on these five themes helps to ensure that you teach all aspects of geography (not just details of location and place) in ways that lead students through levels of abstraction from the simple to the complex. Note, however, that the themes are not meant to be used as unit topics and taught in serial order, one after the other. Instead, they are meant to be organizers of the content taught about unit topics such as states, nations, or regions. Good teaching of most geographic topics requires consideration of several, if not all five, of the themes, with attention to their relationships.

The five themes supposedly are being used to guide revisions of the geographical sections of elementary social studies texts. To the extent that this proves to be true, the texts should improve and you won't have to do as much adapting and supplementing in the future. So far, however, the texts leave much to be desired. Texts for the primary grades tend to emphasize basic geographical concepts and skills, such as the globe, the earth's rotation, daily and seasonal cycles, the cardinal directions, understanding of maps as two-dimensional representations of "bird's eye" views of sections of the earth, and experiences with different kinds of maps. These textbooks are sometimes quite good at introducing and scaffolding students' learning of basic map and globe skills (see the 1988 edition of the Silver Burdett and Ginn series). Unfortunately, these aspects of the program tend to be separated from the rest of the program dealing with families, neighborhoods, and so on.

In the intermediate grades, units on places and cultures tend to include maps and descriptions of physical geography, so that they do at least communicate basic information about where places are located and about the environmental characteristics they offer their human inhabitants. However, the texts usually do not draw on the five themes as much as they should to develop understanding of why places have the characteristics that they do and why humans have adapted to them in the ways that they have. As a teacher, it is important for you to help your students to focus on the most important facts about a place, to see the connections among these facts, and to begin to ask and acquire answers to the "why" questions that geographers ask about the places that they study.

The five themes are useful for understanding not only the physical aspects of places but also their human adaptation and cultural development aspects. When studying past or present societies and cultures, it is helpful to organize content around cultural universals and related dimensions that facilitate comparison and contrast. For example, Hanna et al. (1966) presented detailed suggestions about ways to organize such studies around nine basic human activities:

1. Protecting and conserving life and resources
2. Producing, exchanging, and consuming goods and services
3. Transporting goods and people
4. Communicating facts, ideas, and feelings
5. Providing education
6. Providing recreation
7. Organizing and governing
8. Expressing aesthetic and spiritual impulses
9. Creating new tools, technology, and institutions

Similarly, Fraenkel (1980) suggested that systematic study and comparison of societies can be organized around the following questions:

1. Who were the people being studied?
2. When did they live?
3. Where did they live?
4. What did they leave behind that tells us something about them?
5. What kinds of work did they do and where did they do it?
6. What did they produce or create?
7. What did they do for recreation?
8. What family patterns did they develop?
9. How did they educate their young?
10. How did they govern and control their societies?
11. What customs and beliefs did they hold?
12. What events, individuals, or ideas are they especially known for, and how did these affect their lives?
13. What problems did they have?
14. How did they try to deal with these problems?

Certain key ideas appear repeatedly in sources of advice on how to teach elementary students about societies and cultures. One is the importance of *focusing on cultural universals,* because these are fundamental categories of the human condition that children can understand based on their own prior experiences. A second is the value of *comparison and contrast* across well-chosen examples that illustrate and promote understanding of the variations to be found on key dimensions. A third is the importance of *explaining cultural adaptations within the context of their time and place,* to help students empathize with the people involved and begin to see things from their point of view (as opposed to focusing on the exotic in ways that make the people seem stupid or crazy).

For example, we recommend studying Native Americans within historical and geographical contexts and focusing on a few well-selected tribes in sufficient depth to allow students to develop an appreciation of the similarities and differences in their cultures. We might include an eastern woodlands tribe, a plains tribe, a southwestern pueblo tribe, a Pacific Northwest tribe, and (if not already included) a tribe that lived (or better yet, still does live) in your local area. Key ideas to be developed might include the following:

1. Native Americans are believed to have crossed from Asia on a land bridge now beneath the Bering Strait; they gradually spread through North and South America.

2. Different tribes developed a diversity of cultures, although many of them shared common elements centered around knowledge about living off the land and beliefs featuring respect for natural elements and resources. Seasons of the year and local plants and animals often figured prominently in cultural customs and beliefs.

3. Depending in part on local geography, climate, and resources, different tribes used different forms of shelter (longhouses, tepees, pueblo apartments), clothing (animal skins, woven cloth), food (meat from hunting and trapping, vegetables from farming, seafood from fishing), and transportation (dugouts, canoes, travois pulled by dogs and later by horses). Some tribes were nomadic, moving with the seasons to follow the animals that they hunted; other tribes lived continuously in the same place and emphasized farming supplemented with hunting and fishing.

4. For a variety of reasons, and in contrast to what happened in most of Africa and Asia, discovery of the New World by Europeans led not just to colonization or establishment of trade relations, but also to heavy immigration and ultimate repopulation. First, the land was attractive to Europeans because of its many natural resources and familiar climate and geography. Also, the Native Americans were vulnerable to encroachment by immigrating Europeans. In North America, tribes were mostly small and spread thinly across the continent. From a European point of view, vast amounts of desirable land were there for the taking, virtually unused and unowned by anyone in particular. At first, many Native Americans welcomed these newcomers and enjoyed friendly social and economic interactions with them. Resentments began to accumulate as immigrants kept coming and pushing the frontiers of settlement forward, but there was little that the local tribes whose land was being overrun could do against armies equipped with firearms. Individuals and small groups of Native Americans became assimilated into European

settlements or lived on small, locally negotiated reservations, but the major tribes were continually pushed back beyond the frontiers. Eventually, the settlers occupied the entire continent and the remnants of these tribes, decimated by war, disease, and starvation, were forcibly relocated to reservations established by the U.S. government.

5. Today, many Native Americans still live on these reservations and retain their tribal customs, but many others have moved into surrounding communities and become assimilated into mainstream American culture (elaborate with examples, especially examples of the activities and accomplishments of Native Americans residing locally; conduct inquiry into some of the social and policy issues relating to local tribes).

This treatment of Native Americans is designed to attack stereotypes (e.g., that all Indians lived in tepees and hunted with bows and arrows) and to help students to see the diversity and appreciate the contributions of various tribes and individuals. It is designed also to develop knowledge of where Native Americans came from, what has happened to them over the last 500 years, and where and how they live today. It draws on the basic geographical themes described above, as well as on the principles for developing historical content that are presented in the following section.

GUIDELINES FOR TEACHING HISTORY

The primary foundational disciplines for social studies are usually described as "history and the social sciences." This wording recognizes that history is different from the social sciences. *History* is an interpretive discipline concerned with particulars, not an empirical science concerned with developing theories meant to have broad applicability and explanatory power. Historians do seek to develop explanations, and they follow rules for developing and interpreting evidence. Their explanations focus on particular events in the past. Concerning the drafting of the U.S. Constitution, for example, historians seek to establish the chronology of key events and determine the motives and intentions of the framers, so as to understand how the Constitution came to be written as it did. In the process, they draw on political science concepts and develop information that political scientists find useful for their purposes, but they do not seek to develop and test political science generalizations (e.g., about relationships between divisions of government embodied in constitutions and the ways that these tend to function in practice).

Unlike the sciences, the content of history is not organized into networks of knowledge structured around key concepts and generalizations. Historical information can be organized according to the place or people investigated (e.g., U.S. history or the history of the Seminole tribe) or according to the aspects of the human condition addressed (e.g., the history of medicine or warfare). Even so, the content in each of these "files" consists of an enormous collection of particulars, along with a few generalizations about evolutionary trends over time or common patterns observed in parallel situations. Historical interpretations often conflict, if not on issues of what happened and in what order, then on issues of cause and effect (e.g., the possible causal roles of various factors that may have led to the Civil War and the role the war may have played in causing subsequent events). These features of the historical knowledge base make it very difficult to decide what history to teach in the schools.

Content selection questions become easier to address when history is subsumed within the social understanding and civic efficacy goals of social studies. As Rogers (1987) noted, decisions about what history should be studied are not fundamentally questions about history at all; they are questions about what *things* are important, and therefore which "histories" are most important to study. Traditionally, history has been taught in U.S. schools predominantly as a way to socialize the young into American democratic traditions and prepare them to be citizens. The focus has been on famous people and events, especially those connected with the origins of the nation and its struggles to grow physically, politically, and economically (Sunal & Haas, 1993). This role has been reemphasized lately by William Bennett (1986), Diane Ravitch (1989), and others who fear that U.S. culture risks fragmentation if American youngsters do not learn a body of shared information about the past. These authors claim that history presents a more fundamental and integrative way of developing this knowledge base than other social studies subjects (Thornton, 1994).

Critics of this view object that its approach to history is too concerned with perpetuating the status quo. Social educators who emphasize a global purview and world interdependence want to see U.S. history embedded more clearly within world history, and taught in ways less likely to induce chauvinistic attitudes in Americans. Those concerned with multicultural issues want to see a more inclusive selection of topics, treated in ways that represent more diverse points of view. Those concerned with gender issues would like to see more emphasis on social history and the lives of everyday people (especially women), and correspondingly less emphasis on political and military issues. Social critics would like to see more representation of the activities and views of workers relative to capitalists, oppressed or voiceless minorities relative to the establishment, and so on.

Along with such conflicts over what historical topics to include and whose views to emphasize, there are extreme disagreements about how much history to teach to elementary students. A few social educators prefer to minimize the role of history and instead focus social studies on current events and issues, emphasizing critical discussion and reasoned decision making. Most social educators, however, believe that history deserves an important place in the curriculum for several reasons, including its value as background knowledge that students can draw upon to develop contexts for understanding current events and issues.

For a time during the 1970s, some social educators questioned the feasibility of teaching history to elementary students on the grounds that these students have not yet achieved the levels of cognitive development that are needed to learn history with understanding. However, subsequent debate and data collection led to the rejection of this argument. It is now generally accepted that elementary students can understand general chronological sequences (e.g., that land transportation developed from walking to horse-drawn carriages to engine-powered vehicles) even though they may still be hazy about particular dates, and that they can understand age-appropriate representations of people and events from the past (especially narratives built around the goal-oriented activities of central characters with whom the students can identify) even though they might not be able to follow analytic treatments of abstract historical topics or themes (Booth, 1993; Crabtree, 1989; Downey & Levstik, 1991; Levstik & Pappas, 1992; Thornton & Vukelich, 1988; Willig, 1990).

At the other extreme from the "get rid of history" arguments are the arguments calling for eliminating the social science content of elementary social studies and replacing it with content drawn primarily from history, supplemented by children's literature selections featuring biography, myth, and lore. As noted in Chapter 1, we value history but we also value the social science content needed to develop basic social understandings, especially content relating to cultural universals. Consequently, we reject the notion of eliminating this content from the curriculum in order to make more room for historical content.

We also reject the notion of infusing myth and lore into the social studies curriculum. Myth and lore are worth studying as literature (i.e., within the language arts curriculum), but their value as social studies content is questionable. Stories about Paul Bunyan or Pecos Bill might be interesting to children, and the story of George Washington and the cherry tree might be a convenient fiction to use when teaching them about honesty, but

1. these are fictions, not historical accounts of actual events;
2. at a time when children are struggling to distinguish what is true and continuing from what is false or fleeting, an emphasis on myth and lore is likely to interfere with their efforts to construct a reality-based model of the world;
3. as students discover that they have been taught myth, lore, and other fictions, they may begin to question the credibility of teachers or of social studies as a school subject; and
4. most of the content of myth and lore and the reasons for its development in the first place reflect the thematic preoccupations and entertainment needs of premodern agrarian societies and thus were passé even 50 years ago, let alone today.

Goal-Oriented History Teaching

Recent debates about teaching history within social studies have stimulated renewed interest in the topic and empirical data collection to accompany the theoretical debate. These studies do not support claims that history courses have been supplanted by other courses over recent generations (Jenness, 1990; Thornton, 1994). Social educators agree to some extent that there are deficiencies in U.S. students' knowledge of history; they do not agree that the answer is to teach them more history in the way that it is taught now. Studies indicate that, after two or three exposures to U.S. history, most students remain indifferent to and ill-informed about it (Thornton, 1994; VanSledright, in press).

One reason for this is that American youngsters often view history as "someone else's facts," with little connection to their lives and concerns (Holt, 1990). Given the problems with texts described in Chapter 2, this is not surprising.

To address these problems, we will need to focus not just on what history to teach but on how to teach it. Theory and research are beginning to emerge on how to teach history in ways that promote the social understanding and civic efficacy goals of social studies. These involve coming to understand how the human condition in general and the current social world in particular have developed through time and evolved to their present state, and what this means for personal, social, and civic decision making.

Proposed National History Standards

The National Center for History in the Schools (NCHS) has published standards for teaching history in general in Grades K–4 (NCHS, 1994a) and standards for teaching U.S. history (NCHS, 1994b), and world history (NCHS, 1994c) in Grades 5–12. These documents offer content standards and thinking skills standards. Content standards for K–4 are not stated chronologically but in terms of general understandings that the students should develop during these grades, divided into five general topics:

1. Living and working together in families and communities, now and long ago
2. The history of students' own state or region
3. The history of the nation
4. The history of peoples of many cultures around the world
5. Historic discoveries in science and technology

The content standards for Grades 5–12 contain detailed lists of understandings of chronologically organized developments and associated knowledge about the reasons for them, organized within historical periods.

The thinking skills standards focus on five groups of historical thinking skills:

1. *Chronological thinking:* distinguishing between past, present, and future time; identifying the temporal structure of historical narratives or stories; establishing temporal order in the students' own historical narratives; measuring and calculating calendar time; interpreting data presented in timelines; creating timelines; and explaining change and continuity over time.

2. *Historical comprehension:* reconstructing the literal meaning of the historical passage; identifying the central questions that the narrative addresses; reading historical narratives imaginatively; developing historical perspectives; drawing on the data in historical maps; drawing on visual and mathematical data presented in graphics; and drawing on visual data presented in photographs, paintings, cartoons, and architectural drawings.

3. *Historical analysis and interpretation:* formulate questions to focus their inquiry or analysis; identify the author or source of a historical document or narrative; compare and contrast differing sets of ideas, values, personalities, behaviors, and institutions; analyze historical fiction; distinguish between fact and fiction; compare different stories about a historical figure, era, or event; analyze illustrations in historical stories; consider multiple perspectives; explain causes in analyzing historical actions; challenge arguments of historical inevitability; and hypothesize influences of the past.

4. *Historical research capabilities:* formulate historical questions; obtain historical data; interrogate historical data; and marshal needed knowledge of the time and place to construct a story, explanation, or historical narrative.

5. *Historical issues-analysis and decision making:* identify issues and problems in the past; compare the interests and values of the various people involved; suggest alternative choices for addressing the problem; evaluate alternative courses of action; prepare a position or course of action on an issue; and evaluate the consequences of a decision.

Clearly, these standards documents put forth a challenging agenda, in part because their authors assumed that changes in elementary social studies curricula would increase the curricular "air time" devoted to history. Where this is not the case, attempts to address these standards might not begin in earnest until students begin chronological study of U.S. history in fifth grade.

Bradley Commission Recommendations

The Bradley Commission on History in Schools (1988) advocated that the entire social studies curriculum be built around history and designed to develop knowledge and "habits of mind" acquired through historical study. The knowledge taught would include American history (to tell us who we are and who we are becoming), the history of Western civilization (to reveal our democratic political heritage and its vicissitudes), and world history (to acquaint us with the nations and people with whom we share a common global destiny). "Habits of mind" include understanding the significance of the past to our lives and to society as a whole; distinguishing between the important and the inconsequential; perceiving past events and issues as they were experienced by people at the time (developing historical empathy as opposed to present-mindedness); acquiring a comprehension of both diverse cultures and shared humanity; understanding cause-and-effect relationships in studying how things happen and how things change; recognizing the roles of human intentions but also of unpredictability and chance in affecting developments; appreciating the interpretive and often tentative nature of judgments about the past; resisting temptations to overemphasize "lessons" of history as cures for present ills; recognizing the importance of individuals who have made a difference in history and the significance of personal character for both good and ill; and reading widely and critically in order to recognize the difference between fact and conjecture and between evidence and assertion, and thereby to frame useful questions.

The Commission also suggested that historical study promotes personal growth because history is the central humanistic discipline and can satisfy young people's longing for a sense of identity and a sense of their time and place in the human story. In this regard, it argued that the arts, literature, philosophy, and religion are best studied as they developed over time and in the context of societal evolution. With regard to citizenship goals, the Commission argued that history furnishes a wide range of models and alternatives for political choice in a complicated world, and that it conveys a sense of civic responsibility through its graphic portrayals of virtue, courage, and wisdom—and their opposites.

Other Recommendations

Mere exposure to history will not automatically confer all the benefits envisioned by the Bradley Commission, but it is reasonable to expect these outcomes to result from goal-oriented history instruction that is planned with these outcomes in mind. Others have also written eloquently about reasons for studying history and about how to teach it so that its potential may be realized.

John Dewey (1900/1956) suggested that history for elementary students be approached as an indirect form of sociology—a study of developments in the social aspects of the human condition—and taught with emphasis on its inspirational aspects—the heroic accomplishments of individuals and the inventions that helped people to solve problems and improve their life conditions. Instruction would draw upon genuine historical content or historically based biography and fiction and not on myths or fairy tales featuring fictional heroes solving fictional problems.

Hoge and Crump (1988) identified four purposes for teaching history in elementary school: to make the past seem real; to build insights into present circumstances and events; to develop a love and respect for history learning, including an understanding of its limitations; and to help students recognize their own relationship to history. These authors suggested four guidelines for teaching history for understanding. First, make history real to students by allowing them to manipulate "realia" such as artifacts or primary documents from the past. Struggling to read script in an old mill ledger or to operate an early corn sheller will help the students feel how hard people in earlier times labored intellectually and physically to survive. Second, transport students to the past through constructing, processing, and interacting within simulated environments (making hoe cakes on a hoe over an open fire, tracing origins of words, interviewing older people about home remedies). Third, question the text as a single authority and engage students in collecting information from other sources, discussing discrepancies, and writing their own accounts. Finally, make sure that students get the intended benefits from participating in "hands on" activities by engaging them in reflective discussions about the activities and following up with assignments that require them to think and communicate about what they learned.

Knight (1993) emphasized developing historical empathy as a major goal of history instruction, arguing that the purpose of teaching history "is not directly to teach us lessons, nor to form laws which show the future. Rather, the past is to be studied on its own terms and "from within": The intention is to try to recreate the understandings, the perspectives of people in the different societies which constitute the past. History, then, is a multicultural study. Like geography, its goal is to try to explain (often strange) others on their own terms, within their own cultures, set in their situations, and without the benefit of hindsight" (Knight, 1993, p. 84). He also argued that elementary students are able to recognize that characters in the past had a perspective different from theirs; generate explanations that depend on taking another's perspective; predict outcomes of situations given another's perspective; and make evaluations of historical characters that involve handling evidence that can support more than one judgment.

Low-Beer and Blyth (1983) argued that we should teach history to develop understanding and thought about the human condition, building appreciation of its development through the ages and extending students' horizons from personal experience to that of the wider human society. They emphasized helping children to develop a sense of chronological sequence, of the idea that historical knowledge is based on evidence, and of historical interpretation as a process of meaningful reconstruction from the available sources.

Keep in mind these worthy purposes and goals of historical study as you plan and implement your history teaching. Help your students learn to approach historical episodes or periods not just as chronicles (lists of events in order of occurrence), but as narratives—stories worth learning and thinking about because they relate to important themes or issues.

History as Meaningful and Usable Knowledge

Theory and research on teaching history for understanding suggest several principles that are particularly relevant to elementary teachers. First, *focus instruction on the study of particular individuals and groups of people rather than on impersonal abstractions;* study these people with emphasis on developing understanding of and empathy for their contexts and points of view; and focus on general trends in the evolution of social systems rather than on particular dates or detailed chronologies (Barton & Levstik, 1994; Knight, 1993; Levstik &

Barton, 1994; Low-Beer & Blyth, 1983; Willig, 1990). Children in the primary grades are interested in and can understand accounts of life in the past that are focused on particular individuals or groups (cave dwellers, Native American tribes, the Pilgrims, life on a planation or on the frontier in the eighteenth century). Fifth graders are interested in and can understand an introduction to chronological study of U.S. history. However, the material needs to be represented to them in the form of narratives that depict people with whom they can identify pursuing goals that they can understand. For example, primary-grade children can understand that the "Pilgrims" were persecuted for their religious beliefs and left England because they wanted to be free to practice their religion as they saw fit, but they could not follow an abstract analysis of the theological differences between the "separatists" and the Church of England. Similarly, fifth-graders can understand a discussion of trade routes in colonial times that includes the notion that the colonists sold raw materials to England and purchased finished products manufactured in England, but they could not follow an abstract discussion of "the rise of mercantilism."

Various sources also agree on the value of *exposing students to varied data sources and providing them with opportunities to conduct historical inquiry, to synthesize and communicate their findings, and to learn from listening to or reading biography and historical fiction selections as well as conventional textbooks* (Downey & Levstik, 1988; Harms & Lettow, 1994; Lamme, 1994; Low-Beer & Blyth, 1983; Sunal & Haas, 1993). It is important, however, for you as the teacher to *guide your students in their use of these varied data sources.* Fictional sources should be historically accurate and free from bias and stereotyping (unless they are going to be used as examples of fictionalized or biased portrayals). Elementary students lack a rich base of prior knowledge to inform their efforts at critical thinking and decision making, so they have difficulty knowing what to believe or how to assess conflicting accounts. They will need to learn that textbooks, and even eyewitness accounts or diaries, tend to emphasize aspects of events that support their authors' biases and interests. In studying the American Revolution, for example, it is helpful to expose students to information sources that will help them to realize that King George had a quite different view from that of the American rebels concerning how the events leading to the revolution should be interpreted, and thus whether or not revolution was justified. Similarly, the students might come to see that the Boston Massacre would be viewed (and later described) quite differently by a British soldier seeking to avoid a confrontation than by an American rebel seeking to provoke one.

History-based fiction can be helpful in "making history come alive" for elementary students. For example, the book *Sarah Morton's Day* depicts a day in the life of an English child born in Holland in 1618 who came to Plymouth in 1623. Through engaging narrative and photographs (taken at the reconstructed Plymouth Planation in Massachusetts), the book chronicles what might have been a typical day in Sarah's life. Much of it recounts the many chores that Sarah had to do during most of the time between dawn and dusk, but it also mentions lessons (in the home), social chat and games with a playmate, and excitement at the sighting of an incoming ship. In the process, the book communicates a great deal about what life was like in this colony, especially for children. It is based on an actual child and family and depicts events that are authentic given what is known about the time and place, although the depicted conversations are fictional. Most fifth graders are quite taken with the story, and especially with its details about the life of children in the colony, such as the notion that Sarah had to work on chores almost all day long and had to stand up while eating meals even though her parents were seated.

Comparisons of children's trade books with social studies textbooks indicate that the trade books have a great deal to offer as substitute or supplementary sources of curricular content. One research team that focused on the use of trade books for teaching history noted that the historical trade books' content emphasis on human motives, solving problems, and the consequences of actions compares favorably with the emphasis on facts, names, and dates in the textbooks, and that the trade books' emphasis on ordinary people, the human aspects of famous people, and the effects of world or national events on the lives of common people compares favorably with the textbooks' emphasis on world leaders, famous people, and big events (Tomlinson, Tunnell, & Richgels, 1993).

This same research team also found important differences in the nature of the writing. Texts featured expository writing almost exclusively, but historical fiction featured narrative writing; trade books featured longer and more complex sentences that were nevertheless easier to understand because they offered deeper elaboration of a smaller subset of topics and more cohesion across sentences and paragraphs than the texts did. The trade books were unrestricted by readability formulas, so they offered richer vocabularies, more varied styles, and more descriptive and elaborated language. The texts' use of past tense verbs lent a sense of distance and unreality to the events portrayed and made the people seem lifeless, while trade books presented the people and events as living by using present-tense verbs and dialogue that lent a sense of immediacy and reality. The trade books' were human stories well told which created greater interest, reader involvement, and memorability (Richgels, Tomlinson, & Tunnel, 1993). However, you will need to exercise care in selecting historically based trade books meant for children because many of them offer romanticized rather than realistic portrayals of historical figures and events, feature chauvinistic or otherwise biased interpretations, or reflect other problems in content selection or representation that undermine their value as historical content sources (Tunnell, 1993).

Children need help in keeping fictional sources in perspective, so that they do not confuse the real with the fictional (like the student who named Johnny Tremain as a leader of the American Revolution) or overgeneralize from the specific (like the students who develop the notion that life for all children in all of the colonies was like Sarah Morton's life among the Puritans at Plymouth

Plantation). These examples illustrate how the potential motivational and insight benefits derived from using fictional sources must be balanced against their potential for inducing distorted learnings. Some distortions are inevitable, and most will be cleared up without great difficulty. Still, you should minimize such problems by screening historical fiction sources for authenticity and by helping your students to understand the differences between fictional and historical representations (Levstik, 1989; VanSledright, 1994).

As was the case with geography, virtually all sources of advice on teaching history emphasize the importance of *fostering empathy with the people being studied.* Just as there is a danger of chauvinism when we study contemporary cultures other than our own, there is a danger of presentism when we study people from the past with benefit of hindsight. Children are especially prone to presentism, often believing that people in the past were not as smart as we are today because they did not have all of the social and technical inventions that ease our contemporary lives. You can foster their development of empathy by helping them to appreciate such things as bow-and-arrow hunting, horse-drawn carriages, or butter churns as ingenious inventions that represented significant advances for their times, not just as tools that seem primitive when compared with today's technology.

Along with the sources cited previously, you may wish to consult the following sources for more ideas about teaching history to elementary students. First, you may wish to subscribe to or inspect issues of *Cobblestone: A History Magazine for Young People.* Designed for 8- to 14-year-old students, *Cobblestone* publishes 50-page issues devoted to a particular theme (person, event, period, or place) in American history. Each theme is addressed through nonfiction articles, historical fiction, poetry, and biography, and includes film and book bibliographies. The textual material is accompanied by good illustrations as well as puzzles, games, songs, cartoons, and other material related to the theme. You may want to adapt some of this material for use with your students, but in any case, each issue of *Cobblestone* offers useful ideas about content and activities to include when teaching about its historical theme.

For information about historical trade books and other text supplements for use in teaching history to elementary students, see Brandhorst (1988); California State Department of Education (1991); James and Zarrillo (1989); Lawson and Barnes (1991); and Symcox (1991). For information about using computers and associated technology for teaching history, see Parham (1994), Schlene (1990), and Seiter (1988). Finally, for information about the History Teaching Alliance that offers training and resources for history teaching, see Beninati (1991).

CONCLUSION

Organizations and scholars concerned with geography and history teaching have developed useful guidelines that can help you to teach these aspects of social studies in ways that promote progress toward social understanding and

FIGURE 7.1

Key Ideas That Connect to the Five Fundamental Themes of Geography

UNIT	
Five Fundamental Themes	**Related to the Five Themes**
Location–position on the Earth's surface _____	
▪ Absolute location _____	
▪ Relative location _____	
Place _____	
▪ Physical characteristics _____	
▪ Human characteristics _____	
Human–environmental relations _____	
Movement: humans interacting on the Earth (relationships between places) _____	
Regions: how they form and change _____	

civic efficacy goals. Along with more detailed and subject-specific advice, these sources emphasize the value of

1. replacing parades of facts with coherent networks of knowledge structured around powerful geographic or historical themes;
2. studying people within the contexts of their time and place, so as to develop empathy and avoid presentism or chauvinism; and
3. focusing on causal explanations that will help students to understand not only what happened, but also why, and what this might mean for personal, social, or civic decision making.

YOUR TURN: SOCIAL STUDIES IN THE INTERMEDIATE GRADES

Geography

If the focus of social studies teaching at your grade level is geography, we suggest that you secure a copy of the *Guidelines for Geographic Education* (see references for complete citation). Contact your state's geographic alliance for information and resources to help you. Review the school's curriculum guide at your grade level and carefully examine the textbook, if one has been adopted. If you have developed your own units, you will want to revisit those materials as well.

FIGURE 7.2
Specific Examples to Illustrate

	UNIT I	UNIT 2	UNIT 3	UNIT 4
Develop and present networks of knowledge structured around powerful ideas.				
Instruction should focus on the study of particular individuals and groups of people rather than on impersonal abstractions.				
Expose students to varied data sources and provide them with opportunities to conduct historical inquiry, to synthesize and communicate their findings, to learn from biography, fiction, and texts, etc.				
Bring history to life for students.				
Foster empathy with the people being studied.				
Focus on causal explanations that help students understand what happened, why, and what it might mean for personal, social, or civic decison making.				

As you inspect all of these sources, use the grid shown in Figure 7.1 to plot the key ideas that correspond to the *Five Fundamental Themes.* Once you have identified the weak spots, spend time developing the key ideas for each (see Figure 7.2). This activity will bring you one step closer to geographic teaching in depth instead of breadth.

After teaching a unit using the five themes, interview your students using questions that focus on the themes. Study their responses to determine the degree to which they have acquired the big ideas.

SAMPLE INTERVIEW QUESTIONS

Select questions that match your goals and major geographic understandings for the unit.

1. Using a range of map types such as physical, political, and climatic, describe the Southwest of the United States.
2. Using a road map, plan a trip to Santa Fe, Phoenix, and so on.
3. Using a range of map types, explain what is special about Salt Lake, Tucson, White Sands, Reno, and so on.
4. What specifically have you learned about the people who live in the Southwest? What are some of the groups we have studied about and what is special about each? Explain the settlement patterns of various groups. What are some of their traditions, customs, beliefs, and values?

What types of economic activities would you expect to find in the Southwest? Why?

5. Would you expect high or low population densities in the Southwest? Why? Describe how specific parts of the Southwest have been modified to support large concentration areas.

6. Explain why certain parts of the Southwest are attractive for retirement developments.

7. How has technology influenced life in the Southwest?

8. Why are certain parts of the Southwest growing so rapidly?

9. How would you characterize the Southwest as a region? Compare it to the region in which you live. How are they the same? Different? Which would you prefer to live in as an adult? Why?

History

If the focus of social studies at your grade level is history, we suggest that you obtain and review the *National History Guidelines,* your state's guidelines, and your district's or school's curriculum guide at your grade level. Then carefully examine the textbook if one has been adopted. If you have developed your own units, you will want to revisit these materials, too. As you inspect all of these sources and reflect on what you have read in Chapter 7, use the following grid to plot specific examples that correspond to the principles for teaching history in your classroom. Once you have identified weak spots, spend time revising your program to be reflective of the principles. This exercise will bring you one step closer to presenting a social studies course in history that is meaningful and usable.

Select one of the following options:

After planning a unit using the guiding principles for history teaching outlined in Chapter 7, share your plans with a "history buff." Elicit that person's reactions regarding the "love" of the subject you hope to impart—as well as the "meaningfulness" that you hope will result.

OR

After teaching a unit using the guiding principles established in Chapter 7, interview students to determine their reactions regarding meaningfulness and enjoyment.

SAMPLE INTERVIEW QUESTIONS

Select questions that match your goals and major historical understandings of the unit.

1. What were the big ideas you learned about the history of our (state/region/nation)?

2. Would you have liked to have been one of the early settlers to come to our area? Why? Why not? What do you think life was like for them?
3. What groups of people do you think were the most influential in the development of our (state/region/nation)? Why?
4. If you could meet one historical figure who contributed to the development of our (state/region/nation), who would it be? Why? Describe how you would choose to spend a day with this person.
5. Have a range of data sources available that you used during the unit. Ask students to select those that were most inspiring, enjoyable, meaningful, and so on, and explain their choices.
6. If you could live during the early development of our region or now, which would you choose and why?
7. How do you think learning about the past can help you today? In the future?

(These questions could be discussed in focus groups and tape-recorded for later analysis and reflection.)

REFERENCES

Barton, K., & Levstik, L. (1994, April). *"Back when God was around and everything": Elementary children's understanding of historical time.* Paper presented at the annual meeting of the American Educational Research Association, New Orleans.

Beck, I., McKeown, M., & Gromoll, E. (1989). Learning from social studies texts. *Cognition and Instruction, 6,* 99–158.

Beninati, A. (1991). History Teaching Alliance. *OAH Magazine of History, 6* (1), 46.

Bennett, W. (1986). *First lessons: A report on elementary education in America.* Washington, DC: U.S. Department of Education.

Boehm, R., & Petersen, J. (1994). An elaboration of the fundamental themes in geography. *Social Education, 58,* 211–218.

Booth, M. (1993). Students' historical thinking and the national history curriculum in England. *Theory and Research in Social Education, 21,* 105–127.

Brandhorst, A. (1988). Historical fiction in the classroom: Useful tool or entertainment? *Southern Social Studies Quarterly, 14,* 19–30.

Brophy, J. (1992). The de facto national curriculum in US elementary social studies: Critique of a representative example. *Journal of Curriculum Studies, 24,* 401–447.

California State Department of Education. (1991). *Literature for history-social science. Kindergarten through grade eight.* Sacramento: Author.

Crabtree, C. (1989). History is for children. *American Educator, 13* (4), 34–39.

Demko, G. (1992). *Why in the world: Adventures in geography.* New York: Anchor Books.

Dewey, J. (1900/1956). *School and society.* Chicago: University of Chicago Press.

Downey, M., & Levstik, L. (1991). Teaching and learning history. In J. Shaver (Ed.), *Handbook of research on social studies teaching and learning* (pp. 400–410). New York: Macmillan.

Farrell, R., & Cirrincione, J. (1989). The content of the geography curriculum—a teacher's perspective. *Social Education, 53,* 105–108.

GENIP/NGS. (1986). *Maps, the landscape, and the fundamental themes in geography.* Washington, DC: National Geographic Society.

Geography Education National Implementation Project (GENIP). (1987). *K-6 geography: Themes, key ideas, and learning opportunities.* Washington, DC: Author.

Haas, M. (1991). An analysis of the social science and history concepts in elementary social studies textbooks grades 1-4. *Theory and Research in Social Education, 19,* 211-220.

Hanna, P., Sabaroff, R., Davies, G., & Farrar, C. (1966). *Geography in the teaching of social studies: Concepts and skills.* Boston: Houghton Mifflin.

Harms, J., & Lettow, L. (1994). Criteria for selecting picture books with historical settings. *Social Education, 58,* 152-154.

Hoge, J., & Crump, C. (1988). *Teaching history in the elementary school.* Bloomington, IN: Social Studies Development Center and ERIC Clearinghouse for Social Studies/Social Science Education.

Holt, T. (1990). *Thinking historically: Narrative, imagination, and understanding.* New York: College Entrance Examination Board.

James, M., & Zarrillo, J. (1989). Teaching history with children's literature: A concept-based, interdisciplinary approach. *Social Studies, 80,* 153-158.

Jenness, D. (1990). *Making sense of social studies.* New York: Macmillan.

Joint Committee on Geographic Education. (1984). *Guidelines for geographic education: Elementary and secondary schools.* Washington, DC: Association of American Geographers and the National Council for Geographic Education.

Knight, P. (1993). *Primary geography, primary history.* London: David Fulton.

Lamme, L. (1994). Stories from our past: Making history come alive for children. *Social Education, 58,* 159-164.

Lawson, J., & Barnes, D. (1991). Learning about history through literature. *Social Studies Review, 30* (2), 41-47.

Levstik, L. (1989). Historical narrative and the young reader. *Theory into Practice, 28,* 114-119.

Levstik, L., & Barton, K. (1994, April). *They still use some of their past: Historical salience in elementary children's chronological thinking.* Paper presented at the annual meeting of the American Educational Research Association, New Orleans.

Levstik, L., & Pappas, C. (1992). New directions for studying historical understanding. *Theory and Research in Social Education, 20,* 369-385.

Libbee, M., & Stoltman, J. (1988). Geography within the social studies curriculum. In S. Natoli (Ed.), *Strengthening geography in the social studies* (Bulletin No. 81, pp. 22-41). Washington, DC: National Council for the Social Studies.

Low-Beer, A., & Blyth, J. (1983). *Teaching history to younger children.* London: The Historical Association.

Ludwig, G., et al. (1991). *Directions in geography: A guide for teachers.* Washington, DC: National Geographic Society.

Marshall, B. (Ed.). (1991). *The real world: Understanding the modern world through the new geography.* Boston: Houghton Mifflin.

Muessig, R. (1987). An analysis of developments in geographic education. *Elementary School Journal, 87,* 519-530.

National Center for History in Schools. (1994a). *National standards for history: Expanding children's world in time and space* (Grades K-4 expanded edition). Los Angeles: University of California, Los Angeles.

National Center for History in Schools. (1994b). *National standards for United States history: Exploring the American experience* (Grades 5-12 expanded edition). Los Angeles: University of California, Los Angeles.

National Center for History in Schools. (1994c). *National standards for world history: Exploring paths to the present* (Grades 5-12 expanded edition). Los Angeles: University of California, Los Angeles.

Parham, C. (1994). Ten views of the past: Software that brings history to life. *Technology and Learning, 14* (6), 36-39, 42-45.

Petersen, J., Natoli, S., & Boehm, R. (1994). The guidelines for geographic education: A 10-year retrospective. *Social Education, 58,* 206-210.

Ravitch, D. (1989). The plight of history in American schools. In P. Gagnon & The Bradley Commission on History in Schools (Eds.), *Historical literacy: The case for history in American education* (pp. 51-68). New York: Macmillan.

Richgels, D., Tomlinson, C., & Tunnell, M. (1993). Comparison of elementary students' history textbooks and trade books. *Journal of Educational Research, 86,* 161-171.

Rogers, P. (1987). History—the past as a frame of reference. In C. Portal (Ed.), *The history curriculum for teachers* (pp. 3-21). New York: Falmer.

Schlene, V. (1990). Computers in the social studies classroom: An ERIC/ChESS sample. *History Microcomputer Review, 6* (2), 45-47.

Seiter, D. (1988). Resources for teaching with computers in history. *History Microcomputer Review, 4* (2), 37-38.

Stoltman, J. (1990). *Geography education for citizenship.* Bloomington, IN: ERIC Clearinghouse for Social Studies/Social Science Education. (ERIC Document Reproduction Service No. ED 322 081)

Stoltman, J. (1991). Research on geography teaching. In J. Shaver (Ed.), *Handbook of research on social studies teaching and learning* (pp. 437-447). New York: Macmillan.

Sunal, C., & Haas, M. (1993). *Social studies and the elementary/middle school student.* Fort Worth: Harcourt Brace Jovanovich.

Symcox, L. (1991). *Selected teaching materials for the United States and world history: An annotated bibliography.* Los Angeles: National Center for History in the Schools, University of California, Los Angeles. (ERIC Document Reproduction Service No. ED 350 249)

Thornton, S. (1994). The social studies near century's end: Reconsidering patterns of instruction. In L. Darling-Hammond (Ed.), *Review of research in education* (Vol. 20, pp. 223-254). Washington, DC: American Educational Research Association.

Thornton, S., & Vukelich, R. (1988). Effects of children's understanding of time concepts on historical understanding. *Theory and Research in Social Education, 16,* 69-82.

Thornton, S., & Wenger, R. (1990). Geography curriculum and instruction in three fourth-grade classrooms. *Elementary School Journal, 90,* 515-531.

Tomlinson, C., Tunnell, M., & Richgels, D. (1993). The content and writing of history in textbooks and trade books. In M. Tunnell & R. Ammon (Eds.), *The story of ourselves: Teaching history through children's literature* (pp. 51-62). Portsmourth, NH: Heinemann.

Tunnell, M. (1993). Unmasking the fiction of history: Children's historical literature begins to come of age. In M. Tunnell & R. Ammon (Eds.), *The story of ourselves: Teaching history through children's literature* (pp. 79-90). Portsmourth, NH: Heinemann.

VanSledright, B. (1994, November). *How to read history? The content-form problem in fifth-grade classrooms.* Paper presented at the annual meeting of the National Reading Conference, Coronado, CA.

VanSledright, B. (in press). "I don't remember—the ideas are all jumbled in my head": Eighth graders' reconstructions of colonial American history. *Journal of Curriculum and Supervision.*

Willig, C. (1990). *Children's concepts and the primary curriculum.* London: Paul Chapman.

Winston, B. (1986). Teaching and learning in geography. In S. Wronski & D. Bragaw (Eds.), *Social studies and social sciences: A 50-year perspective* (Bulletin No. 78; pp. 43–58). Washington, DC: National Council for the Social Studies.

Chapter 8

BUILDING A LEARNING COMMUNITY IN YOUR CLASSROOM

The week before school starts, Mrs. Paul's students receive her letter, personally prepared, signed, and mailed. This letter is important to them because it comes from their new teacher. It fills them with anticipation, hopes, and dreams. They are eager to join her in Room 104 to begin building a learning community together. Her letter has given them a preview of the formal curriculum—the content to be experienced and the overarching goals to be achieved, the planned field trips and visits by resource people, and so on. It also has communicated high expectations for all learners. Most importantly, it has addressed the "hidden" curriculum: celebrating differences, fairness, rights and responsibilities, caring, and sharing. It offers a vision that her new students find compelling and curious. They think "Room 104 sounds special," but they wonder, "Will we really play a role in making all of that happen?"

Anxiety, optimism, and uncertainty are written on the students' faces as they come to Room 104 on the first day of school. For many, it seemed as if this day would never arrive. Unlike previous years, with their repeating cadences of teacher rules and regulations, student testing, textbook dissemination, and class introductions, this day greets students with a welcome doormat, soft music, a partially decorated room that includes a special bulletin board depicting the personal history of the teacher, and other unique trappings that reflect the communal voice that is about to be introduced and allowed to grow.

Introductions and organizational matters occupy but a few minutes, soon followed by reference to the learning community that was promised in the treasured letter. Mrs. Paul begins with a description, accompanied by visuals, of her ideal learning community. She is quick to say that this is her "sketch," her "vision," and that she wants to hear about the children's. A lengthy conversation ensues. References are made to real communities, to gardens, and to other natural places where there are plans for building something special with common goals, hopes, and dreams, and where diversity is appreciated. The teacher's storyline is inspiring, authentic, and presented with direction and purpose, yet it contains room for allowances that children view as important and engaging.

Mrs. Paul goes on to explain herself as the teacher who receives a paycheck for assuming the role of head educator who orchestrates learning opportunities for all students. She makes no excuses about being the designated leader in charge, but she likens her role to that of the President of the United States, who needs lots of help to be an effective leader of our country. She explains that a teacher needs lots of cooperation and assistance in order to promote democratic life in the classroom.

The President has a cabinet and Mrs. Paul plans to have one too. Health, education, welfare, and defense are among the communal functions that she draws upon for organization, attachment, and action. Initially, she appoints members to each area, assigning a chair to each post. Over the first two to three weeks of the year, the committees will engage in dialogue about their roles, rights, and responsibilities, how they will function, and how they will monitor their performance. Individual committee meetings coupled with large-group discussions are the secret to effective planning and well-executed efforts. Individual committee role descriptions, student rights and responsibilities, expectations, and so on are developed and posted around the room to ensure effective communication and encourage life applications.

During the course of Mrs. Paul's storyline about learning community and cabinet member efforts from the past year, she shares that the welfare committee wanted to support students with special needs. Consequently, it decided to offer lunch money on an emergency basis for kids who had no lunch—either because they forgot to bring one or lacked the resources to purchase one. This group felt that these kids should "work off" their loans, so the welfare committee found school building tasks that the kids could get paid to do, in order to reimburse the committee. This committee held fund-raisers (i.e., used book sales, popcorn and bake sales) to generate resources. Last year's welfare committee also created a supply trunk with hats, shoe laces, mittens, and other clothing, collected through a donation drive for the purpose of applying "good citizen" actions toward peers who had special needs.

YOUR CLASSROOM AS A LEARNING COMMUNITY

You may want to begin your school year as Mrs. Paul did, by putting forth a vision of your classroom as a learning community. Using past class examples, incidents, and personal stories can engender early interest and inject meaning and context into the building of a learning community, although each new class should be encouraged to generate its own ideas. You need to plan carefully to ensure that every child has classroom (departmental) responsibilities that are within his or her capacity, match committee goals, and fit the learning community vision. You also need to set aside periodic committee and total-class reflection time to ensure that learning community efforts are contributing to social understanding and personal and civic efficacy.

While Mrs. Paul used the President's office and cabinet as her metaphor, you might use the governor of an island or state with a supportive cabinet, a family, a sports team, or a neighborhood for building context and structure into the learning community in your classroom. The main idea is to let your students get a sense of what it means to satisfy needs and wants and to participate in a community where rights and responsibilities are exercised in ways that make community members feel in control of their destinies. The classroom community provides a forum for living informal social studies in a safe and orderly environment. It serves as a natural way of connecting cognitive, socioemotional, and moral development. This also relates to Conway Dorsett's (1993) concept of a good curriculum, which is one that respects and balances the need to educate "three people" in each individual: the worker, the citizen, and the private person. All of these dimensions can be experienced first-hand as a learning community in a "laboratory-like setting" in your classroom.

The story of Mrs. Paul's launching of her learning community is intended to position your thinking about a powerful teaching and learning opportunity that considers knowing, understanding, appreciating, and applying a "hands-on" approach to democratic life. It paves the way for building an environment for addressing the academic subjects of school as well.

The remainder of this chapter will expand on the notion of developing a sense of community, present a series of steps for creating it, and explain how cooperative learning can be a natural outgrowth of a collaborative environment. Your challenge is to connect what you already do within the spirit of building an optimal learning environment using a planned learning-community approach to enhance citizen education in your classroom.

Productive Communication and Interaction Patterns

Research on powerful social studies teaching underscores the importance of establishing a productive context for learning by encouraging the class to function as a learning community. The learning-community approach articulates and follows through on expectations set for both teacher–student and student–student interaction patterns. It calls for an open and supportive classroom atmosphere in which students are encouraged to speak their minds without fear of ridicule of their ideas, or criticism for mentioning taboo topics or voicing forbidden opinions. Students are taught that the purpose of reflective discussion of the meanings and implications of content is to work collaboratively to deepen understandings. Consequently, they are expected to listen carefully and respond thoughtfully to one another's ideas. Students advance their own ideas and respond critically to others by building a case based on relevant evidence and arguments and by avoiding inappropriate behavior. They are challenged to address controversial issues, to participate assertively but respectfully in group discussions, and to work productively with partners or groups of peers in cooperative learning activities. They are expected to develop and assume individual and group responsibilities for managing instructional materials and tasks, and to develop an ethic of caring for the personal, social, and academic needs of every child and adult who is part of the classroom.

Steps for Creating a Learning Community

In formulating a learning community with any age level, the teacher needs to explain the goals. These goals cut across the spectrum of cognitive, socioemotional, and moral development. For example, a cognitive goal might be for students to acquire knowledge, understanding, and appreciation for cultural diversity and apply what they learn from their social studies units to life in the classroom. A socioemotional goal might be to develop the ability to question opinions in responsible ways, and a moral goal might be to treat one another with respect. All of these goals can be realized in a learning-community environment.

After formulating overall classroom goals specific to social education instruction (Step 1), you are ready to move on to Step 2. At this juncture, focus on the physical environment and how to go about creating and maintaining a classroom climate that supports shared responsibility, celebrates diversity, and provides the support needed for the realization of established learning outcomes. Use of physical space, accessibility of instructional materials, and availability of visual controls (such as charts, daily schedules, and the daily agenda and calendar of events) all contribute to the setting. Visual materials promote learning as part of specific content units and provide pictorial support for academic, socioemotional, and moral responsibility. Plants, music, rugs, special chairs, identifiable spaces for reading or writing, manipulative materials, and maps, globes, and computer data all build a sense of engagement and connectedness to the classroom milieu.

Step 3 in building the learning community includes the establishment of norms, roles, rules, and procedures for ways of doing things. These range from communicating with parents to beginning the school day, managing individual and group work, resolving peer conflicts, and promoting appropriate behavior in the classroom as well as on the playground, in the lunch room, and on the school bus.

Step 4 involves returning to the initial metaphor or picture, and as a class, creating a vision of how all of this will function. As part of the dialogue, pose questions such as: What should our classroom look like to its inhabitants? What should it look like to a bypasser? What should it sound like? Feel like? Responses can be captured in words, pictures, and photographs to be displayed as reminders of goals and to serve as self-monitoring aids for achieving them.

Our description of implementation may appear highly structured and sequential, so we hasten to assure you that your style as a teacher, your prior experiences, and your unique teaching situation and students will all contribute to how you begin "growing" your learning community. These steps for building a learning community should be supplemented by a planned daily dialogue that focuses on the learning community as it is evolving. Possible questions that might be a part of those conversations include: What is going well? Why? What needs to be modified? How do we need to change a procedure? Does the physical setting need modification? Do we need more or fewer students on a given committee? Are the tasks clearly defined? Does everyone understand his or her role?

Lots of attention needs to be given to the maintenance of learning community ideals and expectations. Be careful about moving too quickly. After creating an overall vision and plan with the class, work on one facet of the community at a time, such as rules. Then move on, but continuously loop back to previous concepts, steps, procedures, and practices. Think of your learning community as an ongoing, growing process that has existing expectations but is always moving to new heights of understanding and positive actions.

COOPERATIVE LEARNING IN A COMMUNITY SETTING

Once the class begins to feel comfortable with the democratic climate and senses a connectedness, and the steps for learning community implementation are in place, the class is ready to work as a community in a collaborative environment. A great deal of research has been done on cooperative learning concepts and techniques. These are often observed in social studies classes because they fit so well with the overarching goals of the subject, for at least three reasons (Winitzky, 1991). First, social studies teachers tend to use group work more than other teachers, and research on cooperative learning provides practical suggestions for making these activities more effective. Second, important goals of social education, such as cross-ethnic acceptance and interaction and integration of handicapped students, are highly congruent with behavioral outcomes associated with cooperative task and reward structures. Finally, the values underlying democratic classroom climate and cooperative learning also align well with the values promulgated by social studies educators.

Any arrangement that calls for two or more students to work together could be called collaborative or cooperative learning. Most of the research has focused on small-group cooperative learning methods. These methods differ according to the task and incentive structures that are in effect (Slavin, 1983, 1990). To appreciate the implications of research on cooperative learning methods, it is helpful to distinguish among alternative task and incentive structures.

Task Structures

The term *task structure* refers to the nature of the task (its goal, the kinds of responses that it requires, etc.) and the specified working conditions that accompany it. Task structures may be individual, cooperative, or competitive. *Individual* task structures require students to work alone; *cooperative* task structures require them to collaborate in learning or in producing some group product; and *competitive* structures require them to compete, either as individuals or as teams, in various contests, debates, or competitive games.

Members of student teams or groups may cooperate in working toward either group goals or individual goals. When pursuing *group goals*, the members work together to produce a single product that results from the pooled resources and shared labor of the group. For example, the group might prepare a video, skit, or slide display for presentation to the class. When working cooperatively to reach *individual goals*, group members assist one another by discussing how to respond to questions or assignments, checking work, or providing feedback or tutorial assistance. Individual students are responsible for their own assignments but are allowed to consult with one another as they work.

Cooperative task structures also differ according to whether or not there is task specialization. *Task specialization* is in effect when a larger task is divided into several subtasks and different group members work on different subtasks. In preparing a report on a country, for example, task specialization would be in effect if one group member were assigned to do the introduction, another to write about the country's geography and climate, another about its natural resources and economy, and so on.

Incentive Structures

Besides differing in task structure, group activities differ in incentive structure (also called reward structure or goal structure). *Incentive structure* refers to methods used for motivating students to perform the task. These include the nature of the incentives themselves (grades, concrete rewards, symbolic rewards) as well as the rules specifying what must be done to earn them and how they will be delivered. Like task structures, incentive structures can be individual, cooperative, or competitive.

Under *individual* incentive structures, any particular student's performance has no consequences for other students' chances of earning available rewards. Individual students are rewarded if they meet prespecified performance criteria, regardless of how the rest of the class performs. Under *cooperative* incentive structures, individuals' chances of earning rewards depend not only on their own efforts but also on those of other members of their group. The teacher rewards groups according to the levels of performance they have been able to achieve through their members' combined efforts. Under *competitive* incentive structures, groups or individuals must compete for whatever rewards are available.

Cooperative and competitive incentive structures also can be differentiated according to whether they involve group or individual rewards. *Group rewards* are distributed equally to all members of the group. These may involve a single reward to be shared or assignment of the same reward to each group member. *Individual rewards*, on the other hand, are assigned differently to individual students depending on their personal levels of effort and performance. For example, students might be encouraged to cooperate with peers in discussing assignments and preparing for a test, but then be required to take the test individually. Or, they might be asked to serve on a committee, but their individual performance would be assessed.

In a robust learning community, one might see the full range of task and incentive structures used on occasion, with clearly defined goals for each. However, the emphasis would be on cooperative practices. Instead of working mostly alone on seatwork assignments, students often work together in pairs or small groups on guided practice or application-type activities. They have opportunities to listen to one another, question among themselves, and write and revise in a collaborative setting. They also have chances to receive information and feedback from peers in addition to the teacher and the instructional materials. Cooperative learning opportunities provide the forum for socially mediated learning.

Cooperative Learning Programs

Several well-known cooperative learning programs are suited to social studies. Among them are Learning Together (Johnson & Johnson, 1975; Johnson, Johnson, Holubec, & Roy, 1984), Group Investigation (Sharan & Sharan, 1976), and Jigsaw II, an adaptation of the original Jigsaw (Slavin, 1990). Information about these and other cooperative learning programs may be found in reviews by Sharan (1990) and Slavin (1983, 1990). These programs serve as natural additions to a classroom where a democratic community context is in place. Students cannot merely be placed together and told to cooperate; they need to be taught how to work collaboratively, engage in productive dialogues, and provide constructive feedback and help. Having a learning community plan in place prior to the implementation of cooperative learning programs provides the necessary foundation for successful results.

The Learning Together program features diversity within groups among students who differ in achievement level, gender, race, or ethnicity. Groups are expected to turn in a collaborative product and are praised for working well together as well as for good task performance. Traditionally, the Learning Together program has had four features: positive interdependence, face-to-face interaction among all students, individual accountability for mastering assigned material, and instruction in appropriate interpersonal and small-group skills.

Group Investigation works very well when a social studies unit has several natural subtopics. For example, in a unit focusing on a particular region, the teacher might offer a range of subtopics such as environmental concerns, economic priorities, climatic conditions, and so on. Students are formed into two- to six-member groups to work together using an array of instructional materials and applying cooperative inquiry, group discussion, cooperative planning, and cooperative projects. Each member of the group chooses an individual task and carries out the appropriate activities necessary to contribute to a group report on the subtopic.

Finally, Jigsaw II works well when a chunk of textual reading needs to be completed in a short period of time in order to provide context or a data base for further inquiry. Teachers find this technique especially successful in classes where there is a wide range of reading abilities. To be effective, care must be taken to ensure heterogeneity in each subgroup. In using Jigsaw II, all students begin by reading a common narrative but then each member of a given team is assigned a separate topic on which to become an expert. Then, the students (from separate teams) who have been assigned to the same topic meet in expert groups to dialogue, after which they return to their teams, each teaching what he or she has learned to the teammates.

Research on Cooperative Learning

Research on cooperative learning generally has yielded quite positive results. These methods have been shown to be feasible in most classroom situations and likely to have positive effects on achievement and other outcomes. The most effective achievement results come from methods that combine group goals with individual accountability (Slavin, 1988). Achievement effects seem to be positive for all types of students, although especially for minorities.

Effects on outcomes other than achievement are even more impressive. Cooperative learning arrangements promote friendship and prosocial patterns of interaction among students who differ in achievement, gender, race, and ethnicity. They also promote the acceptance of mainstreamed handicapped students and frequently have positive effects on self-esteem, academic self-confidence, and liking for classmates. Students who are taught how to interact in a collaborative environment tend to spend more time on tasks (asking questions, giving feedback, checking answers) and to enrich their answers by providing explanations designed to make sure the listener understands the concept or process.

The Teacher's Role

The teacher's role is multifaceted throughout the developmental process of building a learning community and implementing cooperative learning strategies. It includes but is not limited to

1. creating a climate of mutual concern;
2. teaching specific cooperative learning skills and techniques;
3. showing sincerity and interest in each student's responses, ideas, experiences, and work products;
4. eliciting students' input on a regular basis;
5. giving reasons and thoughtful explanations regarding socioemotional, behavioral, and academic issues;
6. giving students the chance to examine and express the importance of what they do;
7. providing them with opportunities to participate actively in the evaluations of their academic work;
8. minimizing their need for extrinsic rewards and abolishing their fear of punishment; and
9. celebrating their successes, while also engaging with them in ongoing dialogue and reflection regarding their individual and class development.

Many, if not all, of the above elements relate to the teacher's role in generic teaching and learning in the classroom, but they apply especially to powerful social studies teaching. In this role, the teacher has the added responsibility of building appreciation and meaningfulness in all situations related to the human condition and civic efficacy, as well as connecting the unit content to life in the classroom.

CONCLUSION

Building a learning community with cooperative learning approaches for specific tasks must be

1. goals-driven;
2. pitched at the appropriate level of difficulty for the academic and socio-emotional levels of the students;
3. integrated into the total school day as the way of life in the classroom;
4. deliberate in shaping democratic activities and actions to ensure that they support progress toward overall social understanding and civic efficacy goals, as well as relating to the unit goals that are linked to the social science disciplines;
5. maintained and monitored on a regular basis; and
6. culminative in producing students who understand, appreciate, and are willing to apply social studies concepts, processes, and actions to democratic life outside the classroom.

We believe that building a learning community draws on all of the senses, is established on the premise of democracy, and serves to shape constructive human interactions. At the same time, it provides a natural framework for acquiring meaning in the social studies.

Your Turn: Building a Learning Community in Your Classroom

Observe several classrooms and look for evidence that the students are functioning as a learning community. Attempt to interview each teacher afterwards. If you did not see much evidence of a learning community, try to seek explanations. Where learning communities were successfully implemented, talk with the teachers about their insights—and how they have actualized their visions.

Sample Observation Schedule

- How would you characterize the climate of the classroom?
- Does the climate reflect mutual concern? (Evidence?)
- Do you feel like you are "living" in a community? (Evidence?)
- Is there a sense of shared values? (Evidence?)
- Are specific cooperative learning skills and techniques being developed? How?
- Is there a sense of high expectations regarding positive behaviors and academic success? (Evidence?)
- Does the teacher show sincerity and interest in each student's responses, ideas, experiences, and work products? (Evidence?)
- Is student input elicited on a regular basis? (Examples?)
- Does the teacher give reasons and thoughtful explanations regarding socioemotional, behavioral, and academic issues? (Evidence?)
- Do students get a chance to share and express the importance of what they do? (Evidence?)
- Do students participate actively in the evaluation of their behavior? Of their academic work? (Evidence?)
- Do they celebrate their successes while engaging in ongoing dialogue and reflection regarding individual and class development? How?

After reviewing Chapter 8, take a sheet of paper, fold it vertically in half. On one side list things that you can do as a teacher to build a learning community in your classroom, and on the other side list behaviors to avoid because they will detract from your learning community goals. Find a peer who is willing to participate in this exercise. After you have both compiled your lists, discuss them.

After this preliminary activity, revise your list. Then find a quiet spot and, using the list as a starting point, spend at least an hour creating your vision for your classroom learning community. Then, put your response aside, but work on it for 30 minutes every day for a week. Finally, spend time developing a long-range plan for launching the learning community in your classroom. Remember, it is a year-long process. Accumulated experiences will expand your understanding and build your confidence in implementing the learning-community approach to democratic life in classrooms; you will begin anew each year as you meet a new class of students and journey through the process together.

REFERENCES

Johnson, D., & Johnson, R. (1975). *Learning together and alone*. Englewood Cliffs, NJ: Prentice-Hall.

Johnson, D., Johnson, R., Holubec, E., & Roy, P. (1984). *Circles of learning: Cooperation in the classroom*. Alexandria, VA: Association for Supervision and Curriculum Development.

Sharan, S. (Ed.). (1990). *Cooperative learning: Theory and research*. New York: Praeger.

Sharan, S., & Sharan, Y. (1976). *Small-group teaching*. Englewood Cliffs, NJ: Educational Technology Publications.

Slavin, R. (1983). *Cooperative learning*. New York: Longman.

Slavin, R. (1988). Cooperative learning and student achievement. *Educational Leadership, 46* (2), 31–33.

Slavin, R. (1990). *Cooperative learning: Theory, research, and practice*. Englewood Cliffs, NJ: Prentice-Hall.

Winitzky, N. (1991). Classroom organization for social studies. In J. Shaver (Ed.), *Handbook of research on social studies teaching and learning* (pp. 530–539). New York: Macmillan.

Chapter 9

INTEGRATING SOCIAL STUDIES WITHIN THE TOTAL CURRICULUM

Curriculum integration appears to be an obviously good idea. Articles and inservice speakers extol its potential for enhancing the meaningfulness of what is taught, for saving teachers' time by reducing the need to make so many preparations, for reducing the need to cover everything, and for making it possible to teach knowledge and skills simultaneously. For social studies and other subjects that suffered reduced time allocations as a result of the back-to-basics movement, integration is pictured as a way to restore needed content emphasis. In general, integration is seen as a viable response to problems of content balance and as a way to save time and make for more natural and holistic learning.

These seemingly compelling arguments have predisposed most educators to view integration in social studies as a desirable curriculum feature. Indeed, the implicit maxim is "the more integration, the better." A few years ago, we shared this view, and we still find it hard to resist the notion that integration is a good idea—in the abstract. However, we have become more cautious after examining the best-selling elementary social studies series, observing in classrooms, and talking to teachers about their integration practices. We have found some desirable forms of integration, but also many undesirable ones (Alleman & Brophy, 1993; Brophy & Alleman, 1991).

DESIRABLE INTEGRATION

The key to successful integration is that it results in enhanced understanding and appreciation of subject-matter content and processes in ways that promote progress toward social education goals. For example, adding content drawn from another subject can enrich the content of social studies (e.g., reading about and displaying the works of an artist can enhance the study of a historical period).

Adding science content related to technology can enrich understanding of social issues. Using a powerful literary source can add interest and appeal to the study of the Revolutionary War and help develop students' understanding and appreciation of the origins of U.S. political values and policies.

Literary sources need to be chosen carefully, however, so as to develop topics in ways that promote progress toward major social education goals. For example, if the goal in the early grades is to enrich students' understanding and appreciation of family life in the past, *When I Was Young in the Mountains* would be an appropriate selection to include. If the goal is to develop a perspective regarding pioneer life, a chapter or two from *Little House on the Prairie* might be more appropriate. The latter novel describes, among other things, the efforts and dangers involved in digging a well. It is written from a child's point of view—very engaging to a youngster—and it presents a powerful glimpse of pioneer life that enriches the social studies curriculum.

Some forms of subject-matter integration are the result of necessity. For example, certain topics are primarily identified with one subject but require applications of another to be learned meaningfully. Map and globe studies are part of geography, and consumer education is part of economics, but both of these topics require mathematical knowledge and skills.

Probably the most popular form of integration in social studies, however, involves combining social studies knowledge content with processes from a skills subject, typically language arts. This approach can be effective if the students have had previous experiences with the needed skills. For example, students may be asked to interview business people about an urban renewal project as part of a social studies unit focusing on the city. Prior to this assignment, the students should have learned about and practiced the interviewing process.

Accountability Considerations

The focus of the instruction and the accountability pressures placed on students may be on the knowledge, the processes, or both. If students were to write to their political representatives about their legislative roles or policy positions, the assignment would be primarily a social studies activity, although it would include application of writing skills. In contrast, students might write about an imaginary visit to the White House as an exercise in descriptive writing. If the emphasis in structuring and grading this assignment was placed on the functions of the President, it would be mostly a social studies activity. However, if the emphasis was on technical aspects of composition and form, it would be mostly a language arts activity—and should not count against social studies instructional time. Of course, assessment and grading can reflect criteria drawn from both subjects.

As another example, students studying narrative composition skills in language arts and the American Revolution in social studies might write biographies on key Revolutionary figures. This assignment promotes progress toward important goals in both subjects, and is especially appropriate if the goals are clear to the students and the reports are graded separately for compositional features and for historical content.

Examples of Appropriate Integrative Activities

For an activity to be considered part of the social studies curriculum, its primary focus should be on one of the social education goals that have been established for the social studies unit—a goal that would be pursued whether or not this particular activity were included. Other guiding principles that you can use to determine whether an integrative activity is appropriate for social studies include the following: The activity must represent social studies appropriately, and not distort or trivialize its subject matter; the benefits to social education must justify the activity's costs (for both teacher and students) in time and trouble; the activity must be geared to the appropriate level of difficulty; and it must be feasible for implementation within the constraints under which you must work.

Examples of appropriate integrative activities that we have found in social studies materials fall into three major categories:

1. Necessarily integrative activities that focus on topics that draw on content from more than one subject area
2. Authentic applications in which skills learned in one subject area are used to process or apply knowledge used in another
3. Enrichment activities that help personalize content, make it more concrete, enhance learner curiosity, or add an important affective perspective

INTEGRATIVE ACTIVITIES THAT FOCUS ON TOPICS THAT DRAW CONTENT FROM MORE THAN ONE SUBJECT

Some topics inherently cut across subjects. For example, map and globe studies are part of geography, but they also require applications of mathematical knowledge and skills. A map activity for the early grades calls for students to go on a walking trip around the school campus, to make sketches of its key features, and to measure distances. After recording their measurements, students return to the classroom and make a map to scale. After completing the map, they revisit the route and make any necessary corrections. Finally, students add pictures to enhance the sketches and design a legend so that the map will make sense to visitors to the school and to new students who need to be oriented to the school site. Math and geography combined make this a meaningful learning experience.

An elementary social studies unit that focuses on needs and wants includes teaching about an economic decision-making model. A key activity calls for applying this model to a purchase, using knowledge about the diverse options that need to be considered. Students are to decide which bicycle is the best buy: a new model, last year's model, a used bicycle that can be purchased at a garage sale for a mere portion of the original price, or a another used one that is in good condition but needs new tires. Prices are attached to each model. Students use their economics and mathematics knowledge to decide what constitutes the best buy, to discuss alternatives and consequences, and finally, individually and then as a group, to decide which bicycle to purchase.

An activity in an upper-grade unit on technology, where the goal is to develop understanding and appreciation regarding the trade-offs that result from change, calls for students to read a case study and discuss the pros and cons of introducing robotics into a factory setting. Both science and social studies issues are to be examined as a means of illustrating that change often results in problems as well as in fresh and efficient practices.

INTEGRATIVE ACTIVITIES IN WHICH SKILLS LEARNED IN ONE SUBJECT ARE USED TO PROCESS OR APPLY KNOWLEDGE LEARNED IN ANOTHER

If planned carefully, the instruction and the accountability expectations may include both knowledge and processes. For example, in a unit addressing equity in America, assigning a report on a famous American who helped make U.S. society more equitable is appropriate if the students have mastered report writing in language arts. However, bear in mind that new processes and new knowledge should not be taught simultaneously if the content is to be mastered with meaningfulness and with an eye toward appreciation.

The following examples also focus on social studies content goals but integrate skills from other subjects. A history activity calls for students to write an essay explaining how the colonial plantation differed from today's large farms. With proper structuring and scaffolding by the teacher, this activity could be useful in extending understanding and promoting critical thinking about how the nature and economics of farming have changed over time in response to inventions. A creative writing activity calls for students to imagine that they were among the Native Americans forced to endure the Trail of Tears journey and to write diaries describing their experiences, attitudes, and future expectations. This topic provides a good basis for creative writing. The assignment should deepen understanding of the events involved and help students to develop sympathetic and positive attitudes toward Native Americans.

Another activity, part of a unit on the Middle East, asks students to analyze newspaper and magazine articles to identify biases and to explain the points of view expressed and the factors that contribute to developing them. Here, communication skills addressed in language arts are applied to a real-life critical-thinking situation in ways that encourage students to begin to see the power in becoming thoughtful, astute readers.

ENRICHMENT ACTIVITIES THAT HELP TO PERSONALIZE CONTENT, MAKE IT MORE CONCRETE, ENHANCE LEARNER CURIOSITY, OR ADD AN IMPORTANT AFFECTIVE PERSPECTIVE

Enrichment activities can help to personalize content, make it more concrete, enhance learner curiosity, or add an important affective perspective. In an early elementary social studies unit on families, with a goal to develop understanding and appreciation for peoples' needs and wants, literature is used to enhance children's ideas. The teacher reads a story to the students about a person wanting something (Cinderella, King Midas), then poses questions such as Were these people wise to want the things they did? What were the things these people really needed? The teacher continues the lesson by explaining that certain things that people need and want cannot be purchased with money. Students are then to imagine what some of these resources might be (e.g., love, caring, kindness, and friends). This activity provides a nice departure from the often sterile concept of needs and wants, and it appropriately adds an affective dimension that speaks to the ideas that valuable things cannot always be purchased and that there are ways, besides things, to make people happy.

Activities that integrate music, literature, or art with social studies, when connected to social education goals, help to personalize the time and place being studied. For example, in a unit on France, students study Monet reprints, describe how he viewed France, and then, using geography texts, determine the accuracy of his interpretations. This activity is followed by one in which students figure out the time period depicted in his work, citing evidence to support or reject their hypotheses.

Another activity calls for students to read a text or an encyclopedic account of Paul Revere's ride and compare it with the more romanticized, less accurate version in Longfellow's poem. Besides being a natural and useful incorporation of poetry, this is a worthwhile activity for helping students to understand some of the ways in which historiography and fiction differ in goals, processes, and products.

UNDESIRABLE INTEGRATION

Integration is assumed to be productive, but often it is not. Potential pitfalls in applying the concept are often masked by arguments related to the latest trend in curriculum, the goal of getting teachers to be collaborative, the desire to heighten interest, or the attempt to increase the amount of time that can be given to a particular subject. All of these arguments should give cause for pause. From our point of view, all integration of content, skills, or activities into social studies should tie directly to stated subject goals and add meaningfulness to social education. If it does not, we urge you to delete it from the social studies curriculum (although you might want to include it as part of the curriculum for the other subject involved, if it promotes progress toward that subject's major goals).

Characteristics of Unproductive Approaches

The following are examples of integration activities that we view as inappropriate for use in social studies.

ACTIVITIES THAT MASK OR LACK SOCIAL EDUCATION GOALS

Most of the ill-conceived forms of integration that we have seen suggested for social studies classrooms involve activities that draw on content or skills from other subjects. Often these activities lack significant value in any subject and are just pointless busywork (alphabetizing state capitals, counting the number of states included in each of several geographical regions). Others may have value as language arts activities but do not belong in the social studies curriculum (exercises that make use of social studies content but focus on pluralizing singular nouns, finding the main idea in a paragraph, matching synonyms, using the dictionary, etc.). Some are potentially useful as vehicles for pursuing significant social education goals, but are structured with so much emphasis on the language arts aspects that the social education purpose is unclear. We believe that these activities are not cost-effective uses of social studies time.

One fourth-grade social studies manual suggests assigning students to write research papers on coal. The instructions emphasize teaching the mechanics of doing the investigation and writing the paper. There is no mention of social education goals or major social studies understandings such as "humans have unlimited wants but limited resources," or policy issues such as conservation of natural resources or development of energy alternatives. With the task conceived narrowly and the focus on research and report writing, it is unlikely that the 25 or so individual reports would yield enough variety to allow students to benefit from one another's work. Consequently, the social education value of this assignment would be minimal and its cost-effectiveness would be diluted further because of the considerable time required to obtain and read content sources, copy or paraphrase data, and make presentations to the class.

COST-EFFECTIVENESS PROBLEMS

In a unit on families, students were asked to recreate their families by portraying each member using a paper plate decorated with construction paper, crayons, and yarn. The plates were to be used to "introduce" family members to the class and then later combined to make murals. This activity not only is time-consuming but it also emphasizes the artistic dimensions rather than the social studies dimensions. We doubt that art teachers would support this activity as appropriate for art classes either.

In a unit on tropical regions, students were asked to construct examples of homes in tropical areas of the world. Again, such an activity takes a great deal of time, especially if authentic building materials are used, and emphasizes construction skills instead of understanding and appreciating the impact of climate and local geography on living conditions.

Besides time-consuming art and construction projects, role-play is another frequent basis for activities that are either inherently limited in social education value or too time-consuming to be cost-effective. For example, a unit on families calls for students to dress in costumes, play musical instruments, and participate in a parade as a means of illustrating how families celebrate. On the following day, students are to write about the event. This series of activities offers tie-ins with humanities and physical education and provides a stimulus for language arts work, but it lacks a significant social education content base. Students already know that families celebrate holidays, and despite the extensive hands-on features of this activity series, it fails to elaborate usefully on this idea.

Cost-effectiveness problems are also embedded in collage and scrapbook activities that call for a lot of cutting and pasting of pictures, but not much thinking or writing about ideas linked to major social education goals. Instructions for such activities are often given in ways that focus students on the processes involved in carrying out the activities rather than on the ideas that the activities are supposed to develop, and the final products often are evaluated on the basis of artistic appeal. One activity calls for students to cut out articles of clothing and paste them under the appropriate category. Categories included wool, linen, cotton, polyester, and so on. Students can spend a substantial amount of time on this "hands-on" activity without learning anything important about the different fabrics.

We believe that the time spent on activities must be assessed against the time quotas allocated to the subject in ways that reflect the cost-effectiveness of the activities as a means of accomplishing the subject's major goals. You should ask yourself, Is this activity the best choice given the limited time allocated for social studies? Keep in mind that cognitive/affective engagement need not be "hands on"—in fact, hands-on doing can sometimes be a hindrance to "minds-on" learning.

CONTENT DISTORTION

Attempts at integration sometimes distort the ways that social studies is represented or developed. A unit on clothing includes a lesson on uniforms that calls for students to make puppets of people dressed in uniforms. The teacher is to set up situations where two puppets meet and tell each other about the uniforms they are wearing. This activity is problematic because it is time-consuming, emphasizes art activities instead of social studies content, and calls for knowledge not developed in the lesson (which provides only brief information about the uniforms worn by firefighters and astronauts). Most fundamentally, however, it is problematic because it results in a great deal of social studies time being spent on uniforms, a topic that at best deserves only passing mention in a good unit on clothing as a basic human need.

Content distortion was also observed in a unit on pioneer life that included a sequencing-skills exercise linked to an illustration of five steps involved in building log cabins. The last three steps in the described sequence were arbitrarily imposed rather than logically necessary, and in any case, they did not correspond to what was shown in the illustration. It appears that the text authors wanted to include an exercise in sequential ordering somewhere in the curriculum and chose this lesson as the place to include it, rather than seeing the exercise as important for developing key knowledge about pioneer life.

DIFFICULT OR IMPOSSIBLE TASKS

Ill-conceived integration attempts sometimes require students to do things that are difficult, if not impossible, to accomplish. In a fifth-grade unit focusing on the English colonies, students are asked to demonstrate their understanding of the joint stock company by diagramming its structure to show relationships and flow among the company, stocks, stockholders, and profits. Besides being a distraction from the main ideas of the unit, this activity seems ill-considered because the operations of a joint stock company, although relatively easy to explain verbally, are difficult to depict unambiguously in a diagram.

Other examples of strange, difficult, or even impossible integration tasks include asking students to use pantomime to communicate one of the six reasons for the U.S. Constitution as stated in the Preamble; asking students to draw "hungry" and "curious" faces as part of a unit on feelings; and role-playing life in the White House as part of a unit on famous places. None of these activities reflects the key social education understandings of its units, and each will probably leave students confused or frustrated because they are difficult if not impossible to accomplish definitively.

FEASIBILITY PROBLEMS

Activities that call for integration must be feasible within the constraints under which the teacher must work. Certain activities are not feasible because they are too expensive, require space or equipment that is unavailable, involve unacceptably noisy construction work, or pose risks to the physical safety or emotional security of students. One activity attempts to integrate geography, physical education, and music. The teacher posts the cardinal directions appropriately, then the students line up and march around the room to music as the teacher calls out "March north," "March east," and so on. Implementation of this activity in a classroom full of desks and other furniture invites chaos and injury.

CONCLUSION

We acknowledge the value of productive forms of integration in social studies, but we suggest two caveats. First, content, skills, and activities included in the name of integration should be educationally significant and desirable even if they did not involve the across-subjects feature. Second, such content, skills, and activities should foster rather than disrupt or nullify the accomplishment of major social studies goals.

Successful integration comes in many forms. Sometimes the nature of the topic makes integration natural or even necessary. Other worthwhile integration results when the teacher selects learning experiences that fit the established social education goals by allowing students to apply skills learned elsewhere in ways that promote social studies understanding or application or by adding useful affective dimensions that make learning more interesting or personalized.

Teachers cannot depend on the manuals supplied in contemporary market-share social studies series to focus their efforts on integrative activities that meet the criteria we have outlined. Suggested learning activities need to be assessed, not just for whether students are likely to enjoy the activities, but also for whether they offer sufficient educational value to merit inclusion in the curriculum. For judging activities that purport to integrate across subjects, consider the following questions:

- Does the activity have a significant social education goal as its primary focus?
- Would this be a desirable activity for the social studies unit even if it did not feature across-subjects integration?
- Would an "outsider" clearly recognize the activity as social studies?
- Does the activity allow students to meaningfully develop or authentically apply important social education content?
- Does it involve authentic application of skills from other disciplines?
- Do students have the necessary prerequisite knowledge and skills?
- If the activity is structured properly, will students understand and be able to explain its social education purposes?
- If they engage in the activity with those purposes in mind, will they be likely to accomplish the purposes as a result?

YOUR TURN: INTEGRATING SOCIAL STUDIES WITHIN THE TOTAL CURRICULUM

Use the following exercise focusing on a second-grade shelter unit to assess your level of understanding regarding the perspective on integration contained in this chapter. Study the goals carefully, then read each of the activities. Using the guiding principles for productive integration and the questions for making decisions about social studies integration, label each activity "good," "bad," or "conditional." Be prepared to give reasons for your decisions.

Unit Goals

- To build on children's understanding that shelter is a basic need and that different forms of shelter exist.
- To help children understand and appreciate the reasons for different forms of shelter. Shelter needs are determined in large part by local climate and geographical features. Most housing is constructed using materials adapted from natural resources that are plentiful in the local area. Certain forms of housing reflect cultural, economic, or geographic conditions: Tepees and tents are easily movable shelters used by nomadic societies; stilt houses are an adaptation to periodic flooding; highrises are an adaptation to land scarcity in urban areas.

- To help children understand and appreciate how inventions, discoveries, new knowledge, and development of new materials have enabled many people today to live in housing that offers more durability, and better waterproofing, insulation, and temperature control, with fewer requirements for maintenance and labor.
- To help children understand how the development of modern industries and transportation make it possible to construct almost any kind of shelter almost anywhere on earth. It is now possible for those who can afford it to live comfortably in very hot or very cold climates.
- To help children appreciate the energy efficiency now possible in modern homes due to the developments of technology.
- To help children acquire a sensitivity toward the range of factors that contribute to the type of home (shelter) that a family can afford. (This includes consciousness-raising regarding the homeless.)
- To engender in children an appreciation for their current and future opportunities to make decisions about and exercise some control over aspects of their lives related to their shelter needs (choice making, life applications).
- To help children acquire an appreciation for the range of structures that have been created for shelters over time.

Possible Activity Selections

ACTIVITY	GOOD	BAD	CONDITIONAL	REASONS
1. Students read about various forms of shelter, view pictures of these forms, and then discuss reasons why people might select each form.				
2. Students read about a range of workers, their expertise needed in constructing a home, and the order in which their work would be completed. Then they make puppets to represent these workers talking to one another. The focal point of the discussion should be the role each plays in the completion of the shelter and the sequence in which each job would be done.				
3. Students prepare a collage that illustrates all the ways in which people satisfy their shelter needs.				
4. Provide the class with a mural illustrating the range of shelters that exist in your area. Have the students study the mural carefully and count the number of shelters depicted.				

ACTIVITY	GOOD	BAD	CONDITIONAL	REASONS
5. After describing (using pictures) inventions, new knowledge, and the development of new materials used in shelters, ask each student to share with the class the ones he or she thinks are most significant and why.				
6. Students interview members of their households to find out if and how their homes are energy efficient. (A brief interview schedule will be developed for use in retrieving the data.) A guided class discussion will follow.				
7. Give students an opportunity to study a collection of pictures that illustrate how forms of housing reflect cultural, economic, and geographic conditions. Then lead a discussion that addresses these issues. At the conclusion of the discussion, each student will be asked to identify the most important thing he or she learned.				
8. Provide pictures to show changes in shelters over time. Have students work in groups to arrange the pictures in chronological order. Each group will be asked to provide reasons for its response.				
9. Students will bring in pictures of shelters from around the world, make a class mural, create lyrics for a song about shelters, and then make a presentation to parents.				
10. Lead students on a walk around the neighborhood. Focus on the types of shelters that exist and the types of construction materials that are used. Analyze the findings in a follow-up discussion.				
11. Using an outline map of one or two neighborhood blocks, plan a walk with the class to determine the location of each shelter. Plot each shelter. Upon return, have students make a 3-D model representing the area visited.				

ACTIVITY	GOOD	BAD	CONDITIONAL	REASONS
12. Read a story about the White House. Then have groups of students plan puppet shows representing the following scenarios: the day nobody visited, the day a visitor got lost, the day the presidential family moved in, and the day the electricity went off.				

REFERENCES

Alleman, J., & Brophy, J. (1993). Is curriculum integration a boon or a threat to social studies? *Social Education, 57* (6), 289-291.

Brophy, J., & Alleman, J. (1991). Activities as instructional tools: A framework for analysis and evaluation. *Educational Researcher, 20* (4), 9-23.

Chapter 10

EVALUATION

Part Two of this book provides a model of powerful social studies teaching and learning. This chapter focuses on evaluation, the last component of the model. We begin with a set of questions for you to use in examining your current assessment practices:

- Do my assessment practices reflect major social studies goals?
- Is there congruence between how I teach and how I evaluate?
- What messages or values are reflected in what and how I evaluate?
- Are my practices congruent with the notion that evaluation should be ongoing?
- Do I draw content for my formal and informal evaluation activities from a range of sources?
- Do these evaluation opportunities serve as learning experiences?
- Do I teach my students how to monitor and evaluate their social studies learning on their own?

THE PAST: A FOCUS ON OBJECTIVE TESTS

While assessment is now considered to go far beyond testing, testing has always had a place in social studies teaching because evaluation is considered an integral part of curriculum and instruction and because students must be given marks for report cards. Until recently, social studies tests were not seen as especially important or controversial.

After summarizing what was then known about evaluation in the social studies, Dana Kurfman (1982) concluded that teacher-made tests predominated over norm-referenced tests and over tests that came with curriculum materials, that objective tests were used more commonly than essay tests (especially with low-ability students), and that items concentrated on knowledge and skills with little attention to affective outcomes. He also claimed that social studies teachers were not sophisticated about evaluation, did not engage in much of it, and were uninventive in doing so.

During the last several years there has been a shift in perspective. In a 1991 handbook chapter, Kurfman (1991) noted that testing has begun to receive serious attention from social educators because of its potential effects on schools. States have begun mandating minimum competency tests, and concerns are being expressed about the effects of these tests on the social studies curriculum (Larkins, 1981). Also, standardized test scores, formerly used only as aids in grouping individual students, are beginning to be used to evaluate the performance of school staffs as well.

In just a few years, testing in the social studies has shifted from a relatively informal and uncontroversial curriculum component with implications confined to individual classrooms into the much more formal and controversial realm of high-stakes testing. High-stakes tests have important consequences for examinees, and their scores are seen as reflections of the instructional quality of the schools. Once tests achieve this high-stakes status, they often begin to drive the curriculum, for good or ill (Popham, 1987).

Along with state minimum competency tests and various norm-referenced social studies tests, concerns have been expressed about social studies aspects of the National Assessments of Educational Progress and the College Entrance Examination Board's achievement and advanced placement tests. Social studies educators have questioned the extent to which these tests adequately sample the objectives implied by the curriculum guidelines published by the National Council for the Social Studies. The tests are commonly criticized for focusing on knowledge and skills to the exclusion of values and dispositions, and for emphasizing factual knowledge and lower-order subskills but not critical thinking, decision making, or other higher-order applications (Frederiksen, 1984). Consequently, there is widespread concern among social studies educators that high-stakes testing that features multiple-choice questions will narrow the scope of the social studies curriculum.

Theoretically, the use of test results as feedback with potential implications for adjustments in curriculum and instruction is a desirable feature of a well-planned instructional program. An ideal program is goals-driven such that all of its components serve as means for moving students toward accomplishment of major goals, namely the knowledge, skills, attitudes, values, and dispositions to action that are to be developed in students. The entire program is viewed as a means of accomplishing these goals, and all of its elements are aligned with the goals—the content, the instructional methods, the activities and assignments, and the evaluation measures.

This ideal relationship among program components breaks down, however, if the components begin to be treated as ends in themselves rather than as means to accomplish larger goals. This is what happens to the assessment components when high-stakes testing practices take hold. Theoretically, it is never a good idea to have tests (rather than goals) driving the rest of the system. This concern becomes moot if the tests are very well aligned with the goals, but if they are not, there is good reason for concern about high-stakes testing distorting the curriculum in undesirable ways.

THE PRESENT: A BROADER VIEW OF ASSESSMENT AND EVALUATION

Recognizing the need for accountability, the National Council for the Social Studies (NCSS) and leading scholars who have focused on assessment methods have been arguing for social studies assessment that is well aligned with major social studies goals, more complete in the range of objectives addressed, and more authentic in the kinds of tasks included. NCSS guidelines call for systematic and rigorous evaluation of social studies instruction that

1. is based primarily on the school's own statements of objectives as the criteria for effectiveness;
2. includes assessment of progress not only in knowledge but in thinking skills, valuing, and social participation;
3. includes data from many sources, not just paper-and-pencil tests; and
4. is used for assessing students' progress in learning and for planning curriculum improvements, not just for grading (NCSS, 1990).

In a position statement on testing and evaluation in social studies, the NCSS (1991) emphasized that assessment practices should support school restructuring efforts that favor shared decision making and local leadership at the school level rather than a uniform curriculum or accountability defined only by scores on standardized achievement tests. The statement warned against overreliance on machine-scored standardized tests and favored approaches that balance such measures with alternatives such as performance assessments or authentic assessments. The latter assessments include tasks such as speaking effectively about or taking a reasoned position on a controversial social issue. These assessments focus on the process that students use, not merely the answers they choose.

A comprehensive plan for social studies assessment includes appropriate use of both teacher-made tests and standardized achievement tests. Teacher-made tests might include some of the items supplied by publishers of textbooks. Whether adopted test items are from standardized, norm-referenced tests or from publisher-supplied criterion-referenced tests, teachers should ensure that they are closely matched to the goals and objectives of the local social studies curriculum. To the extent that they are not, this information needs to be taken into account in interpreting test data, and the assessment system needs to be adjusted to better reflect locally adopted goals.

The evaluation component of the curriculum should be viewed as much broader than testing. Tests can be augmented with performance evaluations using tools such as "laboratory" tasks and observation checklists, portfolios of student papers, projects done in conjunction with student interviews, and essays focused on higher levels of thinking.

The NCSS's Advisory Committee on Testing and Evaluation (NCSS, 1991) recommended the following guidelines:

Evaluation instruments should focus on stated curriculum goals and objectives; be used to improve curriculum and instruction; measure both content and process; be chosen for instructional, diagnostic, and prescriptive purposes; and reflect a high degree of fairness to all people and groups.

Evaluation of student achievement should be used solely to improve teaching and learning; involve a variety of instruments and approaches to measure knowledge, skills, and attitudes; be congruent with the objectives and the classroom experiences of the students examined; and be sequential and cumulative.

State and local agencies should secure appropriate funding to implement and support evaluation programs; support the education of teachers in selecting, using, and developing assessment instruments; involve teachers and other social studies professionals in formulating objectives, in planning instruction and evaluation, and in designing and selecting evaluation instruments; and measure long-term effects of social studies instruction.

AUTHENTIC ASSESSMENT

Fred Newmann (1990), Grant Wiggins (1989a, 1989b), and other scholars have elaborated on these guidelines to identify ways in which assessment might become more authentic and address a broader range of goals and objectives. We believe that movement in this direction is needed to promote evaluation activities that support the goal of teaching social studies for life application. Wiggins, for example, identified authentic assessment with performance of exemplary tasks that replicate the challenges and standards typically confronted by writers, business people, or community leaders who engage in activities such as making presentations before a school board or city council, writing an opinion column for a local newspaper, or critiquing a report. In the social studies classroom, a task might be considered authentic in the messages the students speak, write, or draw; the products they create (such as posters); or the performances they complete.

The best evaluation activities make an impact on students beyond certifying their level of competence. Thus, if the social studies goal called for students to develop an ecological position grounded in knowledge regarding local community wetlands, writing an editorial for the town newspaper would be more authentic than writing only to show the teacher that one is capable of doing research and organizing it into a coherent paper. If the social studies goal called for students to understand and appreciate the factors that need to be considered in purchasing consumable products, going on a supervised family shopping trip with a set of conditions that included a clearly established list, uses for products purchased, budget parameters, and so on, would be much more powerful and authentic than taking a true/false test. Authentic tasks such as these challenge students not merely to reproduce what they have learned, but also to construct new knowledge that has value and meaning beyond the instructional context.

Authentic assessment displaces outmoded myths such as the idea that evaluation must be accomplished using objective test formats or that it should yield a score distribution that resembles a bell-shaped curve. It also pushes our thinking toward the use of multiple modalities in assessing progress made toward our social education goals.

Walter Parker (1991) recommended the following as attributes of authentic assessments:

1. Tasks go to the heart of essential learnings by asking for exhibitions of understandings and abilities that matter.
2. Tasks resemble interdisciplinary real-life challenges, not schoolish busywork that is artificially neat, fragmented, and easy to grade.
3. Tasks are standard-setting: They point students toward higher, richer levels of knowing.
4. Tasks are worth striving toward and practicing for.
5. Tasks are known to students well in advance.
6. Tasks are few in number but representative of the goals addressed.
7. Tasks strike the teacher as worth the trouble.
8. Tasks generally involve a higher-order challenge for which students have to go beyond routine use of previously learned information.
9. All tasks are attempted by all students.

Parker went on to argue that authentic assessment should be incorporated in benchmarks that occur at major academic transitions. For example, at the end of elementary school, students might write a summary of a current public controversy drawn from school life (such as instituting a dress code or making birth control measures available in schools) and explain how a courageous, civic-minded American whom they had studied might act on the issue. At the end of fifth grade, instead of taking an objective test on the states and capitals, students might sketch a map of the United States that included this information. Authentic assessments also include informal strategies, such as asking students to state or write summaries of what they learned in a lesson or unit, interviewing them, or observing their performance on tasks.

PERFORMANCE ASSESSMENT: THE LABORATORY MODEL

For performance assessment in social studies, the "laboratory" model can be useful. You probably have experienced this model in your high school or college science classes. On "test" day, stations are located at desks, bulletin boards, whiteboards, murals, wall charts, computer screens, or other appropriate places. Each station displays material such as a chart, artifacts, or an open book with a marked passage. Students visit the stations with clipboards, answer sheets, and pencils in hand. When instructed to do so, they move to the next station. Perhaps some time is allowed for returning to stations where questions have been left unanswered. When all the students have finished, answers are checked.

This model can work very successfully as a means of fostering authentic performance assessment in elementary social studies. Of course, like every type of assessment considered, it must be driven by the social studies goals. If one of the goals of a unit on community is to develop understandings related to transportation systems, students might learn to read and interpret bus schedules. Later, during a lab-type assessment exercise, they might solve a series of questions/problems built around a city map and bus schedules provided at one of the testing stations. At another station, students might be asked to read and answer questions related to bike paths. At still another station, they might be asked to find the most direct routes for reaching certain sites.

Given the goals for the community unit, it is likely that manipulations such as charts, murals, passages from books, slides, flat pictures, newspaper ads, student projects, and so on, can be used effectively to develop major understandings. These would be equally appropriate for performance assessment done under the "laboratory" model.

Here are some helpful hints to consider when planning laboratory-type assessments:

- Try to make the exercises similar in length.
- Begin each sequence with an easy question and build toward the most challenging one.
- Consider providing optional questions at some of the stations.
- For younger students, arrange for adults or older students to help with reading items or manipulating materials.
- If you are concerned about having a station for each student, divide the number in half. You can have half of the class take the test while the other half works on a project in the library, then switch roles. Students can later work in pairs to correct their responses.
- Plan a "dry run" of the model before you use it.
- After administering several lab tests in social studies successfully, gradually add student projects at stations. More advanced students can design questions around their individual and group projects based on the goals of the unit. Provide them with guidelines to ensure that they include questions that address higher-order thinking.
- Be open. There are no hard and fast rules for this model, except that the items must be based on your goals and matched to your teaching modalities.

To stimulate your thinking regarding the use of authentic assessments, we have provided sample station plans from two units (Alleman & Roessler, 1988). (See Figure 10.1.)

The materials and types of items that you can use on lab tests are limitless. The number of questions per station and the amount of time to allocate for each station will depend on your objectives and the age and abilities of your students. As you complete final preparations for this model, go through the Lab Test Checklist shown in Figure 10.2. Be able to answer yes to each question.

FIGURE 10.1
Sample Stations

Station 1: *Questions About the Globe*

Turn the globe slowly. Find the country marked with an X.

1. What is the name of this country? _____

2. In what hemispheres is it located? (circle two of these)

| Eastern | Western | Northern | Southern |
| Hemisphere | Hemisphere | Hemisphere | Hemisphere |

3. Is it earlier or later in this place than where you live? _____

4. Approximately how many miles is it from this country to where you live? _____

5. What would be the fastest mode of transportation to take from here to this place?

    _____

6. If you were to travel southwest from here, would you reach this country or the Hawaiian Islands first?

    _____

Station 2: *The Kyoto Billboard*

(A student project of a billboard advertising Kyoto is displayed at this station.)

1. Is Kyoto an old or a young place? _____

2. Is it a country, province, or city? _____

3. If you were a gardener, would you expect to find work here?_____

    Why or why not? _____

4. If you were a deep-sea fisherman, would you find work here?_____

    Why or why not? _____

5. According to the billboard, what is the most unique characteristic of Kyoto?

    _____

6. According to the billboard, what is one thing a tourist could do for entertainment?

    _____

7. (Optional) According to the billboard, what is one thing that Kyoto and (a city near you) have in common? _____

    _____

PORTFOLIO ASSESSMENT

Authentic assessments might include having students develop and then submit portfolios of their work. Most teachers have students develop a composite of work

FIGURE 10.2
Lab Test Checklist

Did you . . .

_____ acquire clipboards for students to use?

_____ match test items to objectives?

_____ match test items to concepts and skills?

_____ design test items that include higher-order thinking?

_____ use the wide variety of instructional materials that you used in teaching?

_____ use student-made materials? (Gradually infuse these after several successful lab experiences.)

_____ provide optional test items for diverse learners at some of the stations?

_____ make provisions for students to catch up in their writing as they progress through the test?

_____ attempt to make items at each station similar in length, or make necessary accommodations?

_____ provide answer sheets that are easily interpreted?

_____ plan for students who complete the test in minimum time?

_____ prepare an effective feedback strategy?

_____ plan a strategy for reteaching? (if necessary)

_____ plan a strategy for collecting and recording student results?

samples from across the subject areas for this portfolio instead of having one for each subject, but we will focus on the social studies section. Examples of work types include research projects on such topics as "Customs from Our Heritage That We Observe in Our Home," "Rosa Parks, a Native of Michigan Who Championed Civil Rights," and "Life in the Swiss Alps"; and essays such as "Why I Would Prefer to Live in the City Versus the Country," "Some of the Hidden Advantages of Cold Climates," and "What I Can Do to Save Our Country Environmentally." Charts, graphs, maps, photos, letters from pen pals across the globe, interview data and analysis, and drawings are among other work samples we have observed.

Potential portfolio contents are limitless and should typify the diversity of reading, writing, questioning, analyzing, and experiences that is evident among the students. The contents should be indicative of the student's continuing development. The social studies section of the portfolio should represent the important things learned in social studies. It should be used as a powerful stimulus for students to articulate the major understandings in the units of study and to evaluate their own work.

Periodically, students are expected to confer with their peers, yourself, and their parents regarding their work. One teacher we observed also has her students confer with the teacher they will have next year, regarding what they have learned this year and what knowledge, skills, understandings, appreciations, applications, and curiosities they will bring to the next grade. Beginning in the early grades, students can conduct conferences with their parents regarding their social studies goals, showing work samples to represent where they are in their development, what aspects they need to work on more diligently, and what types of assistance and support they think they need from the family. We view this approach as extraordinary in building a sense of self-efficacy—the ultimate in social education.

CONCLUSION

Because powerful social studies teaching and learning is goals driven and integrative, value based, challenging, meaningful, and active, its evaluation component should reflect these same features. In the past, teachers and administrators who preferred to de-emphasize assessment in social studies, or to treat it serendipitously, could do so without high-stakes consequences. Now, however, this benign neglect approach risks adverse consequences. Even if the movements toward national tests fail in social studies, the pressures they exert in other school subjects could result in the reduction of curriculum time allocated to social studies or the importance assigned to social studies courses by students and community members. It is essential for social studies teachers to develop goals-driven classes and programs, and in the process, develop assessment systems that support the accomplishment of these goals and solidify social studies as the flagship for citizenship education.

Assessment should be treated as an ongoing and integral part of each social studies unit. The results should be scrutinized to detect weaknesses in the assessment practices themselves, as well as to identify special learner needs, misunderstandings, or misconceptions. The results of the ongoing analysis should be carefully considered when reviewing, and if necessary, adjusting plans for future versions of currently taught units.

YOUR TURN: EVALUATION

Select a social studies unit that you have designed and taught, or one that you have observed being taught. Collect the evaluation materials that were used as preliminary, formative, and summative assessment. Examine them in terms of the following criteria:

- Do the written items reflect the major understandings that were developed?
- Are the items reflective of the unit goals?
- Does student work show a balance between knowledge and skills on the one hand, and values and dispositions on the other?
- If standardized, norm-referenced tests or publisher-supplied criterion-referenced tests are used, do the items closely match the values, goals, and objectives of the local social studies curriculum?

- What evidence is there that authentic assessment is being considered? Formal strategies? Informal strategies?
- What evidence is there that performance assessment is being woven into the social studies curriculum?
- Is social studies finding its way into portfolio assessment?
- Are teachers talking about student-led conferences—and the role they can play in engendering student responsibility and a sense of self-efficacy?

After you reflect on the responses from this exercise, write a paragraph characterizing what you have observed about the evaluation component of the unit. Write a second paragraph describing what you would retain, what you would modify and/or add to "shore up" the evaluation piece in order to more clearly reflect ideal learner outcomes. Select the weakest link in the evaluation dimension of the unit and redesign it accordingly.

Probably the laboratory model for social studies performance assessment is the one with which you have had the least experience in the elementary school classroom. Incorporate it into one of your upcoming units. Start small with a few stations. One might consist of a wall map accompanied by a series of questions, another might be a chart, another an open book with a marked passage, and another might include a hand slide projector, slides, and questions. As students become more acclimated to the lab-like process, and as they become more adept at engaging in higher-order thinking, you can expand the number and nature of the "testing" stations. At some point, at least by fourth grade, you can include their finished products and their questions as a part of the lab test. Our experiences suggest that students are stimulated by this type of assessment and find it more challenging than frightening.

REFERENCES

Alleman, J., & Roessler, M. (1988). PEP Project. (Unpublished)

Frederiksen, N. (1984). The real test bias: Influences of testing on teaching and learning. *American Psychologist, 39*, 193-202.

Kurfman, D. (1982). Evaluation in social studies. In Project SPAN Staff and Consultants (Eds.), *Working papers from Project SPAN* (pp. 3-27). Boulder, CO: Social Science Education Consortium.

Kurfman, D. (1991). Testing as context for social education. In J. Shaver (Ed.), *Handbook of research on social studies teaching and learning* (pp. 310-320). New York: Macmillan.

Larkins, A. (1981). Minimum competency tests: A negative view. In H. Mehlinger & O. Davis (Eds.), *The social studies. Eightieth yearbook of the National Society of the Study of Education, Part II* (pp. 126-150). Chicago: University of Chicago Press.

National Council for the Social Studies. (1990). *Social studies curriculum planning resources*. Dubuque, IA: Kendall/Hunt.

National Council for the Social Studies. (1991). Testing and evaluation of social studies students. *Social Education, 55*, 284-286.

Newmann, F. (1990). Higher order thinking in teaching social studies: A rationale for the assessment of classroom thoughtfulness. *Journal of Curriculum Studies, 22,* 41–56.

Parker, W. (1991). *Renewing the social studies curriculum.* Alexandria, VA: Association for Supervision and Curriculum Development.

Popham, W. (1987). Can high-stakes tests be developed at the local level? *NASSP Bulletin, 71,* 77–84.

Wiggins, G. (1989a). A true test: Toward more authentic and equitable assessment. *Phi Delta Kappan, 70,* 203–213.

Wiggins, G. (1989b). Teaching to the authentic test. *Educational Leadership, 46,* 41–47.

PART THREE

Representative Unit Plans

Chapter 11
A TEACHING UNIT ON SHELTER NEEDS AND LIVING ENVIRONMENTS

Chapter 12
A TEACHING UNIT ON CLOTHING AS A CULTURAL UNIVERSAL

Chapter 13
A RESOURCE UNIT ON MOUNTAIN REGIONS

Chapter 14
A RESOURCE UNIT FOR FIFTH-GRADE U.S. HISTORY:
THE AMERICAN REVOLUTION

The chapters of Part Two put forth a vision of powerful social studies teaching described at the level of general principles and criteria to use in guiding your instructional planning. In Part Three, we offer plans that exemplify the application of these principles to topics commonly addressed in elementary social studies.

Chapters 11 and 12 contain fully developed teaching unit plans that illustrate our ideas about teaching K–3 topics as cultural universals and addressing them with attention to their development through time, the variety of their manifestations across cultures, and the potential implications of this knowledge for application to the students' current and future lives. Chapter 11 presents a teaching unit on shelter and Chapter 12 presents a teaching unit on clothing.

The next two chapters address topics commonly taught in Grades 4–6. Chapter 13 offers ideas for planning a geographical unit on mountain regions and Chapter 14 offers ideas for planning a unit on the American Revolution as part of a U.S. history course. These are briefer resource units rather than the more detailed teaching units presented in Chapters 11 and 12. That is, they do not include specific plans for individual lessons, but they do outline our suggestions about primary goals and content coverage emphases and suggest learning activities and content resources that might be included in the units.

We emphasize that these unit plans are suggestive, offered as illustrations of how we would apply the planning principles and criteria presented in this book, guided by our preferred goal priorities for elementary social studies. Teachers with different goal priorities will prefer different content emphases and different approaches to developing the content. Even teachers who share our goal priorities are likely to prefer somewhat different content emphases and approaches to instruction and assessment, and all teachers will need to adapt plans to their local curriculum guidelines and the needs of their students. Therefore, the unit plans in the following chapters, even the detailed teaching units presented in Chapters 11 and 12, are meant as representative examples of how we apply our thinking, not as models for you to adopt unquestioningly or follow mechanically.

Remember, initiate the planning process by clarifying and prioritizing your goals and using these goals to guide your decisions about social studies content, instruction, learning activities, and assessment methods. Approaching planning in this manner will enable you to construct a more coherent and powerful social studies program than the one that would result if you simply adopted our plans (or anyone else's) uncritically or if you treated our content coverage and activities suggestions as menus to pick and choose from without having first developed a clear set of prioritized goals to guide your selections.

Chapter 11

A TEACHING UNIT ON SHELTER NEEDS AND LIVING ENVIRONMENTS

The goals of this unit on shelter as a cultural universal are:

1. To build on students' already attained understanding that shelter is a basic need by helping them to understand and appreciate key features of contemporary homes, how the forms and functions of homes evolved over time, through space, and across cultures
2. To help students to appreciate the potential implications of this learning for decision making regarding personal housing needs and preferences

Basic social knowledge is about people—what they do and why they do it. It is not about the disciplines or about shelter, except in this context. In teaching about aspects of human social life, we will include a historical dimension (how it evolved over time) and a cultural dimension (how it varies across cultures). In addressing shelter, the historical dimension will emphasize the role of technology and inventions. People have to meet their basic shelter needs. Early on, they were at the mercy of their environments, but as technology developed, they became more able to control or even shape these environments. Today, we have selected and controlled environments suited to our chosen lifestyles, not just "shelter."

The cultural, and to some extent, the economic dimensions of shelter are connected to the distinctions between needs and wants. As architectural styles and technology developed, people could begin to exercise choice in meeting their shelter needs and wants in terms of styles and features. This led to the diversity of styles within and across cultures, and to the development of landscaping, decorating, and so on.

Content selection and development will also reflect other "meta" ideas: human progress over time, making the familiar strange by placing it in historical and cultural context, choices open to students and the trade-offs embodied in these choices, human applications of knowledge and technology to achieve control over the environment (but with trade-offs here too), and the social reality of homelessness.

The lessons are formatted with goals, main ideas to be developed, introduction, lesson development, summary of key points, assessment, and out-of-school learning opportunities. Lessons 1–3 are a series; Lessons 5 and 6 go together; and Lessons 4 and 7 can be interspersed according to teacher preference.

LESSON 1: SHELTER TYPES

GOALS

- To stimulate curiosity about shelter
- To build on children's understanding that shelter is a basic need and that different forms of shelter exist

KEY IDEAS TO BE DEVELOPED

- Shelter is a basic and universal need: It provides protection from the elements, it provides a place to keep our possessions, and it serves as a home base.
- Shelter is universal; however, it takes many forms. Personal needs and wants and available materials are among the reasons for the range of forms.

INTRODUCTION

Read *A House Is a House for Me* by Hoberman (1978), a brisk rhyming book that presents a range of images regarding houses. Follow this with a discussion about shelter. Use a series of pictures to enhance the discussion. Include pictures from the local neighborhood.

We are going to begin a unit on something that is a very important part of your lives—namely, shelter (homes). You are going to have an opportunity to learn about:

- *Why we need homes*
- *How they have changed over time*
- *Interesting features of modern homes*
- *The various kinds of homes people have, depending on their needs and wants — local differences and world differences*
- *The steps in building a home and the many types of skilled people needed to build them*
- *The choices people make, such as the kind of home they want, whether they should rent or buy, where it should be located, the kinds of decorations they select, and so on*

KWL EXERCISE

Let's begin with what you already know about homes. What do you know about homes already? List responses on chartstand. Note misconceptions to be addressed as you return to this prior knowledge list as the unit unfolds.

Now, let's list your questions about homes. As we study about homes, I want to make sure that we investigate your questions as well as others that I've included in our unit. Record student questions on chart paper so they can be revisited as the unit unfolds. If student queries have not included the following, use them as probes:

- *Do people live in homes just because they want to or do they need to?*
- *Why do they need homes?*
- *What about places like Hawaii where it is warm all year round? Do people still need homes there?* Show pictures of homes in warm places.
- *Why are there so many different kinds of homes?* Show a display depicting homes around the world.
- *What kinds of homes do we have in our area? Why?* Show pictures to stimulate interest. *Which of these are found in our area? Which aren't? Why?*

POINTS TO EMPHASIZE

People need a roof over their heads to protect them from sun and precipitation and they need a structure around them to protect them from extremes of heat and cold. To the extent it is secure and fortified, the shelter also provides protection against animal predators or human thieves or enemies. Structures also provide "inside" space that separates people from the outside environment. This space becomes the "home base" for family activities (cooking meals, sleeping, daily routines in and around the home).

SUMMARIZE KEY POINTS

- All over the world, people spend significant time, energy, and money providing and maintaining homes for themselves. Different people build and use very different kinds of homes, depending on their needs (protection), their wants (cultural and personal styles and preferences), the availability and costs of building materials, and so on.
- Sturdy homes are needed in cold, windy climates but little more than a roof overhead is needed in warm, dry areas.

ASSESSMENT

Have students complete a page in a class or individual scrapbook that summarizes the big ideas regarding shelter types.

Have students make entries in their reflective notebooks and share their entries with their classmates.

OUT-OF-SCHOOL LEARNING OPPORTUNITY

Provide the students with a data retrieval sheet for recording their observations about the kinds of homes they locate in the area.

SOURCE

Hoberman, M. (1978). *A house is a house for me*. New York: Viking Press.

LESSON 2: PROGRESS IN SHELTER CONSTRUCTION

GOAL

- To help children understand and appreciate the range of homes that have been created over time, the changes that they have undergone, and the reasons for these changes

KEY IDEAS TO BE DEVELOPED

- In the early days, housing construction reflected the availability of local materials. While this pattern still exists, modern transportation has allowed choices to be expanded.
- New construction techniques and technological improvements get invented and refined over time. Now, besides meeting *needs* to protect people from the elements, modern houses cater to our *wants* for a comfortable living space, hot and cold running water, electric lighting, comfortable beds and furniture, and so on.

INTRODUCTION

Show three dramatic still pictures or slides that depict the far past, the recent past, and today (see Figure 11.1). Discuss what each picture shows and elicit observations about shelter during these periods. Show a simple timeline and as the "story" unfolds, place pictures on the timeline.

Using pictures and objects plus story-like narrative, describe the progress in shelter construction. Use an enlarged visual of each period for creating context.

POINTS TO EMPHASIZE

Early shelters offered only one multipurpose space. The first kind of house was a cave. It had walls that kept out harsh winds and prowling animals, a ceiling that kept out the rain, and a floor on which to sit or curl up and sleep. Cave dwellers depended on rivers for water and on fire for heat and light.

FIGURE 11.1

Chart: Progress in Shelter Construction

	FAR PAST	RECENT PAST	TODAY
People	Cave dwellers	Pioneers	Us
Construction	None (found)	Low tech	High tech
Light	Fire	Candles	Electric lights
Heat	Fire	Stove	Furnace
Water	River	Well	Plumbing
Room differentiation	None	Minimal	High

The cave dwellers were hunters. They lived in caves during the winter and they kept warm by the fire. In the summertime they were free to move from place to place as they hunted. They built temporary homes so they could move quickly. Often these summer homes were made of a framework of young tree trunks covered with birch branches and twigs.

If they lived where there were no existing caves, they had to build their own cave-like shelters. To do that, they scooped out the earth, making a large dish-like hollow. Then they covered the hollow with a roof of branches.

Gradually, people learned how to use the local building materials to create shelters. Animal hides, stones, straw, vines, clay, and logs were among the early materials used. (Show these materials and allow the students to handle them.)

Still other hunters of long, long ago made a tent-like covering of animal skins over the oval (dish-like) hollow. The hearths in which they built their fires were placed in the middle of the floor. Remember, the kinds of shelters people built in the past—and even today, in some cases—depended on where they lived (climate) and how they earned a living. Hunters built shelters that they needed for only a short time.

The Indians who lived in the Great Plains of North America were hunters, too. They lived in tepees. Tepees were made by tying together three or four long poles at one end and standing them up to form a frame. Then about 15 other poles were leaned against the frame. The whole framework was then covered with a carefully fitted buffalo skin. The bottom of the skin was weighted down with stones to keep the wind out. The Indians built their fire near the center of the tepee. The smoke went out through an opening at the top. Whenever they moved to new hunting grounds, they had to take down the tepee and set it up at the new site. They used available building materials and, because they hunted for food and had to follow the buffalo, they created temporary homes.

As people learned how to raise plants and animals, they no longer had to depend on hunting. They got their food by farming and herding. Once people began to plow land and plant and harvest crops, they could build more permanent homes. Again, they used local building materials such as logs, stone, or bricks that they made themselves. Early farmers in our country built homes of logs and mud-like plaster. Logs and plaster formed the walls of the log cabins. The well-chinked thick logs (and the absence of windows) kept the wind out. (Use pictures or slides to illustrate the building of a log cabin. Focus not on sequencing, but on how the shelter was constructed in order to keep out the elements.)

On the day the home was to be "raised," neighbors in all directions arrived. Ground had to be cleared for the log cabin. Many trees had to be chopped down. The logs that were felled were cut to the same length. Notches were made at both ends and the logs were laid in position, ready to be made into walls. The fireplace was started. The foundation was built up of stones and the chimney was erected above it. The hearth was made. The walls of the cabin went up quickly. The notched end of one log fit nicely into the notched end of the next, which was laid on top at right angles. The roof of the cabin was made of smaller logs and pieces of bark. After the roof was completed, moss, leaves, and mud were stuffed into the spaces between the logs so that the wind could not get through the cracks. Oiled paper was used to cover window openings (if they were present). A blanket hung over the doorway (where there were no available tools to make doors).

Little furniture was found in log cabins. What was there was made with crude tools from wood. For example, the cabin might have bunk beds built right into the wall, tables made out of crates, and chairs made out of barrels. (Limited space existed for the whole family. All of the family activities were carried out in the same space.)

Log cabins were heated by burning wood in the fireplace. Sources of light included the sun (through window openings), light from the fire, and candles.

SIMULATE LIVING IN A LOG CABIN

Darken room, condense space, simulate fire, and light candles. *Imagine that we lived in a log cabin in the past. Our light was restricted to fires, primitive torches, and candles. We didn't have windows because we needed to keep as much cold air out as possible. The cabin was never brightly lit like today's homes are.*

Candles were made from animal and vegetable fat as well as from bayberries and beeswax. When the candles burned, they smelled like frying grease unless bayberries were used. Later the light bulb was invented and homes were wired for electricity.

A nearby river or spring served as the source of water for drinking, bathing, and doing laundry. Carrying water was a backbreaking job, so most settlers would dig a well near the house as soon as they could.

In summary, log cabins were more comfortable than cave homes and more sturdy and permanent than tepees. Still, they were built using only local building materials, offered only one large multipurpose space, and had only limited control of heat, light, and water.

After the log house, the plank house was the next improvement in shelter. Like the log cabin, it was built of wood. Planks could be cut by hand but it was a lengthy job, so farmers would to go to saw mills and buy the planks for their houses.

Plank houses were usually two storeys high. The downstairs contained a kitchen, dining room, and parlor. Upstairs were three or four bedrooms. The rooms were usually heated by pipes which carried heat and smoke from the kitchen and living room stoves up two chimneys. The roof of the plank house was usually made of shingles instead of logs. (Shingles were made at the sawmill.)

The kitchen in the plank house often contained a stove instead of a fireplace. Stoves were more useful than fireplaces. They did not let all the heat escape up the chimney and they were easier to cook on. Stoves usually burned wood or coal.

By the time people began building plank houses there were also finishing mills—usually next to the sawmills where rough boards were made smooth. Cabinet makers would use this smooth wood to make furniture.

Plank houses used candles made from animal fat, bayberries, and beeswax for light, and instead of indoor plumbing they used outdoor facilities known as outhouses. The family members bathed in wooden or tin tubs—bringing the water for them from the nearby streams or wells.

Gradually, modern technology developed so that today, our homes have indoor plumbing and controlled heat and light. They are usually made of locally plentiful building materials—although with modern transportation, almost any material can be shipped in from anywhere in the world. Of course, many of these materials would be very expensive and many would not be appropriate for our kind of climate.

Modern homes are designed by architects and built by builders who use the latest technologies. They are able to build very tall apartment buildings with steel beams and concrete, or single-family dwellings out of brick, wood, or other appropriate materials. They are wired for electricity for light, have efficient heating systems, and indoor plumbing. They also feature a much greater range of materials targeted for special use, the use of precision machinery for exact fits, efficient insulation, clear window panes, and finished and decorated interiors.

SUMMARIZE KEY POINTS

- Shelters have changed over time due to inventions.
- Local resources still account for many of the building materials used in modern shelters, but now they are precision-manufactured and shipped all over the world.

ASSESSMENT

Have students complete a page in a class or individual scrapbook that summarizes the big ideas regarding human progress in shelters.

Have students make entries in their reflective notebooks and share their entries with their classmates.

OUT-OF-SCHOOL LEARNING OPPORTUNITY

Encourage students to tour their home with an older family member and make a list of all the ways that the home differs from a log cabin. The list should be brought to class and, as a total group, a master list will be compiled as a means of illustrating human progress in terms of shelter since the pioneer days.

SOURCES

Kalman, B. (1982). *The early family home*. New York: Crabtree.
Scheele, W. E. (1960). *The mound builders*. New York: World Publishing.
Yue, D., & Yue, C. (1984). *The tipi*. New York: Alfred A. Knopf.

LESSON 3: PROGRESS IN CONTROLLING OUR LIVING ENVIRONMENTS

GOALS

- To develop an appreciation for the power and influence of human progress
- To develop a "macro" understanding of features that we currently label as modern conveniences, especially the control of light, heat, and water

KEY IDEA TO BE DEVELOPED

- New knowledge, development of new materials, inventions, and discoveries have enabled people today to live in houses that offer more durability, and better waterproofing, insulation, and temperature control, with fewer requirements for maintenance and labor.

INTRODUCTION

Show objects and pictures reflecting the past and present. Revisit the timeline constructed for the unit.

Materials	Logs ➤ clay, grasses ➤ stone, aluminum siding, finished wood, and so on
Light	Fire ➤ candles ➤ lanterns ➤ windows ➤ light bulbs
Heat	Open fires ➤ Fireplaces ➤ Boilers, furnaces, heat ventilation

In the past, unprocessed raw materials were used as they were found, generally in the local area. Some areas had few building materials, so people had to resort to materials such as sod and adobe.

In the early days, the raw materials were unprocessed and the tools were really low tech. As a result, the materials were crudely cut from wood or stone or fashioned from clay or grasses.

Today, however, we have modern equipment (i.e., saws, presses) and factories for manufacturing building materials and assembling them with precision. The result is that houses look a lot different than they did in the past.

In addition to changes in building materials, modern homes have better lighting and heating, and more efficient water supplies. Explain and depict schematically:

Water   Collection from source → purification → homes → use → waste water management

Electricity Power plants → line → socket → switches

Fuel   Mined → processed → transported to homes, and so on

Electricity is a kind of energy. It is a current that flows through a wire, much like water flows through a hose. An electric current can do the same kind of work a fuel can do. It can make light and heat. Through the work of scientists, electric current was harnessed and supplied to people's homes. Now we control its flow using switches. When light switches are turned on, electricity runs through a tiny wire inside the bulb and makes the wire get hot. When the wire gets hot enough, light is produced. Anything that gets hot enough (a tiny wire in a light bulb, a candle flame, or a log fire) gives off light.

In the past to keep warm, we had open fires and fireplaces. Today we have boilers and furnaces and heat that circulates through pipes and ducts. Some modern homes have fireplaces, too, but they are usually for decoration or "atmosphere," and are not the only source of heat.

In the past, water supply came from streams or wells near homes. Today we have indoor running water and plumbing which is piped from a central source (township or city) or else a water supply is retrieved from our own property and secured by drilling a well. (Using pictures or actual gadgets such as water faucet, meter, thermostat, switch, and so on, discuss changes that have occurred over time.)

Of course, with modern technology comes the need to pay for purified water, energy/electricity, and fuel that are delivered to our homes. Today, utility companies provide us with electricity, fuel, and water. We have to pay to use it. (Show water bill, light bill, and heating bill.)

These advances have made it possible for people to live comfortably in environments that they could not have lived in so comfortably earlier (perhaps not at all). They also have provided more immediate and precise control of light, temperature, and water, with less trouble. (One strategy for sharing this knowledge is to invite one or more mature adults to discuss changes that have evolved in their lifetimes.)

In the past, geography was the primary influence on the choice of building materials. People used the resources that were available locally. However, with modern technology and modern means of transportation, this has changed.

People who can afford it now build almost any type of home anywhere, exercising control over their immediate environment rather than being at the mercy of geography and climate. (On the other hand, some people elect to "revisit" the past by living in a *modern* log cabin or even to live without modern conveniences like the Amish do.)

Build a chart/bulletin board with pictures and words that has as its theme "Progress in Shelter Types and Conveniences." (A section focusing on future developments could be included.)

SUMMARIZE KEY POINTS

- New knowledge, development of new materials, inventions, and discoveries have enabled people today to live in housing that offers more durability, and better waterproofing, insulation, and temperature control.
- Future developments will change the types of materials used in building homes and the types of conveniences that will be available.

ASSESSMENT

Have students complete a page in a class or individual scrapbook that summarizes Human Progress. If done as a class, the teacher could facilitate a class discussion by pulling out key points, recording them on the chart or overhead, and preserving or duplicating the results.

If done as individuals, starter lines for student responses in pictures and words could be as follows:

In the past, people heated their homes by _____

In the past, people's shelters were lighted by _____

In the past, the water supply was _____

Today, we have modern conveniences in our shelters which include

_____

_____

We pay for these modern conveniences. Examples include

_____

_____

Students will be asked to make entries in their reflective notebooks and share their entries with their classmates.

OUT-OF-SCHOOL LEARNING OPPORTUNITY

Encourage students to tour their homes looking for clues that illustrate how their family has taken advantage of modern technology, then draw pictures or bring photographs of examples (furnace, air conditioner, water softener, etc.) to class for sharing and discussion.

Lesson 4: Portable Shelters

GOAL

- To develop an understanding and appreciation of portable shelters

KEY IDEAS TO BE DEVELOPED

- Portable shelters have existed for many, many years.
- Portable shelters are built of a variety of materials, take many forms, and are used for a variety of reasons.
- In the past, portable shelters were a necessity for certain groups; today they range from being a necessity to being used for recreational purposes.

INTRODUCTION

What comes to mind when you think of a portable shelter? Conduct a brainstorming session placing students' responses on an overhead or the board. Have them formulate some big ideas about their list such as there are many types of portable shelters; they are made out of a variety of building materials; they are used for a variety of purposes; and so on.

Show the students pictures that illustrate many of the ideas they generated. Then begin to share some information that suggests the range of portable shelters and how they have developed over time.

Review the tepee and show a portion of the book entitled *The Tipi* by David and Charlotte Yue. Have the students imagine what it would have been like to live in a tepee.

Key points to bring out in discussing this portable shelter include: (1) Tepee covers were made from buffalo hides; (2) they did not last for more than a year; (3) making a new cover was a community project; (4) when trade with settlers made canvas available to the Indians, that material was used instead of buffalo hides (canvas covers were easier to make, the material was lighter and more easily transported, and canvas tepees could be larger); and (5) tepees were pitched frequently because the Great Plains Indians followed the buffalo.

Today, people all over the world use tents as portable shelters. For some, they are a necessity (e.g., Bedouins). For others, they are used during recreational periods. For example, families can live in tents at camp sites for short periods while they enjoy nature, fish, hunt, hike, and so on. In fact, tents are a common portable shelter used by vacationers (show pictures).

Another type of portable shelter is a mobile home on wheels, often referred to as a recreational vehicle. People who own or rent these houses that move travel for fun, not to hunt food.

Ask students if they have ever lived a mobile home, even for a short period. If so, ask them to share their experiences. What are the advantages? Disadvantages?

If time permits, have students in triads draw a portable shelter they would like to live in for a short period—and discuss what it would be made of, how it would be designed, and what modern conveniences it would have? Share the results with the class.

SUMMARIZE KEY POINTS

- Portable shelters have existed for many, many years. They are built out of a range of materials, and take on many shapes. They are used as homes by people who move often.
- Portable shelters include tepees, covered wagons, yurts, igloos, house trailers, recreational vehicles, fold-down tents, canvas tents, and so on.

ASSESSMENT

Have students complete a page in a class or individual scrapbook that summarizes portable shelters.

Have students make entries in their reflective notebooks and share their entries with their classmates.

OUT-OF-SCHOOL LEARNING OPPORTUNITY

Encourage students to discuss with parents why they would or would not like to use a portable shelter on their next vacation. Share the results the following day in social studies class. (A survey could be designed to gather specific input.)

SOURCE

Yue, D., & Yue, C. (1984). *The tipi*. New York: Alfred A. Knopf.

LESSON 5: CHOICE MAKING

GOALS

- To enhance children's understanding regarding the many forms of shelter that are available

■ To develop an appreciation for the opportunities that people may have to exercise choices in meeting their shelter needs and wants

KEY IDEAS TO BE DEVELOPED

■ One of the choices people make is whether to rent or own a home.
■ Other choices include location, size, style (single or multilevel, color of outside, etc.; if apartment, what storey, with or without security system, etc.)

INTRODUCTION

Present a scenario to use as a stimulus for assessing prior knowledge and for setting the stage for the lesson.

The scene is a family meeting about the need to move because the mother's company has asked her to relocate. The family has decided that she should remain with the company and accept the job promotion in _____ . Select a city near you and show a map of the area.

The family consists of mother, grandmother, four-year old Becky, eight-year old Brande, and twelve-year old Michael.

What are the decisions this family will need to make?

Among the responses that might be given are the following: The family will have to decide whether to rent or buy. If renting, should they get a house, a duplex, or an apartment? If buying, should they purchase a house or a condo? Where should they live—city or suburb? Should it be close to mother's job? Close to schools? Close to the interstate? And so on. (List student responses and comment appropriately. At the end of this segment of the lesson, summarize.)

POINTS TO EMPHASIZE

In order to buy a home, a family needs to have money in the bank for a down payment. All of the money for the home is not needed at the time you move in. You can take out a mortgage (loan) from a bank with a promise to pay the money back over an extended period of time. If you do not have money saved to make a down payment, you will have to rent a place to live. Sometimes you can rent a house, but often you rent an apartment.

Some people with money saved elect not to use it to buy a house, so they also rent. Often such a decision is due to a limited stay in an area, uncertainty about where to buy, owning a home someplace else, a desire to save the money, a desire to have the freedom to move at any time without having to wait to sell the house, or not wanting homeowners' responsibilities.

Once the family has made the decision about renting or buying, it needs to decide where to look for housing (location). Choices include but are not limited to the city or the suburbs; near a school; close to the airport or train station (if a family member does a lot of traveling); near a park; near an expressway; near a shopping center, library, hospital, preschool, etc.

LOCATION IS A MAJOR FACTOR IN DECIDING WHERE TO LIVE

If moving to a home, factors that need to be considered include single or multi-storey, size based on number of occupants, types of rooms based on ages and family priorities, color and types of building materials based on family preferences, and so on.

If moving to an apartment, factors that need to be considered include size, entertainment/exercise options (such as a club house, swimming pool, or tennis courts), floor level (ground, second level, or above), laundry facilities, nature of other occupants (families with children versus young adult professionals, etc.), and level of security (some apartments have a security guard, some have outdoor buzzer systems, others merely depend on individual locks on doors). Note that conveniences and "extras" cost the renter more money. Explain that apartment houses usually are owned by a company (group of investors) and that the apartment manager is someone hired to supervise the complex. The families who occupy the apartments pay monthly rent to the manager—or someone in the office who handles the money. This money is used to pay off money borrowed from the bank at the time the apartment complex was purchased. The money is also used to maintain the building, pay for the extras (laundry facilities, cleaning the hallways, outdoor lighting, etc.), and provide the owners with some profit.

SUMMARIZE KEY POINTS

- People make choices about their shelters; among them are whether to rent or buy.
- A major factor in deciding on a home is its location.
- Other choices include size, conveniences, and "extras" such as garages, decks, swimming pools, security systems, and so on.
- Families must pay for the choices they make. The more conveniences and extras, the more the home costs. Not all people choose to spend their money on things beyond the basics. (They may decide to save their money or to spend it on other things such as new cars, travel, education, etc.)

ASSESSMENT

Have students complete a page in a class or individual scrapbook that summarizes the big ideas regarding choice making.

Have students make entries in their reflective notebooks and share their entries with their classmates.

OUT-OF-SCHOOL LEARNING OPPORTUNITY

Encourage students to talk to their families about the choices they have made in deciding whether to rent or buy, location, amount/types of living space, conveniences, and so on. Use the following interview schedule so the data can be graphed. The end product should be a graphic representation of the range of choices the families made regarding their homes.

1. What was the single most important factor we considered in deciding where to live?

_____

2. Does our family prefer renting or buying a home?   _____

_____

Why?   _____

_____

What are the trade-offs?   _____

_____

3. What are three conveniences we decided to have in our home (family room, garage, fireplace, air conditioning, etc.)?

_____

_____

ENRICHMENT

Books that might be read to the class include *An Apartment's No Place for a Kid* and *My Mother's House, My Father's House*. Both point out changes that result from divorce and the adjustments that need to be made.

SOURCES

Christianson, C. B. (1989). *My mother's house, my father's house*. New York: Atheneum.
Knox-Wagner, E. (1985). *An apartment's no place for a kid*. Niles, IL: Albert Whitman.

LESSON 6: DESIGN YOUR IDEAL HOME (DECISION MAKING)

GOALS

- To draw on prior knowledge and acquired appreciation about shelter in order to "design" an ideal home

■ To develop an appreciation regarding the range of considerations that need to be addressed when deciding on the ideal home

KEY IDEAS TO BE DEVELOPED

■ Location, climatic conditions, availability of materials, cost, family size and composition are among the factors to consider when attempting to identify and "design" the ideal home.
■ Individual tastes and preferences enter into the decision-making process.

INTRODUCTION

We have been studying about shelters from the past and present, how they have changed over time, the kinds of building materials that are used, the choices people make such as whether to rent or buy, where to live, type of home, and so on. Today, you and your classmates are going to design on paper your ideal homes. This will be an individual effort due to the value preferences involved.

After students complete the decision-making data sheet (see Figure 11.2) and feel comfortable with the reasons for their decisions, they should consult with others regarding ideas and questions. They may draw or construct the structure. If construction is selected, the work will need to be done at home, during free time at school, or as an art project (only if it matches the art goals and the teacher agrees to the assignment). The construction could be done in groups.

At the end of the project, have students share their ideal home concepts with the class. Encourage them to talk about the reasons behind their decisions.

SUMMARIZE KEY POINTS

■ Many factors such as climate, cost, location, and family size need to be considered when creating an ideal shelter.
■ Decision making is also influenced by one's culture, personal taste/preferences, the experiences one has had, and the specific conditions that exist, such as number of family members, and so on.

ASSESSMENT

Have students complete a page in a class or individual scrapbook that summarizes their decisions regarding an ideal home.

Have students make entries in their reflective notebooks and share their entries with their classmates.

FIGURE 11.2
Decision-Making Data Sheet for Designing Your Ideal Home

Describe the number of members in the family, ages of the children, pets, and so on:

_____

Describe the number of vehicles the family owns: _____

Describe the location of the home:

   City, country, suburb, and so on: _____

   Climatic conditions: _____

What physical features are nearby?

_____ woods _____ lake _____ mountains _____ other

What building materials will be used? _____

_____

TYPE OF STRUCTURE

_____ Ranch _____ Two-storey colonial

Other (describe) _____

How many rooms will your ideal home have and how will each be used?

_____

What special features will your home have? (air conditioning, fireplace, sauna, etc.)
Why? _____

_____

What special outside features will your home have? _____

_____

How much will it cost? _____

Other: _____

_____

OUT-OF-SCHOOL LEARNING OPPORTUNITY

Encourage students to talk to their families about the choices they made in their school work group regarding their ideal home. Then, as a family, design an ideal home on paper. Compare the two. Encourage the students to bring their family's ideal home plan to school and share with a peer, noting reasons for their choices. The major understanding to be drawn from the activity is that "There are many considerations that come into play when deciding what the ideal home would look like. There are also numerous trade-offs."

LESSON 7: HOMELESSNESS

GOALS

- To help children understand that in extreme cases people are unable to pay for a shelter and the net result is homelessness
- To help children acquire a sensitivity for homeless people and a desire to practice citizenship as it relates to assisting others in need

KEY IDEAS TO BE DEVELOPED

- Sometimes people cannot pay for shelter and utilities due to unemployment or underemployment, and the net result could be homelessness. Often these circumstances are due to untimely illnesses, fire, flooding, loss of jobs, accumulation of bills, and so on.
- People who are homeless can secure help from community organizations (i.e., United Way, Rescue Mission, Salvation Army, religious organizations, etc.).
- As members of the community, we can contribute to organizations that assist people in need by donating time, food, money, clothing, and so on.

INTRODUCTION

Pose questions regarding homelessness. Sample questions might include: What do you know about homelessness? Why does it occur? Have you ever had contact with a person who was homeless? Have you ever had a glimpse of the life of a homeless person?

Introduce the children to *Fly Away Home* by Eve Bunting—a story of Andrew and his father who live at the airport. Ask children to imagine they are Andrew, and after listening to the story, to share their feelings with the class.

POINTS TO EMPHASIZE

Fear, uncertainty, frustration, anger, and sadness are among the feelings associated with homelessness.

The airport was selected by Andrew and his father as a temporary shelter because it is a place where there is lots of activity—everybody is on the move—and they would not be easily noticed or singled out (public buildings cannot legally be used as temporary shelters).

Andrew has hope of having a home again. As a young boy, he does not quite understand why other people have homes and he does not.

After reading and discussing the story, share with the children some of the reasons for homelessness such as tornados, floods, earthquakes, untimely illnesses, loss of jobs, and so on. Newspaper articles can be used to add human interest stories.

Using a map, point out places in the community where people in need can secure assistance (i.e., United Way, Salvation Army, Food Bank, churches, etc.).

As a class, discuss what could be done to provide assistance for members of our community who find themselves in a crisis. Using a decision-making model familiar to the students, plan an activity for helping the homeless in the community.

SUMMARIZE KEY POINTS

- Homelessness is often the result of extremely unfortunate circumstances.
- Communities have organizations that provide assistance to people in need.
- One way of practicing good citizenship is helping others.

ASSESSMENT

Have students complete a page in a class or individual scrapbook that summarizes the big ideas regarding homelessness.

Have students make entries in their reflective notebooks and share their entries with their classmates.

OUT-OF-SCHOOL LEARNING OPPORTUNITY

Encourage students to share with their families what they have learned about homelessness and what the class has decided to do to assist people who are experiencing such unfortunate circumstances. Ask for family involvement in the activity (i.e., donating articles of clothing, money, food, etc.).

SOURCE

Bunting, E. (1991). *Fly away home*. New York: Clarion.

YOUR TURN: A RESOURCE UNIT ON SHELTER NEEDS

	SPECIFIC EXAMPLE	SPECIFIC EXAMPLE	SPECIFIC EXAMPLE
Examine the unit carefully for examples of powerfulness. If you detect a void or weakness, make the necessary adjustments. 1. Social studies teaching and learning is powerful when it is meaningful.			

	SPECIFIC EXAMPLE	SPECIFIC EXAMPLE	SPECIFIC EXAMPLE
2. Social studies teaching and learning is powerful when it is integrative.			
3. Social studies teaching and learning is powerful when it is value based.			
4. Social studies teaching and learning is powerful when it is challenging.			
5. Social studies teaching and learning is powerful when it is active.			

After you have critiqued the unit and found or added examples to ensure powerfulness, reflect one more time on what this unit will look like in your classroom if you adapt it to the needs of your students.

Write a letter to the parents of your students describing powerful social studies teaching and learning and what they can expect to see if they visit your classroom during the shelter unit. What behaviors will their children exhibit if, indeed, the teaching and learning is powerful? Explain how you will evaluate the results.

Chapter 12

A Teaching Unit on Clothing as a Cultural Universal

The goals of the unit on clothing as a cultural universal are:

1. To build on students' already attained understanding that clothing is a basic need by helping them to understand and appreciate its functions and how it has changed over time
2. To help students to appreciate the potential implications of this learning for decision making regarding personal clothing needs.

Basic social knowledge is about people—what they do and why they do it. It is not about the disciplines or about clothing, except in this context. The unit will include historical, geographic, cultural, and economic dimensions as they relate to human social life.

There are several functions of clothing: protection from the elements, communication, and decoration. Everyday clothes are differentiated into clothes for work, clothes for play, and clothes for sleeping. Special-function clothes include clothes for sports and special activities and clothes for ceremonies such as weddings and funerals.

Geographic factors that impact the clothing industry include climate, weather, and terrain. These influence the raw materials that can be produced for clothing. Wool, cotton, and flax are featured as examples.

The study of clothing provides opportunities to examine basic land-to-hand relationships and to illuminate the processes involved in making raw materials into cloth. One lesson focuses on wool, tracing the land-to-hand relationships and showing the interdependence of people involved in the industry. Another lesson focuses on cotton and nylon.

Clothing has changed over time due to specially formulated blends and treatments which have produced clothing with special characteristics. We now have clothing that is waterproof, breathable, lightweight yet warm, soft but durable, and so on.

People have choices to make about what they wear. Types of material such as cotton, wool, or linen, as well as style, color, cost, and where to purchase the garment are among the decisions to be made. A lesson addresses this issue.

In the language of the anthropologist, the unit is designed to "make the strange familiar and the familiar strange" to students. It emphasizes applications to the students' current and future lives. Critical-thinking and decision-making activities are included to raise students' consciousness of the fact that they will make choices about clothing both as individuals and as families throughout their lives, as well as to build knowledge about the trade-offs associated with the major choice options.

Lesson 1: Functions of Clothing

GOALS

- To help children understand why people wear clothing: protection, communication, and decoration
- To help children acquire an appreciation for the cultural diversity that exists in the nature and functions of clothing

KEY IDEAS TO BE DEVELOPED

- Clothing is a basic human need.
- Throughout history, individuals have used clothing for protection, communication (self-expression, group identity), and decoration (status, ceremonies), as well as in attempting to conform to codes of modesty.
- People in various cultures dress differently for many reasons. They may need protection from different kinds of weather, use different methods and materials for making cloth, or have different customs or habits of dress.

INTRODUCTION

Pose questions to the children regarding the functions of clothing. Sample questions might include: Why do people wear clothing? Why do they wear different kinds of clothing at different times? How does climate and geography influence the types of clothing people wear? What do you know about clothing designed to protect people from the dangers of work?

POINTS TO EMPHASIZE

After preliminary discussion of these questions, show the class a poster (see Figure 12.1) that you have "started" that depicts the functions of clothing.

Use the following information as introductory material for each category. Encourage the students to bring pictures to add to the appropriate categories over the next several days. As more data become available, both in visual and in

FIGURE 12.1
People Wear Clothing for a Variety of Reasons

PROTECTION	COMMUNICATION	DECORATION	OTHER

written/oral forms, encourage students to share their knowledge and insights. Guided discussions should focus on how and why the cultural universal—clothing—functions as it does.

Protection   Humans lack the natural protection that most animals have. Our skin is easily pierced or bruised. Lacking thick skin or fur, we have to depend on protective coverings to enable us to survive in extreme climates.

In arctic climates, early humans realized that the fur coat that kept animals from freezing to death might also help them survive. Later, people began to wear many layers of clothing to keep warm. Air spaces between the layers served as insulation against the cold.

In warm climates, people wear clothes of lightweight materials such as cotton or linen, which have fairly open weaves. These fabrics absorb perspiration and allow air to flow around the body. Other warm-climate clothes include light-colored clothes that reflect the sun's rays, open sandals that keep the feet cool, and large hats, often made of straw, that protect the face and neck from the sun. In the Arabian desert, for example, people often wear loose, flowing garments as protection from the hot sun.

For thousands of years, most clothing was fashioned from animal skins and leafy vines. As civilizations developed, humans learned how to make thread and weave it into fabric. During the Stone Age, a kind of cloth was made from the fibers of the flax plant. This was known as linen.

Eventually, humans learned to design specialized clothing to protect them when they were hunting animals or fighting against human enemies. Hide or wicker shields and helmets came into use long before the age of metals. Later came quilted cotton armor, metal shields and helmets, leather breastplates, and so on. Much later came camouflage clothing that was designed to blend into the landscape and was made of materials appropriate to the climate.

More recently, we have developed specialized clothing for people in certain occupations, such as surgeons' gowns or auto mechanics' coveralls. Astronauts and deep-sea divers wear special suits and helmets for protection against changes in air pressure and temperature. The hazards of industry and the challenges of space travel have increased the need for special types of protective clothing that are safe, comfortable, and durable.

Communication Another function of clothing is to communicate how people feel. In our society, clothing with bright colors and bold designs may indicate happiness, whereas people in mourning may wear black. Such color designations vary across cultures, however. Many brides in the United States wear white, while in India white is worn for mourning. Sometimes people wear clothes to indicate what they want to be. Children use clothes to play "grown up" and imitate adults in certain roles, and teenagers choose clothes that signify favored values or lifestyles.

Decoration People wear clothing for decoration or because they believe that it makes them look attractive. A person may stop wearing a suit or dress, not because it is worn out, but because it is out of style. People have often worn ceremonial costumes with decorative features. These include feathers, paint, jewels, and so on.

Standards of modesty vary with cultures as well as with changing social conditions. The concept of modesty held by native women of the Congo, where nothing may be worn above the waist, differs greatly from the concept of modesty held by Moslem women who cover their entire bodies and veil their faces. In our part of the world, there is a generally accepted concept of modesty. At minimum, this involves covering our "privates." However, clothing expectations vary from the informality of beaches and ball parks, to the "No Shirt/No Shoes/No Service" rules in many restaurants, to the more formal dress codes that are enforced, or at least expected, at certain restaurants, in certain work places, and at church services, weddings, funerals, and so on.

At the conclusion of the story-like presentation regarding the functional uses of clothing, ask students to share the most interesting ideas they learned from the lesson. Then ask them to indicate questions that they would like to have answered. Post the new questions, and encourage individual and group mini-reports.

SUMMARIZE KEY POINTS

- Clothing serves many functions.
- Some of these functions are universal across time and cultures.
- During one's life, clothing will probably serve all of the functions described in the lesson.
- Protection and modesty are probably the most common functions of clothing among children.

ASSESSMENT

Have students complete a page in an individual scrapbook that summarizes the big ideas related to the functions of clothing.

Have students make entries in a reflective notebook and share their entries in pairs. The entries could also be shared at student-led conferences.

OUT-OF-SCHOOL LEARNING OPPORTUNITY

Encourage students to share with their families what they have learned about the functions of clothing and bring an example of clothing to school that serves one or more of the functions. A display will be created so unique items are desired. The display will serve as the stimulus for an expanded and enriched discussion regarding the purposes and uses of clothing.

SOURCES

Rowland-Warne, L. (1982). *Costume*. New York: Alfred A. Knopf.
World book encyclopedia. (1994). Vol. 4, 686–692. Chicago: World Book, Inc.

LESSON 2: CHANGES IN CLOTHING OVER TIME

GOALS

- To help children understand and appreciate the changes that have occurred in clothing manufactured across time
- To stimulate children's curiosity regarding clothing, styles, customs, and tastes

KEY IDEA TO BE DEVELOPED

- Clothing manufacture has undergone a variety of changes over time. These changes have produced clothes that are more durable, weather repellent, lightweight, convenient to use, and so on.

INTRODUCTION

Introduce the lesson by asking students what they know about clothing of the past and how it differs from today's clothing. Capture all of their responses on a white board, chalkboard, or flip chart.

POINTS TO EMPHASIZE

Since the children probably have limited knowledge about clothing over time, we suggest that you use a story-line approach with a wealth of pictures. The unique features of clothing during the seventeenth and eighteenth centuries should be of considerable interest to the students, along with the inventions that changed the clothing industry. A simple timeline and cut-out pictures to post as the story unfolds could be an engaging approach. Leave enough spaces for students to add more pictures. See timeline for examples. (See Figure 12.2.) We have included some descriptive material to illustrate what might be included. Based on your interest and knowledge regarding the topic, and the

FIGURE 12.2
Changes in Clothing Over Time

VERY LONG AGO	LONG AGO	RECENT PAST	TODAY

interests that students reveal, much more information could be added. We also suggest that twentieth-century clothing might be done as a total-class research project. Pictures should be added as the findings are discussed.

Many Europeans sailed to the New World during the sixteenth and seventeenth centuries and settled on the east coast of North America. Many of these new settlers made their homes in the wilderness. When the clothes they brought were worn out, they had to make new ones. They made their own fabrics from wool, flax, and leather.

For the leather, the colonists tanned animal hides (placed the hide in water and added oak or hemlock bark). The bark released acid into the water. This acidic solution prevented the hide from rotting. The hide was left to soak for several months. When the leather was finally dried, it was stiff. To make it soft enough to wear, the colonists rubbed it with oil or animal fat.

For wool, farmers raised sheep. Each spring they sheared the thick, heavy coats of the animals. They cleaned the wool, removing the dirt, sticks, and burrs, and then greased the wool in order to restore the oils lost during cleaning. After the oils were restored, the wool was ready for carding (combing), spinning (drawing out and twisting fibers into thread), dyeing, and weaving (a process of crossing two sets of threads over and under each other). (If possible, arrange for students to observe or participate in the process of spinning and/or weaving.)

Flax plants were grown and the fibers of the plants were used to make linen. Since linen was lighter than wool, it was ideal for summer-weight clothing. The fine, combed strands of flax were spun into thread and woven into linen cloth.

By the middle of the eighteenth century, clothing became a visible indication of social class. The lower class wore plain garments made of wool or linen in colors such as gray, brown, or white. The middle class wore clothing that was modest yet stylish, and sometimes their Sunday clothes were quite stylish. The upper class (people who owned a lot of land, traders, and those who were born into wealthy families) wore fashionable clothes of silk or other delicate fabrics. Middle- and lower-class women wore simple cotton and linen dresses while wealthy women wore beautiful gowns made from expensive materials.

Many eighteenth-century towns had shoemakers who stayed at the homes of their customers while they made shoes and boots for the whole family. Early pairs of shoes had no right or left shoe. A few were fastened with laces, but most had buckles. There was a range of styles of boots and shoes—determined usually by the role or class of the individual.

There were numerous women's accessories distinctive of this period. Among them were the calash, a large hood-like structure that can be folded down like the convertible top of an automobile. It was used to protect a woman's tall hair style. Other items included masks to protect women's faces from the sun, wind, and cold weather; muffs (short tubes of fur for keeping the women's hands warm); and fans which served as portable air conditioners and also came in handy for flirting. Aprons were popular and used to keep skirts from getting dirty. Fancy hairdos and hats, as well as unique undergarments, were in style during this time period.

Men's styles included stockings, breeches, waistcoats, and long coats with many buttons, and much braiding and brocading. Men's accessories included items such as cravats, hats, canes, and swords. Men often wore wigs. Some people had their own hair cut off and made into a wig. Wigs could be brown, black, or even blue, but most were white or gray. Both the men and the women wore make-up during this time.

Eighteenth-century children dressed much differently than the children of today. Toddlers often wore puddings, which were paddings wrapped around their middles so they would not get hurt if they fell. Some toddlers even wore a padded hat that looked like a helmet which served to protect the child's head. Both boys and girls wore linen dresses until they were five or six years old. Then they began dressing like their parents (reflecting their social class).

Many of the immigrants who arrived in America in the early nineteenth century became farmers. Since they worked outdoors, they needed tough, comfortable clothing. They frequently wore loosely fitted shirts called smocks and trousers. By the middle of the century, they were wearing high-waisted pantaloons held up by suspenders. By the end of the century, they were wearing overalls much like those worn by many farmers today.

In the West, herds of cattle were tended by cowboys. Early cowboys wore denim coats, leather breeches, and tall boots. Later they wore denim trousers or jeans. In 1850, a tailor named Levi Strauss started making and selling Levis. Cowboys wore huge hats that came to be known as cowboy hats. They were classified in gallon sizes, and were actually used for carrying water. Smaller hats were two-gallon hats, whereas the largest hats were called ten-gallon hats. These doubled as a wash basin or a bucket in which water was brought to a thirsty horse.

Rural women wore simple dresses of wool, linen, or linsey-woolsey. On Sunday, they added a shawl or clean apron if they did not own a good dress.

Hats were a part of every outfit. Wide-brimmed sun hats or sunbonnets were worn on sunny days. Indoors, women preferred mobcaps or cotton bonnets. As settlements grew, fabrics became more easily obtained and frontier women could make dresses and simple suits for themselves and their families.

The basic outfit for the women living in towns or cities in the nineteenth century was a combination of the hooped skirt, blouse, and bodice. Tight corsets and bustles gave women a thin-waisted look. Many dresses, blouses, and jackets had leg-of-mutton sleeves. Near the end of the century, women's clothing became more practical. Simple blouse and skirt outfits were worn during the day. Suits became popular among women who worked in offices.

Men's fashions did not change much throughout the nineteenth century. Suits composed of trousers, a waistcoat, and a coat were common attire. Most of the fashion changes were in the styling of the suits. The biggest change was in the length of men's pants. Breeches, the knee-length pants of the eighteenth century, went out of style in the nineteenth century. Instead, men wore either pantaloons or trousers.

For footwear, many villagers were fortunate enough to call on the local shoemaker. There continued to be no left or right shoes. Families often bought shoes several sizes too big for growing children, stuffing the toes with paper or cloth to create a better fit while they grew into them. A range of styles existed according to use. Both men and women wore gaiters to protect their stockings or pants from mud. Gaiters were canvas leggings strapped over the top of the shoe and buttoned up the side or front of the leg (Kalman, 1993).

During the nineteenth century, both men and women wore hats every day. The top hat was the most popular accessory for men, as was the bonnet for women. This brimmed cap came in a variety of styles and was tied beneath the chin. It could be made of fur, velvet, satin, straw, wood, gauze, or cotton.

The hairstyles of the 1800s were very different from those of the 1700s. Wigs and huge hairdos were no longer in fashion. For a time, chignons for women were popular. They were ringlets, braids, or curls that hung at the neck or from the top of the head. By the end of the century, people wore their hair in much simpler styles (Kalman, 1993).

In summary, today's clothing and fashions are much different from those of even 150 years ago. Many changes have occurred. One change is that children of today have a much simpler process of getting ready for school. Children today, in general, put on the following items:

1. Underwear
2. Shirt or a dress
3. Pants
4. Socks
5. Shoes

However, if they had lived 150 years ago they would have had to wear the following items:

GIRLS	BOYS
1. A long frilly undershirt	1. An undershirt of wool or cotton
2. A bodice—a tight girdle with buttons up the back	2. Long underpants of wool
	3. A shirt, often with ruffles and a tie
3. A garter belt to hold up stockings	4. Long black stockings held up by garters
4. Long stockings made of cotton or wool	5. High-buttoned shoes
5. Long underpants that buttoned to the bodice	6. Pants that buttoned on to the shirt
	7. A buttoned-up waistcoat or vest
6. High-buttoned shoes	8. A wool jacket
7. A red flannel petticoat	9. A hat and coat
8. A starched petticoat	
9. A long stiff dress	
10. An apron, called a pinafore, to keep the dress clean	
11. A hair ribbon, tied in a bow	
12. A bonnet, tied under the chin	

Children of the past took half an hour to get dressed, whereas children today take only a few minutes.

Inventions in the middle of the nineteenth century allowed clothing, shoes, and other items to be mass produced in large quantities. One of these inventions was the sewing machine.

As railroads were built, items could be transported to remote places. This led to the founding of mail-order companies such as Sears Roebuck and Montgomery Ward. Clothes could be ordered and shipped anywhere, and as a result, people throughout the country could have the same fashions. More recently, clothing companies have opened retail outlets all over the country or arranged to sell their "brand name" clothes through local outlets.

SUMMARIZE KEY POINTS

- Clothing has changed in a variety of ways over time.
- Styles seem to evolve from very simplistic and practical to quite complicated and unusual and back to more practical.
- People all over the country can wear similar type clothing due to mass production techniques and modern transportation and retailing methods.
- People's work roles and their social class are factors in their selections of clothing.

ASSESSMENT

Have students complete a page in their individual scrapbook that summarizes the big ideas related to changes in clothing over time.

Have students identify the most interesting thing that they have learned regarding the changes in the clothing industry, and explain why. Pictures or line drawings could be added to illustrate and to enhance meaningfulness.

OUT-OF-SCHOOL LEARNING OPPORTUNITY

Encourage children to discuss with their families what they have learned about the changes in clothing over time, using their pictures or line drawings to explain the most interesting things that they learned. As a follow up, they might ask their parents to share a unique article of clothing that they possess and discuss whether or not it would have existed in the past.

SOURCES

Kalman, B. (1993). *Historic communities: 18th century clothing*. New York: Crabtree.
Kalman, B. (1993). *Historic communities: 19th century clothing*. New York: Crabtree.
Rowland-Warne, L. (1992). *Costume*. New York: Alfred A. Knopf.
Tierney, T. (1987). *Famous American women: Paper dolls in full color*. New York: Dover.

LESSON 3: SPECIAL CLOTHING

GOALS

- To develop knowledge, understanding, appreciation, and life application regarding clothing considerations for special situations: jobs, recreational activities, and celebrations
- To develop knowledge, understanding, appreciation, and life application regarding the factors that contribute to "specialness": culture, gender, climate, and economics

KEY IDEAS TO BE DEVELOPED

- People wear special clothing to perform jobs, take part in recreational activities, celebrate holidays, participate in festivals, and express certain emotions at weddings, funerals, and so on.
- Cultures, gender, climate, and economics are all factors related to special types of clothing.

INTRODUCTION

Show students pictures that depict a range of special types of clothing. Ask them, "Why do people wear special types of clothing?" List the responses. Encourage them to bring examples of special types of clothing for a display in the social studies area. Encourage students to share stories about the special types of clothing they brought—when and why they wore the special garments. With help from adult or older student tutors, the students might write short stories about their garments and special occasions when the garments were worn. Share these with the class.

POINTS TO EMPHASIZE

Using the display of clothing and pictures, explain special clothing. You might approach the lesson by talking about special clothing that you have that relates to holidays you celebrate, as well as special clothing you wear for your job, for recreation, and for celebrations. The following information provides a sampling of what you might include. The information can be as expansive as you determine appropriate and effective.

Festivals and carnivals   Festivals are occasions where special clothing is often worn. One that is popular in the United States is the Mardi Gras celebration in New Orleans. People wear costumes and dance in the streets. It is believed to be a time to get rid of the negative acts a person has done during the past year.

Birthdays, mournings, weddings   Some families wear clothing for celebrating their birthdays (e.g., party hats and special "dress up" clothes). It merely adds to the festivity.

Some cultures have special clothing for certain occasions. In North America and Europe, people often wear black clothing or black arm bands when a member of their family dies. In India, China, and other countries, however, people often wear white clothing when someone they love has died.

Weddings are occasions where certain traditions are expressed through clothing. At most Shinto weddings in Japan, brides wear beautiful traditional kimonos and cover their faces with white powder. In America, men wear tuxedos and women wear special bride's and bridesmaids' dresses for traditional weddings (*Childcraft,* vol. 8, pp. 66-65).

Special clothing for recreation   Football players wear special helmets and lots of padding for protection. Their uniforms are made of very sturdy cloth that stretches (spandex), and they wear special shoes with metal cleats to prevent slipping. Team members wear the same uniforms, which helps players to locate their teammates and helps fans identify the players. (The one difference enjoyed among the players is their individual numbers.) Other team sports also use special uniforms.

Skiers, snowmobilers, mountain climbers, and joggers use special clothing for their individual sports. Choices are based on the amount of protection needed, weather and geographic conditions, and the amount of money the individual decides to spend on specialized clothing.

FIGURE 12.3
People's Choices to Wear Special Clothing Are Influenced by Several Factors

CULTURE	CLIMATE	COST	PERSONAL TASTE	GENDER

Special clothing for work Some occupations require special clothing for protection and/or identity. Examples include astronauts, military personnel, police officers, and postal workers. Factory workers often have special protective clothing such as hats, gloves, or masks.

Choices people have People have a lot of choices of what to wear in most situations. Many types of work allow lots of choices in wearing apparel. For holidays, you can decide whether or not you want to "dress up" for the occasion. On the other hand, if you decide to participate in a certain sport, you may be required to wear special hats, shoes, and so on. There are cases where special articles of clothing are needed for protection or identity.

Using a class discussion format, have students complete a chart (see Figure 12.3) to illustrate the key points of the lesson with words and pictures gleaned from magazines and catalogs.

SUMMARIZE KEY POINTS

- People wear special clothing for a variety of reasons such as for protection, identity, and participation in special events such as holiday celebrations, weddings, funerals, and so on.
- Sometimes people wear special clothing by choice, but they may be required to do so if they join a team or an organization that requires special uniforms or dress codes.
- Culture, climate, and cost considerations are among the factors that determine what people wear.

ASSESSMENT

Have students complete a page in their individual scrapbook that summarizes the key ideas related to the lesson or a chart similar to one done in the large group. If the latter option is selected, have them collect the pictures or complete the drawings as an out-of-school learning opportunity.

OUT-OF-SCHOOL LEARNING OPPORTUNITY

Provide the students with open-ended statements or questions to be discussed with their families. Encourage written responses so the data can be shared with the class, probably along with pictures or objects.

Members of my family wear special clothing for _____

The special clothing includes _____

_____

_____

Our family's decisions for special clothing are based on _____

_____

My favorite special clothing is _____ because _____

_____

My favorite outfit is _____ because _____

_____

Here's a story about a recent clothing shopping trip our family took:

_____

_____

Decisions about the clothing we bought included _____

_____

SOURCES

Childcraft. Vol. 8, pp. 62–65. Chicago: World Book, Inc.

Geringer, L. (1987). *A three-hat day*. Mexico: Harper Trophy. (Hats are special clothing items. Pottle the Third has a truly wonderful, extraordinary collection of hats.)

Winthrop, E. (1986). *Shoes*. Mexico: Harper Trophy. (Shoes are special clothing items. There are many kinds.)

LESSON 4: LAND TO HAND—THE STORY OF WOOL

GOALS

- To help children develop an understanding and appreciation of the "story" of their woolen clothing
- To help children develop an understanding and appreciation of the interdependence of people involved in the clothing industry

KEY IDEAS TO BE DEVELOPED

- The kinds of clothing people wear depend on a variety of factors. One factor is climate.
- There is a variety of raw materials used in making cloth for clothing. One of the raw materials used is wool.
- Because of technology and job specialization, people involved in the processing of wool are interdependent.
- The woolen clothing that we wear goes through many processes (steps) known as "land-to-hand" relationships.

INTRODUCTION

Show children samples of wool and articles of children's clothing made from wool. Pose questions to pique their interest and to determine what theories they have formulated regarding the wool-making process. Place their responses on the board or a flip chart. With the use of pictures and a storyboard, slides, or video, share with the children the story of wool. Include the steps described in the lesson development section and describe the interdependence of the people involved in the "chain of events." Embellish the storyline in ways that hold the children's interest but that do not detract from the key understandings.

POINTS TO EMPHASIZE

Sheep are raised in places where there are warm and cold seasons. They often feed on hillside grasses. In some parts of the world, large numbers of sheep are raised on ranches. Spring is the busiest time of the year for ranchers. It is at this time that the lambs are born. Also, sheep old enough to walk are shorn at this time because they no longer need their thick coats. The thick coat that is *sheared* off in one piece is called a fleece. As soon as the coat is removed, a new one begins to grow. The fleeces are rolled up and tied together with twine, then packed in burlap bags and *shipped* to market. After the wool is sold, it is *cleaned* and *sorted*. Machines *comb* out the knotty wool. The wool is *spun* into thread and then *woven* into cloth. Weaving is a process of making cloth by crossing two sets of threads over and under each other. One set is called the warp. It stretches lengthwise on a loom or a frame. To make cloth, the weaver repeatedly pulls (draws) a set of crosswise threads called the weft over and under the warp.

The cloth is manufactured in many different patterns or weaves as well as dyed in many colors. Bolts of material are shipped to fabric shops where people who sew their own clothes can purchase them. Most material remains in the cloth factories where, using a variety of patterns and styles, it is transformed into articles of clothing. The clothing that is manufactured is shipped to stores around the world. Because of modern technology and transportation and communication systems, people throughout the world have access to the same types of clothing—if they choose. Of course, culture, climate, personal taste, and amount of money available enter into the choices people make. Stress the interdependence in the processes that connect "land to hand."

ACTIVITY

Using a series of pictures depicting the processes involved in making wool, have students work in triads to place them in the correct sequence and describe the process in detail. As a group, discuss the results and note how the people involved are interdependent. If time permits—and if children are interested—compare and contrast the wool-making industry of the past with today.

PAST	PRESENT
1. Raise a few sheep.	1. Raise many sheep (ranch).
2. Shear the sheep.	2. Shear the sheep.
3. Clean the fleeces.	3. Package the fleeces and send them to market by truck or train; sell the fleeces; send the fleeces to factories; clean the fleeces.
4. Card the wool.	4. Comb out the knotty wool by machine.
5. Spin the wool into yarn.	5. Spin the wool into yarn.
6. Weave the yarn into cloth.	6. Weave the yarn into cloth.
7. Dye the cloth.	7. Dye the cloth.
8. Using a simple pattern, cut out the cloth; sew the pieces together by hand.	8. Using a range of patterns designed by people who create a variety of styles, sizes, and so on, cut out the pieces for specified garments; use machines to stitch the pieces of the garments together.
9. Keep the garments for family use or sell them locally.	9. Label each garment; package the finished garments; send garments to stores according to specified orders; unpack garments; put them on racks for sale.

The story *Charlie Needs a Cloak* is a simplistic but appealing view of the land-to-hand relationship. An interesting sidelight is that the male is engaged in carrying out the processes—an entry to a class discussion regarding involvement of both genders in the clothing industry.

Other points that might be included in the discussion, depending on the interest and maturity of the children, are as follows:

- Wool acts as a natural insulator protecting the body from extremes of temperature.
- Woolen clothing is found throughout the world.
- Specific costumes made from wool sometimes dictate unique designs and styles that people create by hand (Laplander clothing).
- Some people choose to make clothing by hand or on their own sewing machine as an art form, as a hobby, or as a means of saving money.

If possible, arrange for the students to observe or participate in a spinning and weaving process.

SUMMARIZE KEY POINTS

- There are many steps (processes) and people involved in creating a woolen garment.
- Yarn is spun wool; cloth is woven yarn.
- Technology has greatly changed the clothing industry.
- Technology and modern transportation and communication, as applied to woolen clothing, provide more choices to people. There are still people who elect to make their own clothing. Some create unique articles of clothing for themselves or for sale that are considered art.

ASSESSMENT

Have students complete a page in their individual scrapbook that summarizes "How the Sheep's Coat Becomes My Sweater." The pictures or line illustrations that the children might like to include could be done as an out-of-school activity.

Have students make entries in their reflective notebooks regarding the most powerful, most surprising (etc.) things they learned. Encourage them to share their entries in their triads.

OUT-OF-SCHOOL LEARNING OPPORTUNITY

Encourage the students to work on a picture story at home regarding "The Wool Sweater That Once Was a Sheep's Coat"—emphasizing the visual dimension and sharing the results with at least one family member.

SOURCES

Blood, C., & Link, M. (1990). *The goat in the rug*. New York: Aladdin Books, Macmillan. (This the true story of a weaver and her goat who lived in the Navajo Nation at Window Rock, Arizona.)

de Paolo, T. (1973). *Charlie needs a cloak*. New York: Half Moon Books, Simon & Schuster.

World book encyclopedia. (1994). Vol. 21, pp. 173–175. Chicago: World Book, Inc.

LESSON 5: RAW MATERIALS USED IN MAKING CLOTH—COTTON AND NYLON

GOALS

- To help children understand and appreciate the range of materials that are used for making clothes
- To help children understand and appreciate how technology has influenced the clothing industry

KEY IDEAS TO BE DEVELOPED

- Cloth can be made from animals, plants, and synthetics developed by humans, using a range of specializations and technologies.
- The type of cloth people select for a garment depends in part on its purpose. For example, nylon stretches and does not absorb water. Cost, weather conditions, availability of the material, and personal choices are other factors.
- The label in a garment identifies the type of material that was used and explains how it should be cared for.

INTRODUCTION

Begin the lesson by having students "check out" the labels in each other's clothing (jackets, shirts, blouses, shoes, etc.). Have other articles of children's clothing (such as jeans and skirts) available to ensure a wide sampling of labels. Make a list of the materials used. Using the list, engage students in preparing and discussing a chart (see Figure 12.4) showing types of clothing that fit each category. Encourage the more mature students to locate information about the properties of various materials that affect their clothing functions.

POINTS TO EMPHASIZE

Continue the lesson using the chart that depicts clothing made from animals, plants, and synthetics. If there is a fabric store nearby, take the students on a short field trip to see the range of materials available. The guide could show the various types of cloth and point out some of the unique properties of each (i.e., water repellent, elastic, stain resistant, insulation-like, crease resistant, etc.), as well as share with the class key points about the land-to-hand phenomena of cotton and flax, an explanation about synthetics, and a description of the dyeing process.

With accompanying pictures, the following content could be at reviewed the end of the field trip: While leather goods and woolen cloth come from animals, other raw materials used for clothing come from plants and human-made products. Cotton and flax are among the most common plants used for clothing.

FIGURE 12.4
Raw Materials Used in Making Cloth

ANIMALS	PLANTS	SYNTHETICS	OTHER

Cotton grows in a warm climate. When the cotton fruit is ripe, it pops open. Then the seeds, covered with white fuzz, are harvested. The picked cotton is tied into bales that are sent to the mill. Many machines are used at the mill for the processing of the cotton. Fluffed-up cotton goes into a carding machine which makes its fibers lie side by side. The combed fibers leave the machines as soft ropes called slivers, and these are then twisted together or spun into thread or yarn.

Threads and yarns are usually dyed, either before or after they are made into cloth. A loom or weaving machine weaves the yarn into cloth. (Have children look through a magnifying lens to see the woven pattern of threads.)

In the past, one drawback to growing cotton was the time it took to process the crop after harvesting. Inside the fluffy balls or tufts of cotton were sticky seeds (50 seeds per boll) that had to be removed by hand. In 1793 Eli Whitney solved the problem by inventing the cotton gin. The first cotton gin was a box-like machine that had metal teeth that pulled the cotton through the grate. Seeds could not pass through the grate so they collected there. Meanwhile, brushes pushed the cleaned cotton out of the box.

Another plant that is used for making clothing is flax. It is used to make material known as linen. Stalks of flax plants are dried, scraped, and combed into long strips to be spun into thread.

Not all clothing is made from plant or animal materials. Some is made using types of cloth known as synthetics. Nylon was the first synthetic fiber and was thought to be superior to natural fabrics. It was created in the 1920s. To make nylon, various chemicals are melted and squeezed through small holes to form nylon thread. The liquid hardens when it is exposed to the air. The thread is pulled and stretched by machines that make it stronger and more elastic, then woven into cloth. Nylon cloth can be stretched and is water resistant. Because it does not absorb, it dries faster than cotton or wool.

There are many other synthetics or blends that draw on the latest technologies and scientific discoveries. Rayon, spandex, and ramie are among them.

Not long ago, people used the juices of flowers, berries, and bark to give colors to cloth. Some of these dyes are still used, but most dyes are now made from coal tar. Ultimately, these coal tar dyes come from plants too, because coal comes from trees that died long ago (*World Book*, pp. 1068–1069).

Many people buy cloth by the yard to make their own garments, but most people purchase ready-made clothing at stores. Ready-made clothes are made by machines in factories. (If possible, secure a video or film to illustrate the division of labor and the mass production process that enables people throughout the world to purchase identical garments. Point out that mass-produced articles of clothing can be sewn much faster than those sewn on a sewing machine at home.)

SUMMARIZE KEY POINTS

- Clothing is made from a variety of materials that come from animals, plants, and synthetics.
- People make choices regarding the type of cloth they buy for making their garments. If the clothing is ready-made, the information found in the label is helpful for making decisions about what to buy.
- The making of cloth involves a series of steps and processes, most notably the spinning or drawing of raw material into threads and the weaving of threads into cloth.

ASSESSMENT

Have students complete a page in their individual scrapbook that summarizes "Raw Materials Used in Making Cloth." Encourage students to add samples and pictures. This dimension of the activity could be done at home.

Have students make entries in their reflective notebooks regarding the most powerful thing that they learned at the fabric shop about the materials used for making cloth—or the most powerful thing that they learned from the video or film that focused on mass production of clothing.

OUT-OF-SCHOOL LEARNING OPPORTUNITY

Encourage children to work on the data retrieval chart that focuses on reading labels of clothing—What is it made of? How should I care for it?

MATERIAL	ARTICLES OF CLOTHING	HOW SHOULD I CARE FOR IT?
Cotton	Blouse, shirt	Machine wash
_____	_____	_____
_____	_____	_____
_____	_____	_____

Encourage students to share the results with their peers.

ENRICHMENT

If a field trip to a fabric shop is taken, have students explore, under adult guidance, other aspects of the clothing industry—patterns, thread, and accessories such as buckles, buttons, zippers, velcro, and so on. The key points to be considered are many people are involved in making clothing; some people make their own clothing or sew at home for others and buy the materials at fabric shops; much clothing is massed produced in factories. (At the factory, bolts of cloth, zippers, and all necessary accessories are found in mass quantities.)

Another dimension of the clothing industry is tailoring. While this would not be considered a major arm of the clothing industry today, there are usually tailors in every large town. A field trip to a tailor shop could have appeal to children. *The Purple Coat* could serve as an introduction to the tailor. A discussion focusing on tailoring versus mass production would illustrate another form of choice making.

SOURCES

Hest, A. (1992). *The purple coat*. New York: Aladdin Books, Macmillan.
World book encyclopedia. (1994). Vol. 18, pp. 173–175. Chicago: Scott Fetzer Co.

LESSON 6: CHOICE MAKING

GOAL

- To develop in children knowledge, skills, and application strategies concerning choices that individuals and families make regarding clothing

KEY IDEAS TO BE DEVELOPED

- While climate and weather dictate in part the kinds of clothing people wear, there are still a lot of opportunities for making personal choices.
- People make clothing choices about style, type of fabric, color, how much to spend given their budget, where to buy the items, and so on.

INTRODUCTION

Display a variety of items that could be worn by students in your class. Divide the class into triads—by gender—and ask them to decide (establish a time limit) on which two items they would buy (they have only enough money for two items). Have each triad share its reasoning with the class.

POINTS TO EMPHASIZE

Use a storyline that reflects the lives of your students and the range of choices that their families make about clothing (see Figure 12.5). Use articles of clothing

FIGURE 12.5
People Make Lots of Decisions About the Clothing They Choose to Wear

WHETHER OR NOT TO PURCHASE	WHERE TO PURCHASE	HOW MUCH TO SPEND	COLOR	STYLE	FABRIC	CARE	OTHER

and words to illustrate key points. Depending on your class, you might elect Ben or Barbara—or you may decide to present both to represent the genders.

Ben's Family and/or *Barbara's Family*

Ben/Barbara told his/her parents that s/he needed a new coat. A discussion ensued that included the following questions (add more if you wish, or solicit suggestions from students):

1. *Does s/he presently have a usable coat? If so, why does s/he need another one?*
2. *If an older sibling or relative has outgrown a coat that would fit Ben/Barbara, will that solve the problem? Why or why not?*
3. *If a new coat needs to be purchased, where should the family go to shop—catalog? Department store? Discount store? Second-hand store?*
4. *Is the coat needed now? Or can they wait for a sale?*
5. *If purchased now, what size, color, and style should be selected?*
6. *Should a coat be selected that needs drycleaning care—or should it be one that can be laundered? Advantages? Disadvantages?*
7. *How much can Ben/Barbara's family afford to spend on the coat?*
8. *How should the family pay for it? Cash? Check? Layaway? Credit card?*

After the discussion, ask each student to share one thing he or she learned about the choices that the family needed to consider. List their responses.

SUMMARIZE KEY POINTS

- Cost, style, and color are among the many choices people make regarding their clothing.
- People need to learn how to make good decisions about clothing.

ASSESSMENT

Have students complete a page in their individual scrapbook that summarizes "Choices My Family Can Make About My Clothing Needs." (Encourage the student to select one article such as jeans for illustrative purposes.) The pictures or line illustrations that the children might include can be done as an out-of-school learning opportunity. The completed page should be shared with their peers.

Have students make entries in their reflective notebooks regarding the most powerful, most surprising, most unique (etc.) thing that they learned. Encourage them to share their entries with peers in a paired setting and as part of their portfolios during conferencing.

OUT-OF-SCHOOL LEARNING OPPORTUNITY

Encourage students to work on a picture story regarding "The Choices My Family Makes About Clothing: My Sweater," and share the entire story with at least one family member.

OR

Give each member of the class a version of the short scenario shown below in a handout. Ask each student to share and discuss it with one member of the family or with a baby-sitter. Discuss the range of family responses in class the following day.

Judy's New Jeans

Judy needs a new pair of jeans, but it is December 5th and her mother is not very excited about making such a purchase this close to the holidays. She tells Judy that there will have to be a dollar limit on the purchase if it is made now.

How can you and your family help Judy and her mother make the best decision? How would you go about making this purchase? Please complete the decision-making chart [see Figure 12.6] *and return it tomorrow so that, as a class, we can discuss the results.*

SOURCE

Parton, D. (1994). *Coat of many colors*. New York: Byron Preiss Book, HarperCollins. (The story features a young girl whose mother makes her a coat of rags because the family has few financial resources. The girl, however, experiences richness through love.)

YOUR TURN: A UNIT ON CLOTHING AS A CULTURAL UNIVERSAL

There are several ways to examine our clothing unit. One filter might be the instructional activity perspective developed in Chapter 6. The following exercise

FIGURE 12.6

Judy's Jeans

WHAT INITIAL QUESTIONS NEED TO BE ASKED?	HOW MUCH SHOULD BE SPENT ON JEANS FOR AN 8-YEAR-OLD? (JUDY'S CLOTHING BUDGET IS $200 FOR SCHOOLWEAR)	REASONS FOR AMOUNT YOU AGREE TO SPEND	WHERE SHOULD THE JEANS BE PURCHASED?	WHY?

WHAT DECISIONS WILL YOU MAKE WHILE AT THE STORE? EX: STYLE, COLOR, ETC.	WHY?	METHOD OF PURCHASE? EX: CASH, CREDIT CARD, CHECK, LAYAWAY	WHY?	OTHER

will serve as a framework for applying the principles put forward in that chapter. Identify an example to illustrate application of the principles. If you find voids or disconnects based on your interpretations, substitute for or add to some of the activities we suggested.

INSTRUCTIONAL ACTIVITY AUDIT: CLOTHING AS A CULTURAL UNIVERSAL

After reviewing the clothing unit in general, revisit it with an eye toward the instructional activities. For clarifications, return to Chapter 6.

	YES: EXAMPLE TO ILLUSTRATE	NO: RECOMMENDED ENHANCEMENT
Primary Principles		
Do the activities reflect goal relevance?		
Are the activities at the appropriate level of difficulty?		
Are the activities feasible?		
Are the activities cost-effective?		

	YES: EXAMPLE TO ILLUSTRATE	NO: RECOMMENDED ENHANCEMENT
Secondary Principles (Desirable But Not Necessary)		
Do the activities accomplish multiple goals?		
Do the activities have motivational value?		
Are the activities constructed around current powerful ideas?		
Do the activities reflect whole-task completion?		
Do the activities incorporate higher-order thinking?		
Principles That Apply to Sets of Activities (Consider All the Activities as a Whole)		
Does the set of activities contain a variety of activity formats and student response modes?		
Does the set suggest progressive levels of difficulty or complexity?		
Does the set include life-application opportunities?		
Does the set reflect a full range of goals identified for the unit?		
Does the set include opportunities for concrete experiences?		
Does the set connect declarative knowledge with procedural knowledge?		
Does the set provide for "natural" applications?		

Chapter 13

A RESOURCE UNIT ON MOUNTAIN REGIONS

GOALS

1. Help students to understand the nature of mountains, the physical environments that mountains create, and the advantages and limitations that these environments pose for human activities
2. Help students to learn about mountain regions in the United States, especially those in which they live or which have noteworthy connections to the region in which they live
3. Engage students in personal and civic decision making related to the nation's mountain regions

KEY IDEAS TO BE DEVELOPED

The Physical Geography of Mountain Regions

1. Mountains are not just hills but very high elevations of land. Define mountains in terms of distance from sea level and compare them with plains that are mostly within a few hundred feet of sea level. (Show and explain relief maps and schematic diagrams that name and illustrate the land forms found between sea level and the highest mountains.)
2. Mountains were not "just always there." They were formed by movements of the earth's surface plates or by volcanic activity erupting from

below the surface. Three major causal mechanisms have been identified: (1) Two surface plates clash directly and force each other upwards
at the point of contact (as when you push two clay pancakes together
on a tabletop). This process created most of the major mountain ranges
that feature high and sharp peaks. (2) Two plates come together, but
instead of a direct clash, the edge of one plate slips over the edge of
the other. This creates more rounded ranges, high enough to be considered mountains but not among the highest peaks on earth. (3)
Volcanoes cause upward bulging of the earth while they are still under-
ground, and once they begin erupting above the ground they expel lava
(sometimes millions of tons) that can build up to mountainous proportions over the centuries.

3. Although there are isolated peaks (mostly volcanoes), most mountains
   are parts of ranges (study the globe or sets of maps to locate and discuss the world's major mountain ranges, especially those that form the
   "spine" of the Americas).

4. Physical environments (and the ecologies that they are capable of supporting) change as one moves from sea level toward higher elevations.
   In general, as one continues to move higher, the climate becomes
   colder and there is less variety in plants and animals. Most plants and
   animals (and people) are found at low elevations that feature relatively
   warm climates, flat land, and rich soil. As one begins to move up into
   mountain elevations, the climate cools, the land is mostly sloped, and
   the soil becomes rockier. It becomes harder for people to grow crops
   and for animals to find food. If the mountain is high enough, one eventually will reach a tree line beyond which trees no longer grow. These
   elevations still support bushes and wildflowers that can survive without
   rich soil or a warm climate and animals such as bears, mountain lions,
   marmots, and mountain goats that are adapted to the rough terrain and
   forbidding climate. Still higher up, there is only rock, sometimes covered in part by snow (or even glaciers). Only species such as lichen
   and insects, and perhaps a few wildflowers and marmots, can survive in
   this environment.

5. Prevailing winds blowing into a mountain range create weather patterns
   that may affect entire regions. The mountain range interrupts the flow
   of clouds and moist air, turning it back on itself and building up the
   air's moisture content until it forms precipitation. As a result, there is
   frequent rain or snow on the windward side of the mountain range but
   dry, even desert conditions on the leeward side (illustrate using diagrams taken from textbooks). This is why the northwest coast of the
   United States has a wet climate but the Great Basin east of the mountains
   is very dry (refer to globe or maps to elaborate on this and other examples of mountains' effects on weather and climate, especially effects
   on the local region).

People and Mountains

1. In the past, people who did not live in mountain areas tended to view them as forbidding and unpleasant places to be avoided if possible. Prior to modern paved roads and motor-driven vehicles, mountain ranges were significant barriers to trade and travel, as well as significant protection against invasion. Heavy snows often meant that even passes through the mountains were open only during the warmer months. Even then, mountains were difficult to negotiate because the roads were often sloped. In many places, one could easily slip off the road and either tumble down a steep slope and get hurt or fall off a cliff and get killed. Mountain ranges were significant barriers to westward migration during the pioneer days when people used horses and wagons to cross over the Appalachians into the midwest, and later, to cross the Rockies and the Sierras in the west.

2. Even then, though, some people lived in the mountains. Usually they lived in valleys between ranges or in flat areas such as Jackson Hole that lay between surrounding mountains where some forms of farming and animal grazing were possible. Mountain residents supplemented their diets by hunting and fishing (perhaps embellish here with books or videos on nineteenth-century "mountain men" or other people who have managed to live in mountain areas without benefit of modern housing and transportation).

3. Most mountain regions were (and still are) sparsely populated. However, towns developed in a few places because they became centers for local industry (typically mining or lumbering operations) or transportation hubs (they were located at a key crossroads or served as the point of departure into a major mountain pass).

4. Today, mountain regions are much less isolated than they used to be, and people can drive through them, using modern roads that snake their way around mountains (and sometimes tunnels that go through them). People in our country have good access to the Appalachians, the Ozarks, the Rockies, and the Sierra Nevada ranges by car or train. They also can fly to these areas and to remote areas in Alaska and Hawaii. Many people take advantage of these opportunities: Instead of thinking of mountain regions as unpleasant places to be avoided, most modern people think of them as attractive places to visit to enjoy scenic vistas, hike in national parks, fish in mountain streams, go skiing or mountain climbing, or visit art colonies, historic places, or other tourist attractions. Europeans enjoy visiting the Alps for similar reasons.

5. Even today, however, certain mountain regions are still formidable barriers to travel by land and certain mountain communities are still quite isolated. This is especially true of the Himalayan range and the nations of Nepal and Tibet, as well as various mountain regions in Indonesia and South America.

6. Even in our country and in the Alps, heavy snows and bitter cold make it impossible (or even if possible, economically unfeasible) to keep certain roads or mountain passes open in the winter. Except for ski resorts, mountain communities and national parks that host a great many visitors in the warmer months do not see many outsiders in the colder months.

7. Mountain regions are not heavily populated even today. A major exception is Mexico City—the largest city in the world—located in a "bowl" high in the mountains of central Mexico. There are also a few large cities in mountain areas of the United States that have grown because they are regional marketing and service centers, most notably Denver. However, even the cities in mountain areas tend to be small, and most mountain communities exist for the same economic reasons as in the past (principally mining, lumbering, and cattle or sheep ranching). A major recent addition to the economies of some mountain towns is tourism, notable in ski resorts (Aspen, Park City, etc.) or in towns located near national parks or other places of natural beauty (Jackson Hole, Lake Tahoe).

8. Large cities in mountain regions often suffer from cost-of-living and quality-of-life problems. Food and manufactured items often cost more because they have to be shipped greater distances to remote mountain locations. Local geographic factors sometimes create air inversions or other conditions that limit air flow and thus magnify air pollution problems. Mexico City has a terrible air pollution problem and Denver is developing one.

9. Even though they are sparsely populated, mountain regions make important contributions to our national productivity and quality of life. In some areas, runoff from mountain rain and snow is collected in reservoirs and used to provide vital water supplies—not only for drinking but for irrigation of lands that otherwise would not support farming. The rich central valley of California is irrigated in this way. Mountain regions also supply significant proportions of the nation's lumber and minerals, including some vital minerals that are not found anywhere else in the nation.

Additional Ideas Suggested for Optional Inclusion

1. Humans accustomed to living at lower elevations need to adapt when they visit or move to mountain areas (shortness of breath accompanies physical exertion at high elevations; dry air on the lee side of mountains can lead to dehydration and skin irritation problems; daytime and nighttime temperatures may be much more variable).

2. Along with people who exploit the natural resources found in mountain regions, some people make a living in these regions through occupations that require specialized skills more than abundant raw materials. Many people living in villages in the Swiss Alps make watches or cuckoo clocks. In our country, some people living in mountain communities are artists or crafts workers who make specialized creations.

3. In many parts of the world, farmers cope with sloped land by reshaping it into series of step-like terraces, so that soil and water are prevented from running down the slope.
4. People in mountain areas have learned to construct houses to maximize exposure to the sun, minimize exposure to wind, and cause snow to slide off of their roofs and pile up against the house so as to provide insulation.
5. Mountain climbers using special equipment have scaled many of the world's highest peaks, including Mount Everest.
6. There are active volcanoes in our country, including many in Hawaii and Mount St. Helens in Washington (you might wish to develop a lesson on volcanoes if your curriculum treats this topic as part of social studies rather than science).
7. Many of our highest mountain regions have been reserved as national parks (perhaps show photos or videos from some of these).
8. Some mountain ranges stretch along coast lines (most notably in western North and South America). Often this creates favorable conditions for the development of communities along the coast. Travel between coastal communities is usually easy by land or water, but these communities may be isolated from inland communities on the other side of the mountain range. Some communities in places like Alaska and Chile are accessible only by air or sea.

POSSIBLE ACTIVITIES

1. Start the unit with a story from children's literature about mountain living or with brainstorming about what it is like to live in the mountains.
2. Read children's books or show videos about mountain life in the past and perhaps today in Switzerland or Nepal.
3. Engage students in a research project on how the local area is affected by mountains or is interdependent with mountain regions. Even if located at a great distance from a mountain range, your area probably has some connections via climate and weather patterns, importing of raw materials, visiting of national parks or ski resorts, and so on.
4. Study changes over time in the economy/population of a particular mountain region or community (especially if local).
5. Study and discuss travel brochures or videos that feature tourist options in mountain regions. Invite students to show and tell about vacation trips or other family experiences in mountain regions.
6. Discuss policy issues relating to mountain regions (air and water quality, land and water use, etc.).
7. Have students discuss or write about the trade-offs involved in living in mountain regions and then explain why they would or would not

FIGURE 13.1
Mountain Regions: Sample Page from Unit Overview Chart

GOAL I	KEY IDEAS	SPECIFIC ACTIVITIES TO MATCH THE GOAL	OTHER SUBJECTS INCLUDED	MATERIALS NEEDED
Help students to understand the nature of mountains, the physical environments that they create, and the advantages and limitations that these environments pose for human activities.	Mountains are not just hills but are very high elevations of land. They were formed by movements of the earth's surface plates or by volcanic activity erupting from below the surface. Often people make a living in these regions through occupations that require specialized skills more than abundant raw materials. Mountain features and their cloistered effects often stimulate creativity.	Have students locate the nearest mountain range, first on a physical map, then on a topographical one. Using the scientific method, have the students speculate about how the range was formed. Examine together the line of inquiry. Have students gather data to establish evidence. Then have them gather information about the human activities found in this range. Be wary of "make and take" cutesy-type volcano experiments that are not authentic and detract from the socail studies understanding. Have students investigate the type of specialized skills that people in the mountain region nearest them possess. If possible, have an artist, writer, or musician whose work has been inspired by the mountains visit the class.	Science Art, music, literature	Topographical maps, pictures of mountains, reference books, video of moutain region— acquire from the tour bureau or travel agency and adapt them to the unit goal. Have students observe the characteristics of mountains. Have them, as they observe, imagine the advantages and limitations these environments pose for human activities. Books, paintings, music scores of individuals inspired by the nearby mountain region.

want to live there (or, alternatively, why they would want to visit or move to Denver, Aspen, Lake Tahoe, the Blue Ridge, or some other specific location).

YOUR TURN: A RESOURCE UNIT ON MOUNTAIN REGIONS

There are numerous ways to examine and enhance the mountain region resource unit. We suggest that you develop your plans with an eye toward the integrative aspects because the content naturally lends itself to more than one subject for the development of "meaningfulness." Remember, content, skills, and activities included in the name of integration should be educationally significant, desirable, and authentic. Such content, skills, and activities should be selected because they foster rather than disrupt or nullify the accomplishment of major social studies goals.

We have provided a framework and an example for you to use as you expand your unit in Figure 13.1.

After you have completed the framework, review it carefully using the following guiding questions for successful integration:

- Does the integrated activity clearly match the social education goal?
- Would an "outsider" clearly recognize the activity as social studies?
- Does the activity allow students to meaningfully develop or authentically apply important social studies content?
- Does it involve authentic application of skills or knowledge from other disciplines?
- Will students understand its social education purpose?

Chapter 14

A RESOURCE UNIT FOR FIFTH-GRADE U.S. HISTORY: THE AMERICAN REVOLUTION

Although conceived as part of a chronologically organized introduction to U.S. history for fifth graders, this unit is designed to focus on a connected set of key ideas developed in depth rather than to offer broad coverage of the details of the revolutionary period. In support of the citizen education goals of social studies, it concentrates on the conflicts over governance issues that developed between England and the colonies, and the ways in which the colonists' views on these issues shaped the ideas expressed in the Declaration of Independence and the forms of government established through the Articles of Confederation and the U.S. Constitution. Many of these ideas about government are relatively abstract and new to fifth graders, so unit plans concentrate on developing appreciation of the ideas themselves without getting into the philosophy that led up to those ideas. Nor do the unit plans call for detailed study of the war itself, because we do not view this content as central to our major goals. However, teachers who wish to incorporate material on the war (because it is highly interesting to many students) can easily do so.

GOALS

1. Help students come to understand the conflicts that developed between England and the 13 colonies, how these led to the Declaration of Independence, how independence was secured through the Revolutionary War, and how all this resulted in the establishment of a new nation (federation).
2. Help students come to appreciate the political values and governmental ideals that emerged during this crucial period as keystones of American

political traditions, as expressed in the Declaration of Independence, the Articles of Confederation, and the Constitution.

KEY IDEAS TO BE DEVELOPED

Recommendations about key ideas to emphasize have been informed by the findings of McKeown and Beck (1990) and VanSledright, Brophy, and Bredin (1993) concerning the prior knowledge that needs to be in place and the primary storylines that need to be developed to enable students to construct coherent understandings of the nature and implications of the American Revolution. Suggestions about key historical events to emphasize in this unit were taken from Crabtree et al. (1992) and McBee, Tate, and Wagner (1985).

The Colonies' Relationship to England Prior to 1763

Either in previous units or in the introduction to this unit, students will need to understand the following key ideas as context for their learning about the American Revolution.

1. More than 150 years elapsed between the founding of the first English colonies at Jamestown and Plymouth and the Declaration of Independence on July 4, 1776. During that time, the English colonies in America grew from a few isolated settlements to 13 large and populous collections of communities that became the original 13 states. Also, ties with England gradually weakened as the colonists developed identities as Americans.
2. Although they were located in America, the colonies were governed by England through governors and other officials appointed by the king.
3. Colonists were considered British subjects, so they enjoyed British protection but also were governed by British laws. They elected their own leaders and made some of their own laws at the local community level, but unlike British citizens living in England, they did not vote in Parliamentary elections. They were unable to send representatives to Parliament to specifically represent their interests.
4. Yet, they were subject to British laws and regulations. Like other colonial powers of the time (most notably France, Spain, and the Netherlands), England had built up an empire by claiming lands in other parts of the world, defending them militarily, and sending people to colonize and govern them. Colonies served as sources of raw materials for the mother country's factories, as well as markets for its manufactured exports.
5. Through a system of laws and taxes, England pressured the colonies to trade only with or through England. The colonists were supposed to buy things only from England (even if they could get them cheaper from somewhere else) and sell their crops or raw materials only to England (even though they might have sold them elsewhere, perhaps at greater profit).

Tensions Build After 1763

1. England fought wars against France and other European nations that competed with them in their efforts to build empires around the world. British conflict with the French over land in North America (what we call the French and Indian War) was part of this competition. Between 1740 and 1763, the British were too busy fighting these wars to enforce their economic restrictions on the colonies, and colonists began to trade more freely than the British wanted them to.

2. However, the Treaty of Paris in 1763 established peace for awhile, so England began to pay closer attention to the colonies. It also needed money to pay off war debts, including debts accumulated fighting the French and their Indian allies in North America. Between 1763 and 1770, England imposed a series of taxes on the colonies, viewing this as a way to get the colonists to pay a reasonable share of the war debts (after all, British-paid soldiers had fought the French and Indian War partly on their behalf and were continuing to protect their borders). However, the colonists resented these taxes, not only because of the financial burden but because they were imposed by a Parliament in which the colonists were not represented. This was expressed in the phrase "no taxation without representation," which became a rallying cry against British policies. The British position was that members of Parliament represented not just the people who voted them into office but all British citizens everywhere, including in the colonies, but many American colonists did not accept this.

3. Besides imposing taxes, the British did several other things that angered the colonists: They tried colonists accused of certain crimes in British courts (thus depriving them of the right to a trial by a jury of their peers); forbade them to settle west of the Appalachian Mountains (in an attempt to keep the colonists separated from the Indians, and thus to reduce the need for soldiers to prevent frontier conflicts); forbade them to print their own money, and where necessary, required them to provide living quarters for British troops.

Resistance and Punishment, 1770–1774

1. Anger and political protests built up as the British kept imposing new taxes and restrictions, sometimes leading to attacks on tax collectors or other government officials. Tensions were greatest in Boston, where England sent troops in 1768 to protect government officials. Local citizens sometimes harassed the troops by yelling and throwing things at them. One such incident in 1770 got out of hand and became the "Boston Massacre."

2. Following the Boston Massacre, England sought to reduce tensions by removing the troops to an island in Boston Harbor and by repealing all taxes except the tax on tea. Much of the anger dissipated and things settled down between 1770 and 1772.

3. However, the tea tax stood as a symbol of imposed British restrictions, and many colonists continued to oppose the notion of taxation without representation. Tensions flared up again in 1773 when the British East India Company was given a monopoly over the tea trade in the colonies. Colonists resisted this by refusing entry of "monopoly" ships into colonial ports, and they destroyed the cargo of one such ship that had docked at Boston by staging the Boston Tea Party in 1773.

4. Angered at these developments, the British passed a series of Acts of Parliament (called the Intolerable Acts by the colonists) designed to punish Boston and the Massachusetts colony. These acts revoked self-government, closed the port of Boston, and forcibly quartered troops in people's homes. In effect, Boston was occupied and put under martial law, and steps were taken to reorganize the Massachusetts government.

5. In turn, the British actions alarmed the colonists, leading them to establish the First Continental Congress in 1774 to discuss how to respond to the developing crisis and to arrange for the 13 colonies to act as a united group. Talks continued at the Second Continental Congress held in 1775, culminating in decisions to organize resistance to Parliament's actions and to petition the king for repeal of measures viewed as tyrannical, especially the "Intolerable Acts" directed against Boston and Massachusetts.

Revolution and Independence

1. Attempts to work out a peaceful settlement failed. The king ignored the colonists' petition, sent more troops, and announced further restrictions. In the colonies, verbal resistance spilled over into armed conflicts, including battles at Lexington, Concord, and Bunker Hill.

2. Giving up on attempts to compromise, the Congress accepted a motion to declare independence on July 2, 1776, and issued the Declaration of Independence two days later. In the process of listing grievances against England that justified the declaration, the document put forth some important basic principles concerning human rights that governments ought to respect and also identified actions that governments ought not to take. Many of these reflected the colonists' recent experiences with the king and the Parliament.

3. The declaration meant war with England. The colonies established themselves as a federation through the Articles of Confederation, recruited George Washington to command the army, and began raising money to recruit, equip, and train soldiers.

4. The colonists were fighting the world's foremost military power, but several factors working in their favor enabled them to prevail in the end. England was involved in empire building and armed conflict all over the world, so it could allocate only limited resources to the conflict in America. England had to ship soldiers thousands of miles away to the colonies, but the colonists were fighting on their home ground. England's enemies, most notably France, helped the colonies by sending needed materials and in some cases military assistance. Finally, there was considerable division of opinion in England about the war against the colonies, so that governmental leaders were less eager to pursue it and more willing to conclude a peace agreement than they might have been otherwise.

5. For the most part, the war involved relatively small battles between relatively small armies, nothing like what occurred later in the Civil War. Early battles were mostly in New England and New York, and were mostly inconclusive or won by the British. Later battles were mostly fought farther south, and more often won by the colonists. Hostilities climaxed with a major American victory at Yorktown in 1781, and the war ended after a long period of peace negotiations was concluded in 1783.

6. The united colonies were now an independent nation. The new nation still operated under the Articles of Confederation at first, but this form of federal government proved to be too weak to be effective and was soon replaced by the U.S. Constitution (these events will be the focus of the next unit).

POSSIBLE ACTIVITIES

The nature of the content (past history) and the students' lack of much background knowledge limits opportunities for experiential learning or independent inquiry (except for research assignments based on textbook or encyclopedia accounts of the Revolution or biographies of Revolutionary figures). However, students can use teacher-provided summaries of key information items or historically based children's literature selections as a basis for dramatic reenactments, debates, simulations, or writing assignments that involve taking the role of an individual who was involved in some way in the Revolution. Representative activities include the following:

1. Have students pretend to be journalists or pamphleteers writing about the Boston Massacre or the Boston Tea Party. Have some individuals or groups pretend to be Sam Adams or another colonist seeking to foment rebellion, others to pretend to be a newspaper reporter seeking to write a neutral or balanced account, and still others pretend to be a Tory dismayed by unjustified defiance of legitimate authority.

2. Have the class simulate a town meeting (or a Continental Congress meeting) called to decide whether, and if so how, the group should support the people of Boston in resisting the Intolerable Acts.

3. Simulate a debate or trial concerning whether or not the American Revolution was justified. Include arguments or testimony by King George and other defenders of the view that British actions prior to the Revolution were not only consistent with established laws and customs but reasonable and respectful of the colonists' concerns, as well as by Tom Paine and other defenders of the view that the colonists were justified in breaking away from England to form an independent nation.

4. Have small groups of students simulate family discussions of whether or not the father or one of the sons should join the Continental Army. Assign different geographical locations and life circumstances to different groups (a Boston shop owner, a Massachusetts farmer, a farmer in rural Pennsylvania, a plantation owner in Georgia, a former slave now living in New York City).

5. Have students pretend to be citizens of Boston beginning to get caught up in the events preceding the Revolution, discussing among family members or writing to friends elsewhere about their experiences and how they might respond to them (a family forced to quarter British troops, a family whose son threw a rock at British troops and barely escaped when they gave chase, a Tory family trying to decide what they will do if conflict with England continues to escalate, formerly close friends who find that disagreement over political issues is ruining their friendship).

Other possible activities for this unit include the following:

1. Map activities highlighting key items of information such as the role of the Appalachians as a barrier to westward expansion of the colonies; the long distances and travel times between the colonies and England and between the northern and southern colonies (which created delays of weeks or months in communications); and the locations of major cities and battle sites.

2. Essays or class presentations on why we celebrate the Fourth of July.

3. Discussions or class presentations focusing on comparison and contrast between the issues that led the colonies to declare independence from England and the issues involved in more recent struggles for independence (satellite nations versus the U.S.S.R. prior to its breakup; former component nations within the U.S.S.R. versus Russia since the breakup; Quebec).

Print Resources for Potential Use in This Unit

Avi: *The Fighting Ground*.

James Lincoln Collier and Christopher Collier: *War Comes to Willy Freeman*.

Ingri and Edgar Peres D'Aulaire: *George Washington*.

S. Edwards: *When the World's on Fire*.

Esther Forbes: *Johnny Tremain*.

Jean Fritz: *Where Was Patrick Henry on May 29th?; Can't You Make Them Behave, King George?; Will you Sign Here, John Hancock?; Why Don't You Get a Horse, Sam Adams?; And Then What Happened, Paul Revere?; What's the Big Idea, Ben Franklin?; Shh! We're Writing the Constitution.*

Robert Lawson: *Ben & Me*; *Mr. Revere & I*.

Elizabeth Levy: *If You Were There When They Signed the Constitution.*

Ann McGovern: *If You Lived in Colonial Times.*

Scott O'Dell: *Sarah Bishop.*

Edwin Tunis: *Colonial Living.*

Cobblestone magazine (issues dealing with the Revolutionary period).

YOUR TURN: A RESOURCE UNIT ON THE AMERICAN REVOLUTION

The nature of the content and the students' lack of much background knowledge limit opportunities for experiential or independent inquiry, but the American Revolution provides a very fruitful forum for structured discourse, the topic of Chapter 5. Also, writing can be a natural outgrowth of the discussions, as well as a contributor to subsequent dialogues. Keeping this in mind, we recommend that you expand this resource unit into a teaching unit using discourse and writing as the key modalities. The writing pieces can serve as major entries for the student portfolio, a very appropriate authentic assessment measure given the nature of the goals, content, and strategies for developing meaningfulness. The net result should be powerful social studies teaching and learning.

Figure 14.1 is a "worksheet" to help guide your planning of structured discourse.

FIGURE 14.1

The American Revolution

GOAL I	MAJOR UNDERSTANDING	CONTENT SOURCE	ENGAGING STUDENTS IN REFLECTIVE DISCOURSE
To enhance children's understanding and appreciation of the circumstances that transpired between 1620 and 1776, setting the stage for the Declaration of Independence	During the 15 years between the founding of the first English colonies and the Declaration of Independence, ties with England gradually weakened	Textbook account and/or story with pictures presented by the teacher focusing on the conditions, issues, chain of events, and so on	Review the end-of-chapter material in Chapter 5. Incorporate each of the types of questions into this plan for structured discourse. **POSSIBLE QUESTIONS** • What did you know about the time period from 1620 to 1776 prior to reading about it or hearing the "story" presented by the teacher? • What did you know about the English?

GOAL I	MAJOR UNDERSTANDING	CONTENT SOURCE	ENGAGING STUDENTS IN REFLECTIVE DISCOURSE
To enhance children's understanding and appreciation of the circumstances that transpired between 1620 and 1776, setting the stage for the Declaration of Independence	During the 15 years between the founding of the first English colonies and the Declaration of Independence, ties with England gradually weakened	Textbook account and/or story with pictures presented by the teacher focusing on the conditions, issues, chain of events, and so on	• What did you know about the colonists? • Do you remember hearing anything about England—its people? leadership? If so, explain. • What did the American Revolution make you think of when you heard of it for the first time? • If you were a colonist, how do you think you would feel about what was happening? • Who was right? Wrong? Why do you think so? Do you think there were circumstances beyond either group's control? • Do you think there was any single event or issue that really broke things wide open between the two groups? Explain. • If you had lived during this time period, who would you like to have known? Would you have tried to influence that person's reactions regarding the conflict? If so, how? If not, why not? • How do you think the Declaration of Independence addressed the problem between the two groups? Was it necessary? Why? (Why not?) How else might the differences between England and the colonists have been handled?

Select questions that focus on your goals and address the key understandings. Early in the discussion you will want to assess prior knowledge and determine apparent misconceptions. However, do not allow students to "wallow in ignorance" for too long. Textbook accounts, supplemental materials such as children's literature and information available on CD-ROM, as well as audio and video commentary are among the content sources that can be used as vehicles for launching fruitful discussions with focus, boundaries, and interaction.

PORTFOLIO SUGGESTIONS FOR THE AMERICAN REVOLUTION UNIT

The potential portfolio contents for social studies are limitless but those selected for emphasis should typify the powerful teaching and learning experiences that the students have had during the unit. Portfolio contents should be indicative of their continuous development. The portfolio should serve as a powerful stimulus for students to use as they articulate major understandings about the American Revolution and evaluate their own work.

We have included some sample writing entries that reflect Goal 1 identified on our "worksheet."

GOAL I	SUGGESTED POSSIBLE PORTFOLIO ENTRIES
To enhance students' understanding and appreciation of the circumstances that transpired between 1620 and 1776, setting the stage for the Declaration of Independence	Preunit—What does the American Revolution mean to you?
	Postunit—Repeat entry, drawing on what has been learned. What does the American Revolution mean to you?
	Imagine that you lived in England throughout the 150-year time period (between 1620 and 1776). Explain what life was like.
	OR
	Imagine that you lived in America during that same time period. Explain what life was like.
	OR
	Adopt the role of the King of England during this time period. Explain the situation from your perspective.
	OR
	Imagine you are a colonist. Write a letter to a relative in England explaining what your life in America was like in the mid-1700s.
	OR
	Imagine you are a journalist. Explain the trade-offs that occurred because the colonists were considered British subjects.
	(Encourage students to share their entries with their peers. If they wish to illustrate their writing, suggest they do it at home or when they have completed all of their assignments.)

Student-led conferences using the portfolios as springboards can serve as nice culminating activities for the learning. If structured properly, such conferences will provide powerful learning opportunities for students, especially with regard to key understandings about the American Revolution that they probably will not develop by studying disconnected facts to prepare for a conventional test.

REFERENCES

Crabtree, C., Nash, B., Gagnon, P., & Waugh, S. (Eds.). (1992). *Lessons from history: Essential understandings and historical perspectives students should acquire.* Los Angeles: National Center for History in the Schools, University of California, Los Angeles.

McBee, T., Tate, D., & Wagner, L. (1985). *U.S. history. Book 1: Beginnings to 1865.* Dubuque: William C. Brown.

McKeown, M., & Beck, I. (1990). The assessment and characterization of young learners' knowledge of a topic in history. *American Educational Research Journal, 27,* 688–726.

VanSledright, B., Brophy, J., & Bredin, N. (1993). *Fifth-graders' ideas about the American Revolution expressed before and after studying it within a U.S. history course.* (Elementary Subjects Center Series No. 81). East Lansing: Center for the Learning and Teaching of Elementary Subjects, Michigan State University.

Index